Astrology

My best Tool

Joni Patry

Learn Vedic Astrology at: www.universityofvedicastrology.com
Contact Joni Patry at: www.galacticcenter.org

Copyright 2023 by Joni Patry
All rights reserved. No part of this book may be reproduced, stored in a database or other retrieval system, or transmitted in any form, by any means, including mechanical, electronic, photocopy, recording, or otherwise, without prior written permission of the publisher.

Published by Madeline Zech Ruiz

ISBN: 978-1-952114-67-0

Book cover design by Aleksandar Petrovic – vajsman@gmail.com
Typesetting by Goran Skakic – gskakic@gmail.com

ASTROLOGER'S SECRETS

My Best Tools and Techniques

JONI PATRY

Acknowledgments

I would like to personally thank both Shreekala Ram and Madeline Zech Ruiz for their dedication and support of my efforts to bring this book to the world. Their time and energy spent helping me to edit and publish this book are both a gift and a blessing to me. Thank you from the bottom of my heart to both of you for your love and support.

Dedication

I would like to dedicate this book to all of my students and clients who have blessed me with all of their charts over the years. It has been a blessing and a privilege to read your charts and interact with each and every one of you over the years!

Contents

Introduction 1

Chapter 1
Setting the Foundation:
Houses, Ascendant, Four Aims in Life, Planets 5

Four Aims of Life 6
12 Houses: In depth meanings 7
Planets 9
Outer Planets 11
Nakshatras 11

Chapter 2
The Moon in Vedic Astrology
Moon's Yogas, Isolated, Conjunct Rahu, Ketu 13

Isolated Moon 13
Moon with Rahu 15
Moon with Ketu 16
Moon in Cancer 16
Moon in Taurus and Scorpio 16
Kemadruma Moon 17
Moon in the 10th house: Fame 17
Isolated Moon conjunct Rahu 20
Kemadruma Moon 29
Moon conjunct Rahu 30

Chapter 3
Mercury and the Moon 39

Chapter 4
Debilitated Planets 44

    Jupiter Debilitated 47
    Debilitated Mars 48
    Debilitated Venus neecha banga 55
    Debilitated Mars NO neecha banga 55

Chapter 5
Planet's Houses and Rulers- 1st House 60

    1st House: Death and Endings 60
    1st House: Death of pets 61
    Death of pets 62

Planet's Houses and Rulers- 2nd House 63

    Ruler of 11th in 2nd or ruler of 2nd in 11th Great gains 65
    2nd House: The Voice 69
    2nd House: Eating Disorders 70

Chapter 6
Planets in Houses and ruling houses: 3rd house 73

    3rd House: Entertainers 73
    Exalted and Debilitation degrees of the planets 76
    Ruler of 3rd in 5th house: Entertainers! 84
    3rd House: Technology 85
    3rd and 5th house: Creativity, Expression, Writing 87

Planet's Houses and Rulers: 4th house Chapter 90

    4th House: Ruler of 4th in 12th or ruler of 12th in 4th
    – Live in foreign country 90

Chapter 7
Planet's Houses and Rulers: 5h house 91

    5th House – Final Dispositor in the 5th – Creativity 91

Chapter 8
Planet's Houses and Rulers: 6h house 93

    The 6th house -Health and stomach issues – Moon in 6th house 93

Chapter 9
Planet's Houses and Rulers: 7ʰ house 98
7th- house grandmother (4th from the 4th) 98
Client Chart – parivartana with ruler of the 7th house with 8th house ... 99
Private Client Chart... 100

Chapter 10
Planet's Houses and Rulers: 8ʰ house 101
The 8th House
8th House: Scandals, Disgrace, Charisma 101
8th House Scandals, Disgrace and humiliation 103
8th house Research and Investigation............................ 108

Chapter 11
Planet's Houses and Rulers: 9th house 111
Religious Beliefs: 9th House
Jupiter Ruler of 9th house in 9th house 111
Religious Beliefs change with transiting Saturn in Sagittarius....... 112
Private Client 113

Chapter 12
Planet's Houses and Rulers: 10th house 114

Planet's Houses and Rulers: 11th house 117
Separation and loss of the mother: 11th house
8th from the 4th house 117

Chapter 13 120
Planet's Houses and Rulers: 12th house 120
Alienation, ostracized, exiled................................... 120
12th House – exiled.. 121
12th house – Loss or separation of children (8th from 5th).......... 123
12th house: Problems with children 125
Venus in 12th – Wealth 126
Private Client 128

Venus in 12th house   Great wealth, comes from the mother,
Venus/Moon in Uttara Bhadrapada 128
Fixed Stars 129
Rigel: 23–24 degrees Taurus/Scorpio
Wealth and Money 129
Rigel: 23–24 degrees Taurus/Scorpio
Wealth and Money 132
Regulus-leaders: 5–6 degrees of Leo..........................138
Spica-29 Virgo-0 degrees Libra: overnight sensation.............139
Algol 2–3 degrees Taurus.....................................141

Chapter 14
Planet's Important combinations and Aspects 143

Saturn conjunct Mars. Diligence and power to achieve,
overcome obstacles 143
Venus conjunct Rahu: Marriage to a Foreigner 144
Mars conjunct Ketu can be an injury 145
Mars/Ketu: Injury 145
Mars/Ketu: Accident...146
Jupiter aspecting Rahu 147
Rahu trine Jupiter: Loss of a Son 150
Jupiter trine Rahu: Joseph Kennedy Sr. 152
Rahu conjunct Saturn 152
Karmic indicator 152
Saturn/Rahu: Greatness and Extremes in house they occupy 153
7th house marriage partner 153
Saturn conjunct Rahu
9th house of Father 154
Saturn and Ketu 155
Saturn and Ketu: Unique talent or loss, Gift, Curse or Spirituality ...157

Chapter 15
Rahu and Ketu Fated Destiny 159

Ketu on Ascendant 159
Ketu on Ascendant – Great Losses 161
Rahu on Ascendant – A Fated Life or Destiny 161

Benefic planets, Jupiter or Venus in their own sign or exalted with Ketu
manifests greatness for that house 163
Planets Combust or Cazimi – Stationary Planets 165
Cazimi planet: Venus 168
Stationary Planets 168
Mercury Stationed: Brilliant Mind............................ 169

Chapter 16
Eclipses 170

Eclipses of 1998 and 2016 – Scandal for Clintons 18 ½ years later ..171
Eclipse on Chelsea's Sun: 8th from her Moon 173
Hilary's Vice President: Tim Kane Eclipse on his Sun 174
Eclipses over Hilary's Moon at time of elections 174

Chapter 17
Vedic Astrology Concepts that work!......................... 175

Lakshmi Yoga, Pancha Maha Purusha Yoga, Sade Sati,
Gandanta Planets, Saturn Return 175
Lakshmi Yoga 175
Pancha Maha Purusha Yoga................................. 176
Sade Sati 177
Sade Sati: Jordan Spieth won The Masters Golf Tournament 178
Transiting Saturn was 5 degrees Scorpio 178
Saturn's Return 179
Gandanta Planets 180
Natalie Wood Drowned 11/29/1981........................... 181
Natal Mercury 29 degrees Cancer 181
Transiting Ketu 29 degrees Sagittarius........................ 181
Dennis Wilson: Drowned: 12/29 1983 182
Natal Ascendant 29 degrees Cancer 182
Transiting Mars 29 degrees 182
Transiting Ketu 22 degrees Scorpio........................... 182
Titanic went down: 04/15/1912 184
Natal Rahu 28–29 degrees Pisces 184
Hurricane Harvey 184
Mars and Rahu 0 degrees Leo 184

Chapter 18
Outer Planets – Uranus, Neptune, and Pluto conjunct natal planets: Intense results according to planet they conjunct **185**

    Uranus conjunct Sun..185
    Uranus/Rahu conjunct Sun: Unusual career 185
    Uranus conjunct Moon 186
    Uranus conjunct Jupiter opposed Mercury/Sun
    – Brilliant Mind, Electricity 188
    Pluto conjunct Planets: Betrayal, death 189
    Uranus conjunct Venus: multiple marriages 192
    Mars Conjunct Neptune can be delusional 194
    Neptune between Sun and Moon – Secrets and murder in Family ..195

Chapter 19
Shastastaka (6/8 Relationship) **198**

    American Airlines Flight 11 199
    Natal Moon 8/6 Venus 199
    Transiting Mars/Ketu: 8 degrees Sagittarius 199

Chapter 20
Dashas **201**

    How maha dasha and bhukti are analyzed
    to predict life experience 201
    Maraka planets: Conor Clapton
    – Died in Jupiter Maha dasha Venus Bhukti 204
    Rahu 7th from planets: Rahu Dasha changes in relationships 205
    Special Features of Dashas.....................................207
    Transits during a maha dasha and bhukti 209

Chapter 21
Prediction with Transits **211**

    What the Planets Represent 213
    Planet's Speed 214
    Prediction with transits 216
    Counting from the transiting planet to the natal planet 216

Chapter 22
Astrological realizations from my experiences 229
    Sudarshan Chart, Bhava Chart, Declination
    and Out of Bounds, Aspects to the houses......................229
    Aspects to a house 233

Chapter 23
Final Interesting Clues 235
    Look for positive in a chart....................................237
    Closing 238

Introduction

I went on quite an interesting journey, in my search to find the best astrology and techniques to answer all my questions about life. Astrology was always my quest in life. I began this journey in my teens. I have no idea why I was always so fascinated with it. I suppose past lives and an early sense of purpose had to have something to do with this.

My mother always had astrology books around the house and since her Sun sign was the same as mine, I began reading them early on, maybe 12 years old. Our Western Sun sign was both Scorpio. I was always wondering about everyone's Sun signs after reading Linda Goodman's Sun signs.

The only astrology available at the time was western astrology. I found a teacher while in college that taught us to calculate charts, there was no internet or computers, so we calculated the charts by hand with many technical books, ephemeris, log rhythms, and time change books. I loved it!

My favorite things in the world to do are travel and learn astrology. I became a flight attendant just so I could travel to study under the famous astrologers at the time. I did my first astrological conference in 1980 in New Orleans. At the time I studied and followed all the great astrologers of the day in the U.S., Robert Hand, Noel Tyl, Steven Arroyo, and Alan Oken to name a few.

My quest and greatest interest were always predictions. I studied it all, specializing at one point in Uranian astrology with the transneptunians, because it was the most predictive, but it was like finding a needle in a haystack. Then studied the fixed stars, asteroids, declination and even heliocentric astrology. I got good results, but it wasn't complete, something was always missing and sometimes didn't work. But I knew it had to work, something had to be wrong or missing with the techniques I was using.

Then I heard Vedic – Indian astrology gave the kind of predictive results I was searching for. So, I sought out a teacher. Come to find out they are opposed to using the planets that gave me the best results in prediction, the three outer planets. I couldn't imagine leaving out the best predictive tools I had found in Western astrology. Then the language barriers with the Indian teachers and the Sanskrit words, and nakshatras seemed impossible. I would have to relearn so much more that was so foreign.

Finally, I found American teachers and they used the outer planets and found the certification programs that gave me the structure we all need to learn this. As I continue with Vedic astrology, I found that the entire system makes more sense and absolutely gives the predictive tools I was searching for. The house rulers using the tropical chart never seemed to work for me. The planets ruling the houses are supposed to indicate the events that are happening, but they didn't. I was always stumped with this, until the rulers of the houses with Vedic truly worked. It was a real aha experience. When we begin looking at the houses of the famous individuals in the many examples in this book, you will be a believer too.

When I first realized all the many more meanings the houses have in Vedic, I thought I could never learn and remember them all, but as I kept studying it all came together and actually made more sense. It began to give me an understanding of the world and how everything works together. These realizations changed my perception and opened my mind to self-realization and deeper profound understandings of myself and the world. As above so below, as within so without.

With this brief introduction if you follow through all my astrological discoveries you will go through the deep realizations as I did and come out of this book with new tools and most of the understanding that will change your perspective and your life.

There are so many rules in Vedic astrology and many of them don't work. In my 40 years of practice, I have come to terms with what really works. These are all the gems I have taken away in my many years of trials and errors. If you use these tools, you will become the best astrologer you can be.

Let me take you through a journey of all my discoveries that I have found work. It will amaze and captivate you as you begin to understand the power and awakenings of astrology, which is the science of all sciences.

Chapter 1

Setting the Foundation:
Houses, Ascendant, Four Aims in Life, Planets

There are 30 degrees to each sign and with 12 signs in the entire zodiac it equals a total of 360 degrees. In Vedic astrology we use whole sign houses, meaning an entire sign is in the house. Even though the ascendant rising degree is 29 degrees, the last degree of a sign the entire first house will be one whole sign. The house systems used in Western astrology calculated shorter and longer signs and the beginning of signs can be within the houses, therefore there are two signs in a house, sometimes three signs, called intercepted houses. This complication is eliminated with equal whole sign houses. But there is a system called the Sripati system which uses the western calculation that has more than one sign in a house. This will be explained in a section in this book. Otherwise, all the charts will have a whole sign per house.

The sign rising is the starting point in a chart. It is the sign that is rising on the eastern horizon at the time of birth. The rising sign called the ascendant in Vedic astrology is called the lagna. It is so important because it sets up what planets will rule each house. This is imperative because each planet according to the houses it rules will carry with it the meanings of the houses it rules, so it determines which planets cause difficulties or blessings according to the houses it rules.

For example, Mars is very difficult for Virgo rising because it rules the 3rd and the 8th house. The 3rd house rules siblings, and the 8th house is the most difficult house in the chart. Based on this Mars can bring problems through siblings based solely on knowing the ascendant. The house Mars sits in will be problematic based on the houses it rules because it rules the 8th and 3rd houses. If the ascendant is Pisces, Venus rules the 3rd and 8th houses therefore Venus even though it is a natural benefic will bring the same problems Mars does for Virgo ascendant because it rules houses 3 and 8. The house Venus sits in will bring problems to that house based on the houses Venus rules.

The houses are the foundation of a chart. The houses rule all areas of life and a thorough understanding of what the houses rule is vitally important to be a good astrologer. The houses are called the bhavas in Vedic astrology which means "field of action". In Vedic astrology there is a more extensive knowledge of the meanings with the houses. All these meanings must be memorized and understood to be able to make accurate predictions. Essentially you will begin to understand the meanings of life when the areas of life of each house are deeply understood.

Understanding each house is a progression in life and rules areas that pertain to the four Aims in life. The numbers of the houses also relate to the element and sign that is associated with the house from the natural zodiac. You will better understand these concepts as we go through the four aims in life, their elements and signs.

Four Aims of Life

Dharma – fire signs: Aries, Leo and Sagittarius – 1, 5 and 9th houses purpose, expression, and spirit

Artha – earth signs: Taurus, Virgo, and Capricorn 2, 6 and 10th houses money and work and career

Kama – Air signs: Gemini, Libra, and Aquarius 3,7 and 11 desire for relationship, siblings, marriage and friends (3,7 and 11 houses),

Moksha – water signs: emotions Cancer, Scorpio and Pisces 4, 8 and 12 spiritual liberation – beginning and end of life

12 Houses: In depth meanings

1st house
Entrance into the world, birth, self, personality, ego, confidence, physical body, head, physical appearance, accidents, death of pets

2nd house
Early childhood, family, wealth and money earned, self-confidence based on early upbring, voice, mouth in terms of speech and foods we eat and drink, what we consume, teeth, face, eyesight, particularly the right eye, partner's inheritances, divorce

3rd house
Communication skills, all areas of connection to others, such as telephones, computers, technology, internet, thinking mind, brothers and sisters, hands, arms and lungs, writing, creativity, performers and entertainers, courage, life force, drive and ambition, will power, travel usually short trips by car, learning and education especially early education

4th house
Security, home, real estate, mother, family, end of life, heredity, happiness, past, soul, heart, blood flow to the heart, breasts, chest, seat of power, stomach, degrees obtained – doctorates, family provides opportunity for education

5th house
Children, creativity, theater, authorship, past life good karma due in this lifetime, talent, intelligence, giving advice to others, astrology, investments, stock market, need to express yourself, heart blood flow from the heart, dating, courtship, opening the heart, mother's wealth

6th house
Health, nutrition, diet, health practices, fitness, exercise, work in terms of conditions around work – coworkers and

employees, healers, service industries, restaurants, flight attendants, pilots, doctors, nurses, counselors, therapy, open enemies, lawsuits, struggles, debts, intestines, ability to digest foods, pets, children's wealth

7th house
Marriage, business partners, partnerships that have contractual agreements, how we relate in a relationship, marriage partners, business success, kidneys and external sexual organs, grandmothers

8th house
Death, money through others such as inheritance or marriage partner, psychological depth, psychology, metaphysics, past, disgrace, humiliation, what is beyond this world, life after death, mediums, psychics, suicide, murder, unnatural death, rape, scandals, research, detectives, deep scientific analysis, transformation, rebirth, change, need to be in control, addictions, astrology, shadow side, manipulation, large sums of unearned money, settlements, insurance, lotteries, marriage partner's wealth, sexual organs and colon – elimination system

9th house
Beliefs, spirituality, laws, legal pursuits, legal system, lawyers, justice, judges, judgment, professors, teachers, father, and everything pertaining to him, luck and fortune, travel – long distances, higher learning – university, grandchildren, hips

10th house
Career, sense of purpose, profession, reputation, how the world sees you, social standing ownership of business, the boss, experiences with career work and your boss, father's money and success, fame and recognition for abilities and work, knees

11th House
Friends, groups and organizations, important influential people you know, great gains especially from your work or career, ability to organize and manage people, the oldest sibling, mon-

ey that comes in large one lump sums, sales of large items such as real estate, humanity, house of wealth, mother's psychology, loss and death of the mother, ankles and legs

12th house

Endings, end of life, losses, deep spiritual realizations, anything pertaining to the past, places of escape or confinement, sleep, dreams, hospitals, prisons, ashrams, foreign travel, vacations, foreigners, movies, movies theaters, outer space, what is beyond this world, death as in end of life, forgiveness, spiritual healing, healers, working in hospitals, loss of children, retirement, feet

Planets

The planets are the energy in a chart. The planets have a certain power and represent certain things in a chart aside from what house they are in or rule. Below are the pure meanings of the planets. But again, a big feature concerning the planets is that they will carry the meanings of houses to the houses they sit in. Below is the pure energy the planets are. They are called karakas in Vedic astrology meaning what they are the indicator of.

Here are the planet's natural rulership's and energy

Sun: Natural malefic:
Father, Spirit, life force, physical body, health, heart, ego, vitality, sense of self, fame, authority, bosses

Moon: Natural benefic:
Mother, mind, consciousness, emotions, security, feelings, past, caring for others, popularity, home, subconscious mind

- Exception; it is believed the Moon is not as benefic when it is a dark Moon, and more benefic if it is a bright Moon, this is according to the phase of the Moon being dark- new Moon, bright – full Moon.

Mercury: Natural benefic:
Communications, speech, writing, thinking process, thoughts, school, education, travel, intelligence, sense of humor, youth, twins, analytical mind, aunts and uncles

Venus: Natural benefic:
Wife in a male's chart, feminine spirit, creativity, arts, beauty, grace, charm, refinement, luxuries, wealth, love, romance, relationships, sexual attraction, comfort

Mars: Natural malefic:
Siblings, Masculinity, energy, action, passions, courage, athletics, motivation, determination, competition, attacks, aggression, anger, violence, accidents, injury, enemies, war, weapons, fire, selfishness, real estate

Jupiter: Natural benefic:
Children, Wife's spouse, professors, expansion, opportunities, wealth, fortune, luck, optimism, generosity, teachers, spirituality, truth, laws, religion, college, long distance travel

Saturn: Natural malefic:
Discipline, order, structure, endurance, karma, oppression, separation, pessimism, worry, death, disease, setbacks, delays, land, sorrow, concentration, dependable, limitation, bondage, endings, fear, poverty

Rahu: Natural malefic:
Desire, worldly success, fame, power, prestige, inner turmoil, addictions, extremes, obsessive behavior, foreigners, foreign lands, collective trends, alcohol, drugs, fear

Ketu: Natural malefic:
Loss, negation, lack of confidence, fantasies, death, indecision, spirituality, psychic ability, fire, injury, accidents, wisdom, liberation, illusions, fear

Outer Planets

They affect and change the planet's energy that they aspect, conjunct or opposition, they infuse the personal planets with their intensity and meaning, but they do not rule signs or houses. They mainly have a malefic influence but can bring some benefic qualities.

Uranus: Change, invention, great awakening, electric, rebellion, erratic behavior, sudden and unexpected events, accidents, shock, lightening, earthquakes, computers, airplanes, astrology

Neptune: Illusion, deception, scandals, fog, confusion, denial, photography, films, movies, drugs, alcohol, glamor, romance, spirituality, fantasies, devotion, cults, oil, gas, water, psychic, sensitivity

Pluto: Explosiveness, power, control, manipulation, surrender, transformation, big money, sex, big government, compulsions, underworld, birth and death, secrets, rebirth

Nakshatras

Indian (Vedic) astrology is true to the stars! What I mean about this is, that the actual movement of the stars in procession of the equinoxes keeps the fixed stars in the portions of the zodiac that they are so relative to. Procession of the equinoxes is why the sidereal placements (used in Vedic astrology) are the true placements astronomically of the planets and stars. Tropical astrology used in Western astrology does not take this movement into account. This is why the placements of the stars and planets are different for both systems. At this point in time, the sidereal placements have moved 23–24 degrees backward in the zodiac from the tropical placements used in Western tropical astrology. The stars are continually moving one degree backwards in the zodiac every 72 years.

Tropical Western astrology is based on the Sun which creates the seasons that stay constant year after year. Sideral (Vedic) astrology is based on the movement of the stars.

The meanings of the stars stay true as the fixed stars remain in the signs that the stars give their powerful meanings, such as the fixed star Regulus, which is the heart of the Lion always gives the sign Leo its kingship, as well as the star Antares which is the heart of the Scorpion will always remain in Scorpio. And Aldebaran the red star will always be the red eye of the bull in Taurus. Western tropical astrology places these stars in other signs now, which does not make sense.

These important stars and the groupings of all the stars are divided up in the heavens in sections of 13 degrees and 20 minutes in Vedic astrology. The entire zodiac of 360 degrees divided up in these segments equates to 27 divisions and these are what Vedic astrology called the 27 nakshatras. Their rich meanings (nakshatras) are essentially derived from the stars in their portions. The nakshatra Rohini which is in Taurus is called the "Red One" in reference to the red star Aldebaran which is the red eye of the bull – Taurus.

We will touch on some of the meanings of the nakshatras in this analysis throughout this book. The nakshatras are true Indian astrology as they are each also ruled by a planet. The nakshatra's planetary rulership is furthermore used in the predictive system used in Vedic astrology called the Dashas. There are many dasha systems used inVedic astrology but the one used most often by most Vedic astrologers is called Vimshottari dasha system, and this will be referred to throughout this book as well.

With the basics explained, we are ready to explore my unique findings that I have discovered in my many years of practice and experience.

Chapter 2

The Moon in Vedic Astrology
Moon's Yogas, Isolated, Conjunct Rahu, Ketu

The Moon is so important in Vedic astrology. It is a lunar based system because the dasha system that gives the outline of when events are due to play out in our lives is based on the Moon. Western astrology's core is based on the Sun. Since the Moon rules our mind, consciousness and especially how we feel it is imperative to study a chart from the Moon as the ascendant. You will begin to discover how multi-faceted astrology is as we will look at all the planets as the starting point. It is a hard concept to understand in the beginning so let this slowly sink in as you go through all my concepts. Our lives are multi-dimensional, and we have many layers in our psyches.

Now we are going to cover the depth of meaning of the Moon and you will understand why it is so very important.

Isolated Moon

Since the Moon rules our feelings, it likes to feel connected to other planets, giving us a feeling of connection to others. An isolated Moon is when the Moon is on one side of the chart with no planets around it. If there are no planets in the sign/houses before or after the Moon it is considered isolated.

The Moon is the planet that is karaka (meaning indicator of) the mother. So, planets associated with the Moon can also give indications of the mother and her life experiences.

When the Moon is isolated the person feels alone, isolated without the support of others. A sense of abandonment keeps one feeling alone at some point in life, particularly as a child, alienated by others.

The Moon is involved in many Yogas based on other planets surrounding or aspecting the Moon. These are very important in understanding how a person feels throughout life.

When planets are in the 2nd house/Sign from the Moon it is Sunapha yoga, which means gains financially and connection to others. When planets are in the 12th house/sign from the Moon, Anapha yoga it pertains to release or letting go of things in life, and when there are both planets 2nd and 12 houses from the Moon, surrounding the Moon a person feels supported and has a positive give and take in life, this is called Durudhara yoga. The Moon loves to be connected to other planets.

When natural benefics are in an angle (kendra) from the Moon it is also a very benefic experience for the Moon. When Jupiter is in houses 1,4,7 and 10th from the Moon it is called Gaja Kesari yoga which gives power, leadership and prestige in life. Also, Venus in the 10th from the Moon is Amala yoga (when a natural benefic is in the 10th house from the Moon). This brings great advantages to the career and success. Therefore, the positioning of planet's placements from the Moon are imperative to a person's ability to achieve success and happiness in life.

The nodes of the Moon, Rahu and Ketu are not planets and do not create good yogas with the Moon. They are detrimental to the mind and consciousness of the person and can make things worse when there are no planets surrounding the Moon, meaning in the same house or the two houses surrounding the house the Moon and Rahu or Ketu are in.

But Rahu and Ketu can form a Raja yoga (yoga of kings – great prestige and power) when they sit together in a kendra (1, 4, 7, or 10) or a trikona house (1, 5. And 9) and the planet that is conjunct with them rules a Kendra or trikona. There must be a combination of each, meaning if they sit in a kendra then the planet must rule a trikona or if they sit together in a trikona then the planet rules a kendra. Raja yoga is when there is the combination of a kendra and a trikona. The kendras are the most powerful and strong houses while the trikona houses are the fortunate and lucky houses, together they give rise to luck, power and fortune. The 1st house can be used as a kendra or a trikona, to complete the requirements of a raja yoga.

In the case of the Moon with Rahu, if they are together in the 10th house (kendra) and the Moon rules the ascendant (Cancer rising), then the Moon rules a trikona. This Rahu with the Moon would produce positive lucky events instead of difficult results.

The Moon is also associated with the public and masses of people. A strong Moon can bring attention or fame as we will see in the charts to be analyzed. The Moon in the 10th house can represent fame as the 10th house is our career, reputation and being in the public eye.

Moon with Rahu

The Moon is our emotions, how we feel and the mind as to how we think and believe predominately from childhood experiences. Rahu is a malefic in Vedic astrology and can cause paranoia and extremes in behavior. Both nodes rule intense fear, but Rahu can also rule intense desires. Rahu with the Moon will always bring extremes with deep feelings and reactions.

The sign/house that the Moon is in will bring extremes according to this area of life. Intense desires bring over the top reactions throughout life to achieve goals in life, but with an unrealistic extreme to achieve what they want. The mother can be an extremist in some way, extreme desires and needs or a personality that is bigger than life.

Moon with Ketu

Ketu is the indicator of losses and when conjunct the Moon there is an inner search. Wherever Ketu is by house/sign there seems to be a feeling that something is missing in that area of life, where it never feels whole or complete. There may be a disconnect with the mother or the mother had a difficult life. Sometimes it can indicate a very spiritual mother, searching for answers due to the great difficulties in her life.

Moon in Cancer

The Moon rules Cancer and when the Moon is in this sign it intensifies the emotions and feelings to the maximum point. The house it sits in becomes an emotionally intense area of life. This house will be a focus throughout life.

Moon in Taurus and Scorpio

The Moon is exalted in Taurus. This means the Moon is strongest for good results in this sign. Taurus is the sign of money and sensuality and those with a Taurus Moon love anything pertaining to the senses, food, beauty, sexuality and the good things in life. The Moon here can bring wealth and happiness and help in achieving their goals. The house the Moon is in will be important, intensifying the area of life this house rules. This placement is good for the mother.

The Moon in Scorpio is debilitated which means it is weak, and the results and desires are delayed and sometimes problematic. The sign Scorpio is very intense with deep desires that can at times give dissatisfaction with life's results. The sign Scorpio will give wealth and affluence but sometimes the wealth doesn't give happiness. This placement is not easy or good for the mother.

Kemadruma Moon

This is when the Moon has no association to other planets, no Moon's yogas or any aspect to other planets. The Moon is isolated with no connections. The person feels totally unconnected and isolated from other people. The mind is deranged in some way due to loneliness, isolation and no support from others. The house it is in will be where the deep-seated problems will be felt the most.

Moon in the 10th house: Fame

The Moon in the 10th house of career, recognition, social standing, reputation and fame proves very powerful as many actors have come into great fame and stardom with the Moon in the 10th house. This can represent the masses of people seeing these people as great stars. Those with a Moon in the 10th house will be noted in their field of expertise and will be well known, maybe in their community or possibly worldwide.

9th h.	10th h.	11th h.	12th h.
☓ ♓	♈ ☊ 00:19 Ash ☽ 21:14 Bha	♉ ♂ 15:40 Roh ☿ 17:08 Roh	♊ ☉ 07:34 Ard ♅ 07:35 Ard ♀ 25:16 Pun
8th h. ♒	Meryl Streep Wed 06-22-1949 08:05:00 Summit, NJ, New Jersey USA Timezone: 5 DST: 1 Latitude: 40N43'00 Longitude: 74W22'00 Ayanamsha: -23:08:58 Lahiri		⊕ ASC 09:35 Pus ♀ 21:42 Asl 1st h.
7th h. ♑ ♃℞ 07:22 USh			♌ ♄ 08:25 Mag 2nd h.
♐	♏ ☋ 00:19 Cht	♎	♍ ♆℞ 19:14 Has
6th h.	5th h.	4th h.	3rd h.

17

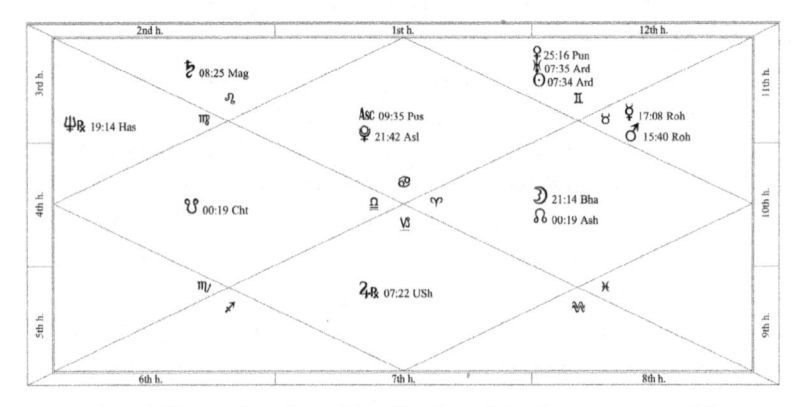

Meryl Streep is often described as "the best actress of her generation", Streep is particularly known for her versatility and accent adaptability. She has received numerous accolades throughout her career spanning over four decades, including a record 21 Academy Award nominations, winning three, and a record 32 Golden Globe Award nominations, winning eight. She has also received two British Academy Film Awards, two Screen Actors Guild Awards, and three Primetime Emmy Awards, in addition to nominations for a Tony Award and six Grammy Awards.

Her Moon is with Rahu in the 10th house. Being with Rahu the Moon is radically expanded. This must be the reason why she can immerse herself in her roles, making her one of the best in her field. The Moon rules her first house with Cancer rising. The ruler of the 1st house is the focus of life and the house it resides in will be the life's focus. When the ruler of the 1st is in the 10th house her life is defined by her career.

An important Moon's yoga is the Sunapha yoga, where planets excluding the Sun or Rahu/Ketu are in the 2nd house from the Moon. Mercury and Mars are in the 2nd house counted from the Moon. This gives her powerful earning capabilities. The Moon is also supported with this Moon's yoga. She has felt supported in childhood, and this gives emotional support and security. This even applies to the Malefics Mars and Saturn. Additionally, these two planets in the 11th house of great gains add to her earning power. Remember the 11th house is the 2nd house from the 10th house meaning the ability to make money from one's career.

In this case the Moon conjunct Rahu in the 10th house is extremely powerful for fame and her acting career. The Moon with Rahu forms a raja yoga, because with Cancer rising they reside in the 10 house which is a kendra and the Moon rules the 1st house which is a trikona creating a raja yoga.

Her Moon and Rahu in the 10th house of career brought her fame and fortune.

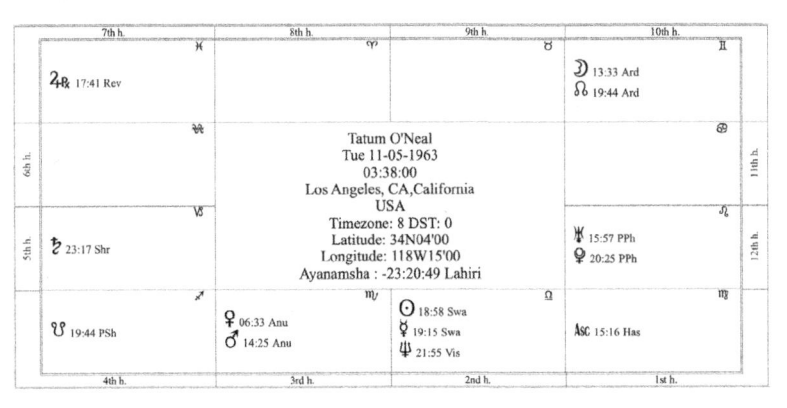

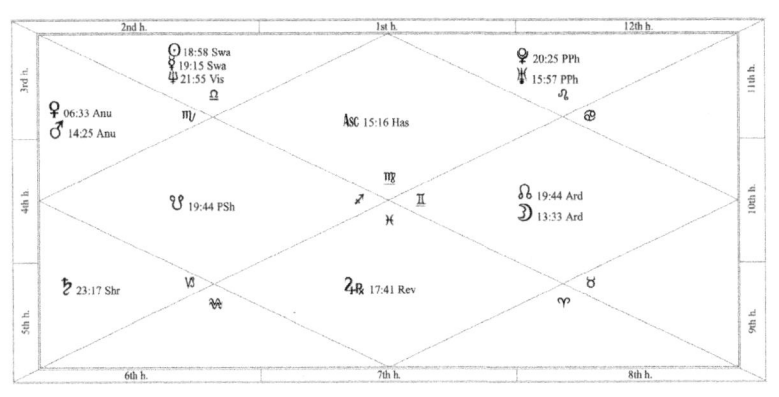

7th h.	8th h.	9th h.	10th h.
♓ 4℞ 17:41 Rev	♈	♉ ☽ 13:33 Ard ☊ 19:44 Ard	♊
6th h. ♒	Tatum O'Neal Tue 11-05-1963 03:38:00 Los Angeles, CA, California USA Timezone: 8 DST: 0 Latitude: 34N04'00 Longitude: 118W15'00 Ayanamsha: -23:20:49 Lahiri		11th h. ♋
5th h. ♑ ♄ 23:17 Shr			12th h. ♌ ♅ 15:57 PPh ♀ 20:25 PPh
4th h. ♐ ☋ 19:44 PSh	3rd h. ♏ ♀ 06:33 Anu ♂ 14:25 Anu	2nd h. ♎ ☉ 18:58 Swa ☿ 19:15 Swa ♆ 21:55 Vis	1st h. ♍ Asc 15:16 Has

2nd h.	1st h.	12th h.
3rd h. ♀ 06:33 Anu ♂ 14:25 Anu ♏	☉ 18:58 Swa ☿ 19:15 Swa ♆ 21:55 Vis ♎ Asc 15:16 Has	♀ 20:25 PPh ♅ 15:57 PPh ♌ 11th h.
4th h. ☋ 19:44 PSh	♍ ♐ ♓	☊ 19:44 Ard ☽ 13:33 Ard 10th h.
5th h. ♄ 23:17 Shr ♑ ♒	4℞ 17:41 Rev	♉ ♈ 9th h.
6th h.	7th h.	8th h.

19

Isolated Moon conjunct Rahu

Tatum is the youngest person to ever win an Academy Award, winning at age 10 for her performance in *Paper Moon* (1973) opposite her father, Ryan O'Neal. But her childhood experiences were far from normal as she was the daughter of very famous movie stars in Los Angeles. Her mother was actress Joanna Moore who went into a gradual but deep decline after her divorce from O'Neal. Depression set in and she developed a severe amphetamine and alcohol addiction. Multiple arrests over time for drunk driving (one much later resulted in the loss of three fingers) led to her losing custody of her children in 1970. In her book, Tatum detailed that she had been through hunger, neglect, underage drinking, underage driving, car crashes, suicide attempts, and had a history of drug addiction.

The isolated Moon in the 10th house with Rahu represents the extremes of isolation and neglect she experienced with her family. The Moon indicates the mother and her mother had problems with addictions which she passed down to Tatum. Rahu in many cases can indicate addictions. The Moon in the nakshatra Ardra is especially troublesome as this nakshatra is said to be severe and cause sadness as its symbol is a teardrop. The Moon in this nakshatra will indicate overall sadness, particularly for the mother.

Other planets aspecting the Moon always add to the way individuals express themselves as well as to how they think. In her case Mars fully aspects her Moon with its 8th aspect. Mars' full Vedic aspects are 4 and 8 signs from where it is located. This can add to the mind being agitated and disturbed as Mars can indicate anger.

Furthermore, when Rahu is in the 10th house then Ketu is in the 4th house, and wherever Ketu is in a chart indicates that something is missing or not whole or complete. It also can mean loss and her home and mother left her feeling no sense of security. It is no wonder Tatum turned to drugs at such an early age with no security, abuse, and love from both of her parents.

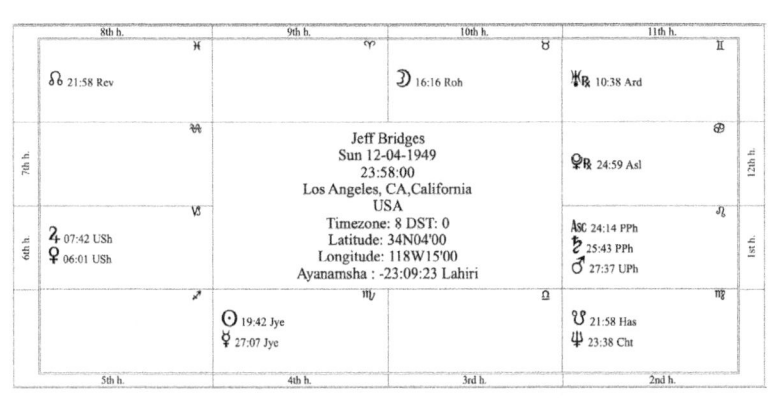

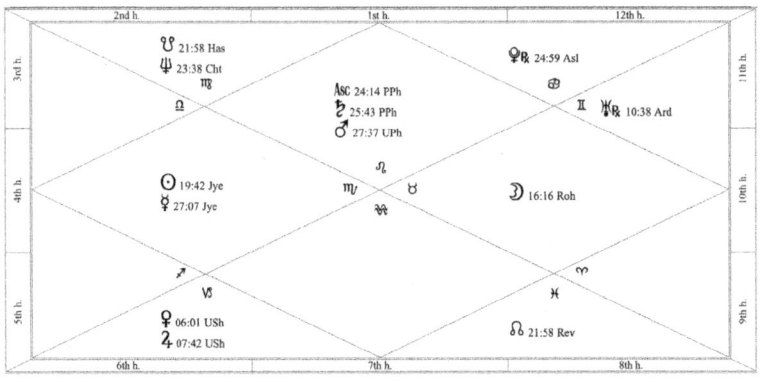

8th h.	9th h.	10th h.	11th h.
☊ 21:58 Rev		☽ 16:16 Roh	♅ R 10:38 Ard
	Jeff Bridges Sun 12-04-1949 23:58:00 Los Angeles, CA, California USA Timezone: 8 DST: 0 Latitude: 34N04'00 Longitude: 118W15'00 Ayanamsha: -23:09:23 Lahiri		♀ R 24:59 Asl
♃ 07:42 USh ♀ 06:01 USh			Asc 24:14 PPh ♄ 25:43 PPh ♂ 27:37 UPh
	☉ 19:42 Jye ☿ 27:07 Jye		☋ 21:58 Has ♆ 23:38 Cht
5th h.	4th h.	3rd h.	2nd h.

Jeff Bridges comes from a prominent acting family and appeared on the television series *Sea Hunt* (1958–1960) alongside his father, Lloyd Bridges, and brother, Beau Bridges. He received the Academy Award for Best Actor for his performance as an alcoholic singer in the 2009 film *Crazy Heart*. And two Golden Globe awards. His acting career has been extremely successful. He appeared in almost a hundred movies with great success, being nominated for academy awards numerous times. He is also a noted musician and recording artist.

Bridges has studied Buddhism and has described himself as "A Buddhistly bent guy." On most days, he meditates for half an hour before beginning work on a film set. He has learned Transcendental Meditation.

His Moon is in the 10th house exalted in Taurus. This placement is superior for career success. Even the nakshatra Rohini is the best placement for the Moon. This catapulted him into fame and gave him great success.

But as a child his older brother Beau was said to have to look after him. The isolation of this Moon can represent the lack of a mother's attention. Even though the Moon is isolated it is a full Moon meaning it is in opposition to the Sun. A full Moon is considered a bright Moon which is very auspicious because it means the mind is bright and full of light and conscious awareness. This adds to the power and success this Moon produces.

His Moon may be isolated, but it receives many aspects from other planets, Mercury, Jupiter and Saturn. Saturn's full aspect is 3 and 10th signs from where it is placed, and Jupiter is 5 and 9 signs from where it is placed. This adds to the manifestation power of his conscious and aware Moon indicating his mind. Another interesting feature is when Mercury and the Moon aspect each other by either conjunction or opposition the mind is over stimulated. This means those with this aspect over think everything and cannot turn off the thinking mind, in other words the mind is on overdrive all the time.

Chapter 2

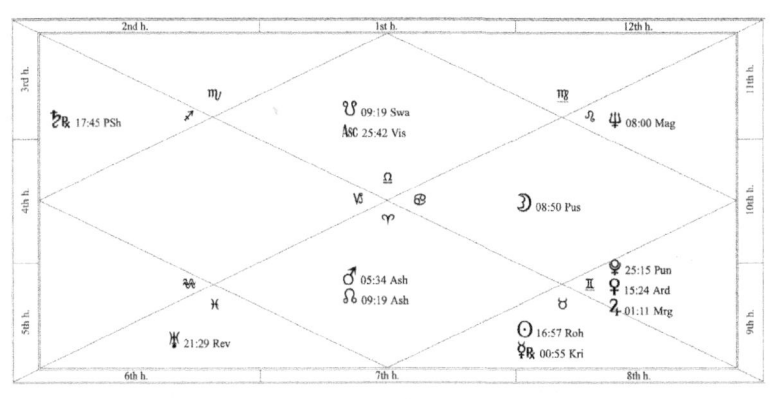

6th h.	7th h.	8th h.	9th h.
♅ 21:29 Rev (♓)	♂ 05:34 Ash / ☋ 09:19 Ash (♈)	♀R 00:55 Kri / ☉ 16:57 Roh (♉)	♃ 01:11 Mrg / ♀ 15:24 Ard / ☿ 25:15 Pun (♊)
(♒) 5th h.	Clint Eastwood Sat 05-31-1930 17:35:00 San Francisco, CA, California USA Timezone: 8 DST: 0 Latitude: 37N47'00 Longitude: 122W25'00 Ayanamsha : -22:52:57 Lahiri		☽ 08:50 Pus (♋) 10th h.
(♑) 4th h.			♆ 08:00 Mag (♌) 11th h.
♄R 17:45 PSh (♐) 3rd h.	(♏) 2nd h.	☊ 09:19 Swa / Asc 25:42 Vis (♎) 1st h.	(♍) 12th h.

Clint Eastwood, actor, director and producer is another example of the Moon in the 10th house which can denote success in the career and give a sense of life purpose. He has been recognized with multiple awards and nominations for his work in film, television, and music. His widest reception has been in film work, for which he has received Academy Awards, Directors Guild of America Awards, Golden Globe Awards, and People's Choice Awards, among others. His career has spanned from the 1950s till today at the age of 92 his most current release 2022 'Cry Macho".

In this case Eastwood's Moon is in Cancer the most sensitive sign of all as it is in its own sign of rulership, and it being in the 10th house means it is the ruler as well of this career house empowering his sense of purpose in his field of work. The Moon's nakshatra is also one of the best and very spiritual nakshatra, Pushya. In 1975, Eastwood publicly proclaimed his participation in Transcendental Meditation when he appeared on *The Merv Griffin Show* with Maharishi Mahesh Yogi, the founder of Transcendental Meditation. He has meditated every morning for years.

His Mars is very powerful conjunct Rahu, and Mars aspects the Moon by its 4th full aspect. This gives drive, ambition and perseverance in his work as the Moon is activated in the 10th house.

His success is due to the strong placement of the Moon and the very auspicious Anapha yoga. This is when planets are in the 12th house from the Moon. He has both Jupiter and Venus in the 12th house from the Moon (Pluto is not counted). This represents someone who is very generous and giving. And he is doubly blessed as there are two benefics 12th from the Moon. He feels powerfully surrounded and supported by others.

11th h.	12th h.	1st h.	2nd h.
☊ 29:47 Rev	♂ 28:49 Kri	ASC 17:24 Roh	
10th h. ☽ 23:37 PBh	Michael Jackson Fri 08-29-1958 23:30:00 Gary USA Timezone: 6 DST: 1 Latitude: 41N35'36 Longitude: 87W20'47 Ayanamsha : -23:16:55 Lahiri	♅ 20:13 Asl ♀ 23:59 Asl	3rd h.
9th h.		☿℞ 02:03 Mag ♀ 08:53 Mag ☉ 13:01 Mag	4th h.
8th h.	♄ 25:50 Jye	♃ 05:17 Cht ♆ 09:17 Swa	☋ 29:47 Cht
	7th h.	6th h.	5th h.

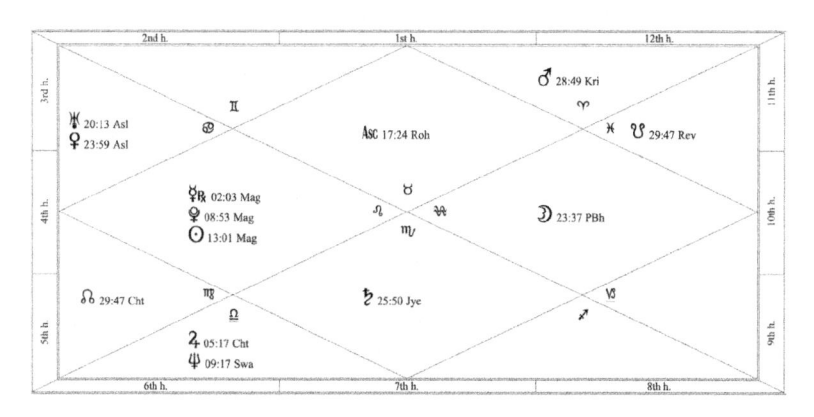

```
        | 2nd h.              | 1st h.                          | 12th h.           |
3rd h.  |                     |         ♂ 28:49 Kri             |          11th h.  |
        |  ♅ 20:13 Asl   ⊕    |            ♈                    |  ♓  ☋ 29:47 Rev  |
        |  ♀ 23:59 Asl        | Asc 17:24 Roh                   |                   |
        |                     |                                 |                   |
4th h.  |     ⚷℞ 02:03 Mag    |        ♉                        |                   |
        |     ♀ 08:53 Mag     |   ♌       ♒                     |  ☽ 23:37 PBh     |
        |     ☉ 13:01 Mag     |        ♍                        |           10th h. |
        |                     |                                 |                   |
        | ☊ 29:47 Cht    ♍    | ♄ 25:50 Jye                     |        ♑          |
5th h.  |               ♎     |                                 |    ♐     9th h.   |
        |  ♃ 05:17 Cht        |                                 |                   |
        |  ♆ 09:17 Swa        |                                 |                   |
        | 6th h.              | 7th h.                          | 8th h.            |
```

Another wildly famous personality that everyone worldwide knows is Michael Jackson. He needs no introduction! I have always used the time of 11:30 pm even though there are many reports of different times for his birth. Many years ago, I met an astrologer at a conference, Basel Farrington, who was a dedicated fan of Jackson attending many of his concerts. He told me that at one of his concerts he got very close to the stage and asked Jackson "what time were you born?" He replied clearly "before midnight!" This time of course places his Moon in the 10th house of fame.

This chart makes the most sense since his Moon in the 10th is isolated, meaning feelings of isolation and lack of emotional support. He was born on a full Moon which brings power and brightness to the Moon representing a bright Moon. It is in the sign Aquarius denoting an unusual unique talent and personality, and the nakshatra is Purva Bhadrapada which can be a visionary but can at times represent that there are two sides to his personality or possibly two-faced.

His Moon in the 10th house is a bit like Jeff Bridges in that it is a Full Moon in the 10th house aspected by both Mercury and Jupiter, but the sign and nakshatra give a completely different disposition. The Full Moon in the 10th house aspected by Mercury and Jupiter give a mind on overdrive and opportunities for success.

Probably the most profound feature in Jackson's chart is that Pluto is opposed to the Moon and conjunct the Sun. Pluto can indicate control, manipulation, and abuse, as his father controlled and abused him. The Sun is the indicator of the father and the Sun conjunct Pluto in the 4th house of the family and home indicates a perverse condition with his family and home. It is known that the father used to whip the kids with a belt if their performances were not perfect. His father controlled the family while he had many affairs while still married. Michael was never allowed to have a normal childhood, working constantly he yearned for childhood experiences developing his obsession with young boys. His emotional problems lead to his demise of disgrace and humiliation. Pluto is associated with obsessions, disgrace and humiliation and it is conjunct Mercury which rules the mind and thinking. Plus, it is conjunct the Sun and opposed the Moon, the two luminaries representing the mind and spirit and the father and mother.

12th h.	1st h.	2nd h.	3rd h.
	♅℞ 05:41 Ash Asc 12:17 Ash		
	CHARLES MANSON Mon 11-12-1934 16:40:00 CINCINNATI USA Timezone: 5 DST: 0 Latitude: 39N09'43 Longitude: 84W27'25 Ayanamsha: -22:57:03 Lahiri	♀℞ 03:04 Pun ☋ 11:10 Pus	
♄ 28:48 Dha ☊ 11:10 Shr ☽ 11:03 Shr		♆ 21:17 PPh ♂ 21:52 PPh	
		☿ 10:02 Swa ♃ 14:09 Swa ♀ 25:21 Vis ☉ 26:52 Vis	
9th h.	8th h.	7th h.	6th h.

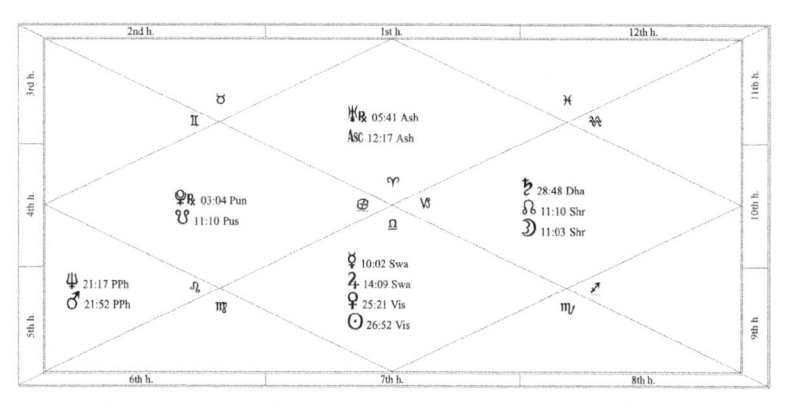

The Moon in Vedic Astrology Moon's Yogas, Isolated, Conjunct Rahu, Ketu

Chapter 2

```
| 2nd h.                          | 1st h.                          | 12th h.                         |
|                                 | ♅℞ 05:41 Ash                    |                                 |
|           ♉                     | ASC 12:17 Ash                   |           ♓                     |
|           ♊                     |                                 |           ♒                     |
|                                 |                                 |                                 |
|                                 |          ♈                      |  ♄ 28:48 Dha                    |
|   ♇℞ 03:04 Pun                  |    ⊕        ♑                   |  ☊ 11:10 Shr                    |
|   ☋ 11:10 Pus                   |             ♎                   |  ☽ 11:03 Shr                    |
|                                 |                                 |                                 |
|                                 |  ☿ 10:02 Swa                    |                                 |
|   ♆ 21:17 PPh                   |  ♃ 14:09 Swa                    |                                 |
|   ♂ 21:52 PPh    ♌              |  ♀ 25:21 Vis                    |     ♐                           |
|                  ♍              |  ☉ 26:52 Vis                    |     ♏                           |
| 6th h.                          | 7th h.                          | 8th h.                          |
```

Charles Manson is famous with the Moon in the 10th house, or should I say infamous. His notoriety is not because of his accolades but the cult and murders he instigated. He led the Manson Family, a cult based in California, in the late 1960s. The members committed a series of nine murders at four locations in July and August 1969. In 1971, Manson was convicted of first-degree murder and conspiracy to commit murder for the deaths of seven people, including the film actress Sharon Tate. The prosecution contended that, while Manson never directly ordered the murders, his ideology constituted an overt act of conspiracy.

His mother was an extreme alcoholic prostitute and imprisoned while he was a child. Since the Moon indicates the mother, his Moon is very afflicted, influenced by the conjunction with Rahu and conjunct Saturn. As with Tatum O'Neal he has the Moon and Rahu in the 10th house and Ketu in the 4th house indicating neglect that was abusive while a child. But in his case, he also has Pluto in the 4th house in opposition to his Moon, Rahu and Saturn. Pluto in the 4th house as seen in Jackson's chart dealt with abuse in the home. Pluto is associated with obsessions and disgrace, but also can contribute to a certain charisma that gave him the ability to mesmerize, hypnotize and control his followers. Home, family, and mother are totally afflicted as the Moon representing consciousness

27

is destroyed, and because it is in the 10th house, he became very famous for his cult and murders.

The Moon is exactly conjunct Rahu, and the closeness of degree will intensify any aspect. Rahu conjunct the Moon will intensify the effects of extremes with obsessions, mother and internalized fears, but of course his Moon is compounded with the aspects of Saturn and Pluto. His Moon is in Capricorn and the nakshatra Shravana can be very intelligent, but the aspects of Rahu and Saturn in Capricorn and the opposition of Pluto affect the nature of this Moon tremendously.

Mansion was given the death sentence but as the death sentence was overturned in the state of California, he was given life in prison, he died in incarceration in 2017 at the age of 83.

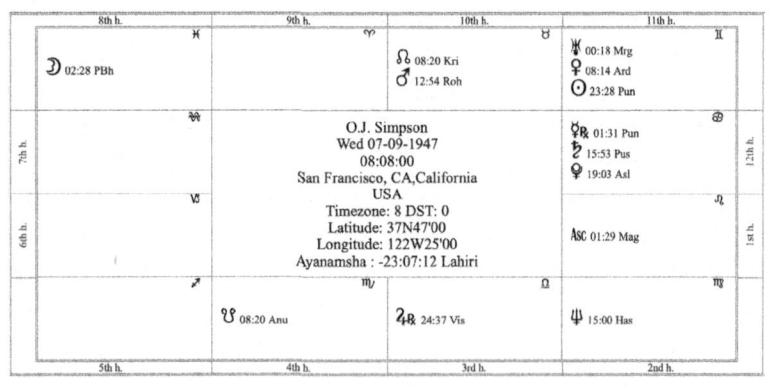

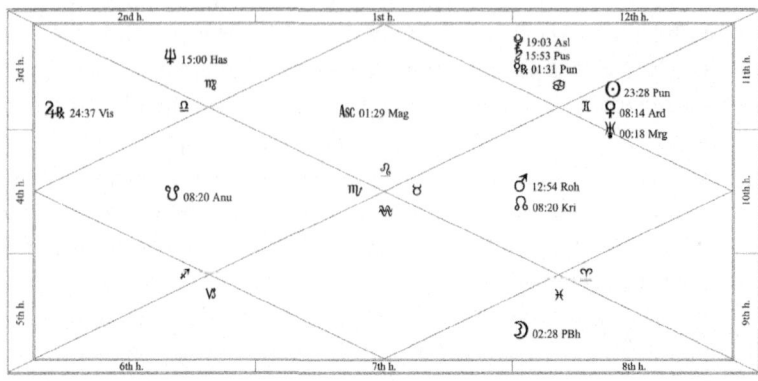

Kemadruma Moon

This is another important situation for the Moon that can totally take on extreme karmic implications. Kemadruma Moon is rare as it is when the Moon is totally unassociated or aspected by other planets. It is totally disconnected from any connections to the other planets. This gives a very dysfunctional mind and disturbed emotions.

OJ Simpson has Kemadruma Moon, explaining why his life is fraught full of emotional discord with relationships and now a life of emotional isolation. He was an American football running back, actor, and broadcaster. Once a popular figure with the U.S. public, he is now best known for being tried for the murders of his former wife, Nicole Brown Simpson, and her friend Ron Goldman. Simpson was acquitted of the murders in criminal court but was later found responsible for both deaths in a civil trial. The civil court awarded a $33.5 million judgment against him in 1997 for the victims' wrongful deaths. In 2000, Simpson moved to Miami, Florida to avoid paying on the liability judgment, which, as of 2022, remains mostly unpaid.

OJ's Moon sits completely alone isolated from all the planets in his chart. It doesn't even participate in any of the Moon's special Yogas. It is in Pisces in the nakshatra Purva Bhadrapada like Michael Jackson, which can be a very sharp and difficult nakshatra, as it is known to have two sides to the personality which can sometimes be conflicting and appear two faced.

But the most telling part of all is that the Moon is in the 8th house, which is the most difficult house of the chart and can denote disgrace and humiliation. As it sits alone, he feels isolated, unconnected with a lack of relationship with others. The 8th house even rules murder, death, and scandals. He must feel emotionally disconnected with lack of feeling or conscience or a psychopath, which is someone with no feeling of compassion for others.

Other indications that add to his behavior is that Neptune is opposite the Moon (Neptune is an outer planet not considered in this yoga). Neptune represents confusion, deceit, lies and scandals which is certainly a major part of his life. Another major indicator of the negative results in his life is that the Moon in Pisces and Purva Bhadrapada, both are ruled by Jupiter and Jupiter sits in the 8th house from the Moon, which accentuates further all the meanings of the 8th house.

On December 14, 2021, Simpson was released from parole early for good behavior, releasing him from the previous conditions of his release and effectively making him a completely free man. But many clubs and organizations have banned his participation, and he is not fully accepted back in society.

Moon conjunct Rahu

The Moon in the 10th house indicates fame or recognition in their area of expertise. Rahu conjunct the Moon always intensifies the Moon, which rules our mind, consciousness and awareness. It will give intense desires, need for attention, and possibly a famous or over-the-top personality for the mother. Rahu can also cause a paranoid mind with an obsessional quality. In some cases, this indicates an addictive personality therefore problems with addictions. When the Moon is conjunct Rahu, remember this always places Ketu in the 7th house, indicating problems in relationships.

The next set of charts with Rahu conjunct the Moon will prove out the qualities of Rahu conjunct the Moon.

The Moon in Vedic Astrology Moon's Yogas, Isolated, Conjunct Rahu, Ketu

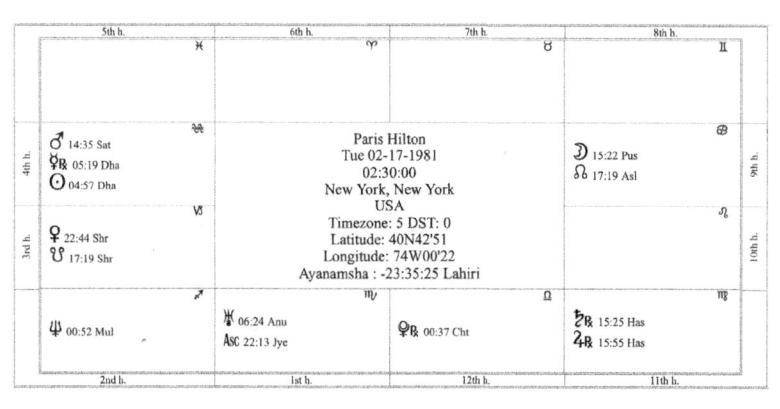

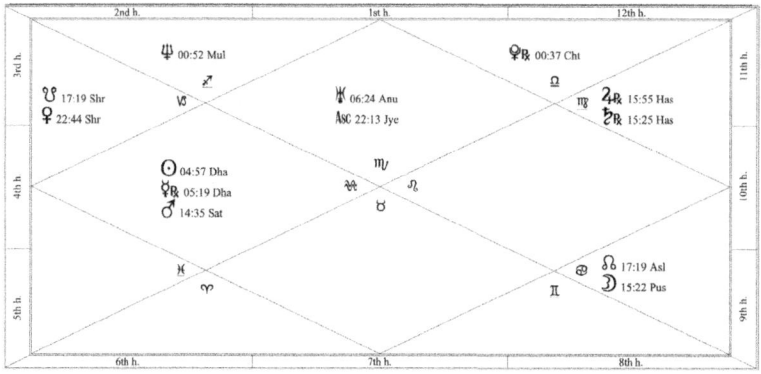

Chapter 2

5th h.	6th h.	7th h.	8th h.
♓	♈	♉	♊
♂ 14:35 Sat ☿ ℞ 05:19 Dha ☉ 04:57 Dha ♒ ♀ 22:44 Shr ☋ 17:19 Shr ♑	Paris Hilton Tue 02-17-1981 02:30:00 New York, New York USA Timezone: 5 DST: 0 Latitude: 40N42'51 Longitude: 74W00'22 Ayanamsha : -23:35:25 Lahiri		☽ 15:22 Pus ☊ 17:19 Asl ♌
♐	♍	♎	♍
♆ 00:52 Mul	♅ 06:24 Anu ASC 22:13 Jye	♀℞ 00:37 Cht	♄℞ 15:25 Has ♃℞ 15:55 Has
2nd h.	1st h.	12th h.	11th h.

2nd h.	1st h.	12th h.
♆ 00:52 Mul ♐ ☋ 17:19 Shr ♀ 22:44 Shr ♑	♀℞ 00:37 Cht ♎ ♅ 06:24 Anu ASC 22:13 Jye	♍ ♃℞ 15:55 Has ♄℞ 15:25 Has
☉ 04:57 Dha ☿℞ 05:19 Dha ♂ 14:35 Sat	♏ ♒ ♌ ♉	
♓ ♈	♊	☊ 17:19 Asl ☽ 15:22 Pus
6th h.	7th h.	8th h.

Paris Hilton is a media personality, businesswoman, model, entertainer, and socialite, but it was a leaked 2001 sex tape with her then-boyfriend, later released as *1 Night in Paris* (2004), catapulted her into global fame.

Hilton's unorthodox rise to fame coincided with society's increased fixation on celebrity and the internet becoming a more accessible medium. These factors, along with Hilton's own public profile, facilitated the insurgency of an unprecedented type of celebrity —which was initially promoted by reality television and has since intensified with the growth of social media. Today much of Hilton's wealth comes from numerous endorsements as well as her retail business, which includes 45 stores and 19 product lines, and has generated sales of over 4 billion.

Hilton has a very tight Moon and Rahu conjunction in the 9th house in Cancer. The 9th house is the house of the father, and it was her father that was the grandson of Conrad Hilton. Her great-grandfather was Conrad Hilton, who founded Hilton Hotels. The massive wealth came from her father's side of the family. Although the Moon represents the mother, her mother was a fashion designer, actress, and television personality and her sisters, Paris' maternal aunts are television personalities Kim and Kyle Richards. Her Moon with Rahu represents extremes with both the father and mother. The Moon in Cancer also exaggerates this because it is strong in its own sign of rulership and as it is in the extremely auspicious nakshatra Pushya. She had everything money and wealth provides. But her Moon is isolated which means she did not feel supported as a child as many socialites of wealthy families do not have time for their children, plus she was the oldest of four children. Paris was sent to boarding schools due to her rebellious ways; rebellious children are acting out for attention.

The Moon conjunct Rahu represents very strong desires, many times for attention and fame. At the same time Ketu is in the 7th house from the Moon representing problems in relationships and marriage. She was involved with many movie stars, singers, powerful businessmen, and engaged many times calling it off. She finally got married in 2021 to Carter Reum.

Her Venus is what magnifies her attractive charisma as it is with Ketu opposed her Moon and Rahu. Venus is in the 3rd house of media and the entertainment business. It is intensified by being with Ketu which means Venus and the Moon are tied up in the nodal axis of Rahu and Ketu. The Moon's aspect with Venus gives wealth and beauty and confers great luck in many aspects of life.

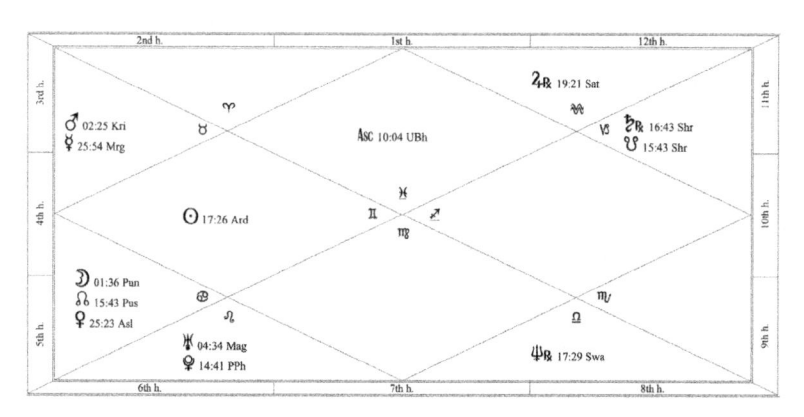

1st h.	2nd h.	3rd h.	4th h.
Asc 10:04 UBh ♓	♈	♂ 02:25 Kri ☿ 25:54 Mrg ♉	☉ 17:26 Ard ♊
12th h. ♃R 19:21 Sat ♒	Tom Cruise Tue 07-03-1962 00:21:00 New York, NY, New York USA Timezone: 5 DST: 1 Latitude: 40N42'51 Longitude: 74W00'23 Ayanamsha : -23:19:47 Lahiri		☽ 01:36 Pun ☊ 15:43 Pus ♀ 25:23 Asl ⊕ 5th h.
11th h. ♄R 16:43 Shr ☋ 15:43 Shr ♑			⛢ 04:34 Mag ♀ 14:41 PPh ♌ 6th h.
10th h.	9th h. ♐	8th h. ♍ ♆R 17:29 Swa ♎	7th h. ♍

Tom Cruise is an American actor and producer. He has received various accolades, including an Honorary Palme d'Or and three Golden Globe Awards, in addition to nominations for three Academy Awards. His films have grossed over $4 billion in North America and over $11.1 billion worldwide, making him one of the highest-grossing box office stars of all time.

Cruise has Rahu conjunct the Moon with Venus in Cancer. This is reminiscent of Paris Hilton's Moon with Rahu opposed Venus. They are both magnetic and fascinating to the public and very fortunate. His Moon, Rahu and Venus conjunction are in Cancer in the 5th house of creativity. Moon in Cancer as with Hilton is powerfully intense. His nakshatra is Punarvasu, which means "return of the light" and refers to those who make major comebacks throughout life. He will always return to being on top with his creative talents. Interestingly, his Venus in the 5th house of creativity rules the 3rd house of entertainers. Talented entertainers often have a connection with the 3rd and 5th house. Also he has both Mercury and Mars in the 3rd house of entertainers and performers.

Rahu is conjunct the Moon opposed Saturn and Ketu. This is detrimental for marriage. He had relationships with Melissa Gilbert, Rebecca De Mornay, Patti Scialfa, Cher, Penélope Cruz, just to name a few, and married Mimi Rogers, Nicole Kidman and Katie Holmes. He seems to fall in love with his costars. The Saturn with Ketu is a very difficult conjunction that occurs about every 11 years. Those that have this conjunction have a very difficult karmic retribution that must be paid. Depending on the house it sits in, this will be the area of life that causes the most pain. For Cruise it sits in the 11th house of friends, organizations and groups. This could concern the problems with the Scientology group. He has been known to preach his beliefs in Scientology which has continually got him into trouble. But of course, the other sore spot is relationships, as this conjunction sits in the 7th house from the Moon. Furthermore, Saturn is not only conjunct Ketu, but it also opposes Moon and Venus. Saturn's aspect to the Moon can make one very serious and determined, and opposing Venus makes one lonely and adds further upsets to relationships. They say it is lonely at the top and I am sure Cruise would agree to that.

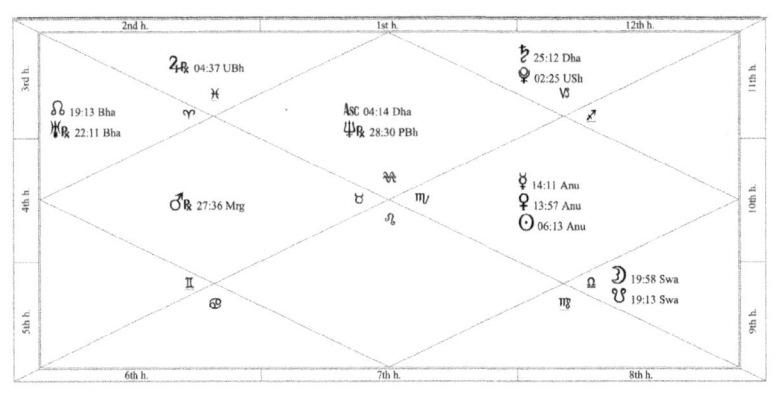

6th h.	7th h.	8th h.	9th h.
♅℞ 18:27 Rev (♓)	☽ 02:44 Ash (♈) ☊ 24:54 Bha	♃ 16:42 Roh (♉) ♀ 28:54 Mrg	♀ 25:30 Pun (♊)

5th h. (♒)			10th h. (♋) ☿ 09:31 Pus ☉ 12:17 Pus
4th h. (♑)	Jacqueline Ken Onassis Sun 07-28-1929 14:30:00 Southampton, New York USA Timezone: 5 DST: 1 Latitude: 40N53'03 Longitude: 72W23'22 Ayanamsha : -22:52:13 Lahiri		11th h. (♌) ♆ 07:16 Mag ♂ 21:57 PPh

3rd h.	2nd h.	1st h.	12th h.
♄℞ 01:46 Mul (♐)	(♏)	☋ 24:54 Vis (♎) Asc 25:05 Vis	(♍)

2nd h.	1st h.	12th h.
3rd h. ☊ 19:13 Bha ♅℞ 22:11 Bha	♃℞ 04:37 UBh ♓	Asc 04:14 Dha ♆℞ 28:30 PBh	♄ 25:12 Dha ♀ 02:25 USh ♑	11th h.
4th h. ♂℞ 27:36 Mrg	♉ ♍ ♌		☿ 14:11 Anu ♀ 13:57 Anu ☉ 06:13 Anu	10th h.
5th h. ♊ ♋		☽ 19:58 Swa ♎ ☋ 19:13 Swa ♍	9th h.
6th h.	7th h.	8th h.

Jackie Kennedy also does not need an introduction as the wife of President Kennedy and Greek tycoon Aristotle Onassis. What is fascinating is the fact that both her husbands were extraordinarily wealthy and famous, and she has Moon conjunct Rahu in the 7th house of the spouse. Also, this means Ketu is 7th from the Moon furthering the problems and loss around marriage. Aside from the great tragedies she had experienced in her life, she was blessed with great wealth as can be seen in the Moon's Sunapha yoga, which is when planets are in the 2nd house from the Moon. This yoga gives a sense of great support from others but because she has both benefics Jupiter and Venus in the 2nd house from the Moon she received a double dose of great wealth. It also helps that both planets Venus and Jupiter are in the 8th house from the ascendant meaning wealth through others.

Her Moon is in the nakshatra Ashwini, which is ruled by Ketu and usually indicates some emotional issues and losses. She most certainly suffered great losses as her Ketu even sits exactly on her ascendant degree. She had a life with a certain destiny with Ketu on her ascendant. When either Rahu or Ketu sit on the ascendant individuals have a life that is fated. There was karma and difficulty through marriage with Ketu 7th from the Moon.

Ashwini is called "the horse woman". Jackie grew up surrounded by horses and was an accomplished equestrian. Many times, those with this nakshatra prominent love horses.

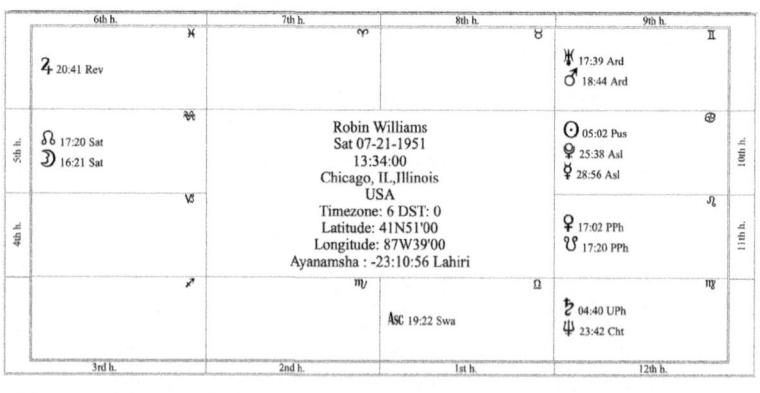

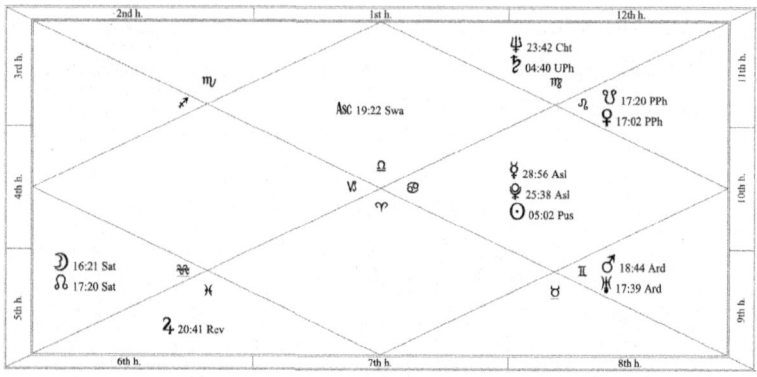

6th h.	7th h.	8th h.	9th h.
♃ 20:41 Rev		♅ 17:39 Ard ♂ 18:44 Ard	
☊ 17:20 Sat ☽ 16:21 Sat	Robin Williams Sat 07-21-1951 13:34:00 Chicago, IL, Illinois USA Timezone: 6 DST: 0 Latitude: 41N51'00 Longitude: 87W39'00 Ayanamsha: -23:10:56 Lahiri	☉ 05:02 Pus ♀ 25:38 Asl ☿ 28:56 Asl	
		♀ 17:02 PPh ☋ 17:20 PPh	
	ASC 19:22 Swa	♄ 04:40 UPh ♆ 23:42 Cht	
3rd h.	2nd h.	1st h.	12th h.

Robin Williams was an actor and comedian. Known for his improvisational skills and the wide variety of characters he created on the spur of the moment and portrayed on film, in dramas and comedies alike, he is regarded as one of the greatest comedians of all time. He struggled throughout life with addictions and mental issues. The Moon with Rahu causes extremes with the mind and in the nakshatra Shatabisha there is a very strong tendency with addictions. Sometimes it represents addictions associated with loved ones in the family, but other times it is the individual that has addiction themselves.

At age 63 Williams died by suicide at his home. His autopsy revealed undiagnosed Lewy body disease, which is a form of dementia. Shatabisha rules hard to cure diseases, and addictions and dementia are hard to cure mental diseases, but many believe all the years spent in his addiction contributed to the early onset of this disease.

His Moon and Rahu are in the 5th house of creativity and the arts. Williams attained a full scholarship to the Juilliard School 1973–1976 in New York City. He was one of 20 students accepted into the freshman class, and he and Christopher Reeve were the only two accepted into the Advanced Program at the school that year. Since the Moon rules the 10th house of career he couldn't avoid a career in the performing arts.

He has Venus opposed his Moon conjunct Ketu. Paris Hilton has this exact combination but in different signs and houses. Venus is the planet that can confer massive wealth, and its aspect opposed the Moon indicates a beautiful wealthy mother. Williams was from a very affluent family, and he was actually very uncomfortable amongst friends who didn't have his level of wealth. His mother, Laurie McLaurin, was a former model from Jackson, Mississippi, whose great-grandfather was Mississippi senator and governor Anselm J. McLaurin. His father, Robert Fitzgerald Williams, was a senior executive in Ford's Lincoln-Mercury Division. Tom Cruise has Venus conjunct Rahu and Moon, but the opposition of Saturn indicates he had to earn his wealth himself, he didn't have the safety net of family wealth.

Venus and Ketu are in the 7th house from the Moon indicating problems in marriage and financial losses through marriage. Williams was on the verge of bankruptcy around the end of his life. He blames his financial situation on two costly divorces.

Rahu conjunct the Moon in the 5th house in Shatabhisha opposed Venus, denoting so much information concerning his talents and the major events that influenced his life.

Chapter 3

Mercury and the Moon

After exploring the effects of the Moon with Rahu now let's look at the effects that the Moon fully aspected by Mercury by conjunction or opposition will produce.

Both the Moon and Mercury rule different aspects of the mind. When they fully aspect each other the mind is in overdrive, unable to stop thinking and processing information. It can lead to an obsessional quality. There is too much activity in the thinking mind. Because of this over stimulation, the mind is obsessed and sometimes worries excessively, overthinking everything, and can have problems getting to sleep at night.

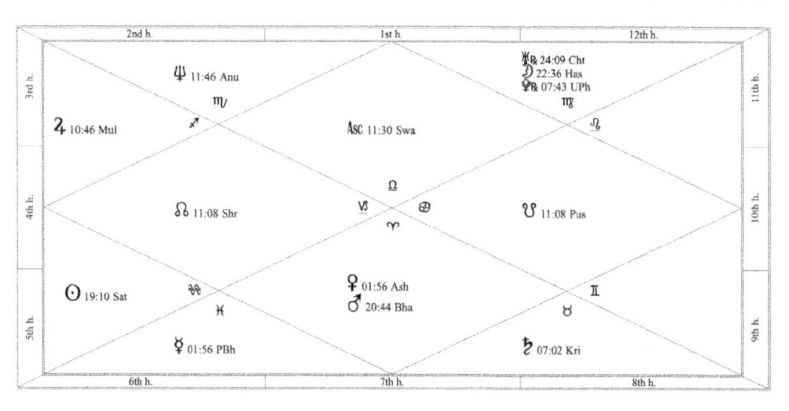

John Salvi was an anti-abortion extremist who carried out fatal shootings at two abortion facilities in Brookline, Massachusetts on December 30, 1994. The shootings killed two and wounded five. An insanity defense at his trial was not successful and he was convicted of two counts of murder and sentenced to life in prison without the possibility of parole. He died in 1996 in what was officially ruled a suicide in his jail cell.

The Moon which rules the Mind is opposed to Mercury, even though there is a wide orb the aspect of a full sign definitely works. In this case, Mercury is debilitated in Pisces and the Moon is in Virgo. Debilitated planets are considered weaker. There are many ways the condition that a debilitation can be lessened, but in this case, Mercury is very weak, another factor is the Moon is in Virgo which is ruled by Mercury connecting this issue of overthinking and obsessing about ideologies. A Moon in Virgo is very critical in their thinking. Even though the Moon sits between two outer planets, this Moon is considered isolated, as the outer planets do not serve in the makeup of the Moon's yogas.

The nakshatra Mercury sits in the Hasta, which is symbolized by the hand, and is known to fixate onto ideas and not to let go. Hasta is ruled by the Moon, so it even intensifies these effects.

It cannot be ignored that the Moon sits between the two outer planets Pluto and Uranus. This causes the mind to be further upset by extreme ideas. These effects are also directed to Mercury causing a deranged mental capacity. Pluto conjunct the Moon but tightly opposed Mercury causes deep and dark thoughts and the need to control things, but Uranus tightly conjunct the Moon can cause irrational behavior and unpredictable thoughts and actions. Salvi was diagnosed with schizophrenia by the defense's psychiatrist (which contradicted the prosecution), he did not receive treatment for his illness in prison. This combination therefore can be an indication of mental disease. In

Mercury and the Moon

my books on the three outer planets Uranus, Neptune and Pluto I discovered that many that have their personal planets tightly conjunct or opposed outer planets will leave a legacy or be remembered after their death. It doesn't matter if it is for good or bad just that their name lives on.

The Moon between Pluto and Uranus sits in the 12th house, which rules imprisonment or prisons. Salvi was found dead in his prison cell with a garbage bag over his head tied around his neck. Salvi was found under his bed with his hands and feet tied up. Salvi was rushed to the hospital where he was pronounced dead. The official report states that Salvi's death was a suicide.

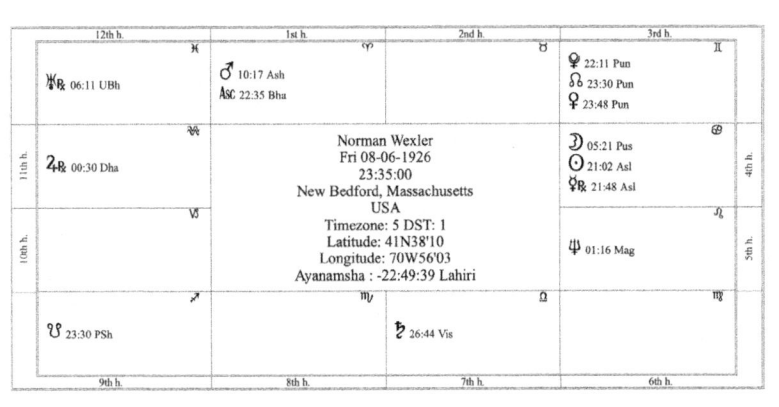

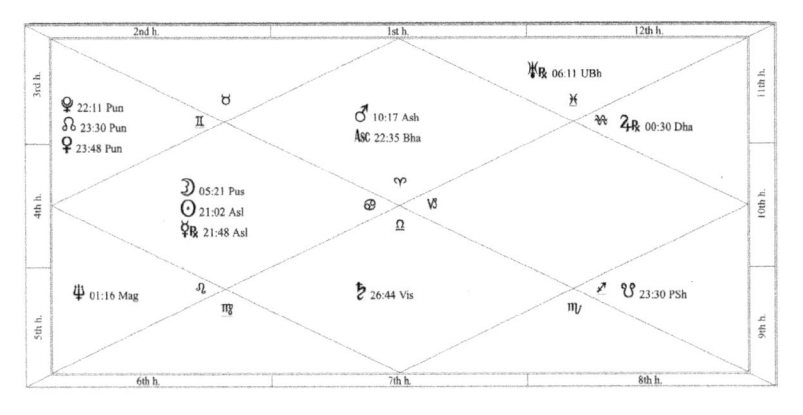

12th h.	1st h.	2nd h.	3rd h.
♅℞ 06:11 UBh	♂ 10:17 Ash ASC 22:35 Bha		♀ 22:11 Pun ☊ 23:30 Pun ☿ 23:48 Pun
♃℞ 00:30 Dha	Norman Wexler Fri 08-06-1926 23:35:00 New Bedford, Massachusetts USA Timezone: 5 DST: 1 Latitude: 41N38'10 Longitude: 70W56'03 Ayanamsha: -22:49:39 Lahiri		☽ 05:21 Pus ☉ 21:02 Asl ♀℞ 21:48 Asl
			♆ 01:16 Mag
☋ 23:30 PSh		♄ 26:44 Vis	
9th h.	8th h.	7th h.	6th h.

41

Norman Wexler wrote the screenplays for several hit films, most notably *Joe*, *Serpico*, *Mandingo* and *Saturday Night Fever*. He received Oscar nominations for *Joe* and *Serpico*. His Moon, Sun, and Mercury are conjunct in Cancer, which causes the over processing of mental information. When the Moon is in Cancer it intensifies the sensitivity of the Moon. His life was steeped with controversy, great talent but a deranged mind. The Moon's nakshatra Pushya is wealthy and nourished. He did achieve great wealth from his creativity, but the Moon is very damaged.

There is another variable that exists here that can never be overlooked, that is that the Moon is very dark, meaning he was born right before the new Moon. This combination in the 4th house can make him very introverted, as the 4th house is the midnight of a chart. In Western astrology it is said to be a balsamic Moon. The dark Moon in Vedic astrology is thought to be a very weak Moon or malefic, but I find it to be very introspective. The Moon as it represents consciousness, and the mind is believed to not see outside of one's own thoughts as in a dark mind without mental brightness. During this phase of the Moon, it is not seen at night, and because it sits behind the Sun the day before the new Moon it is an ending phase before the new beginning of the new Moon.

Venus in the 12th from the Moon is an Anapha yoga, but the nodes, Rahu and Ketu disturb and somewhat cancel this yoga. But Rahu, Pluto and Venus in the 3rd house give him powerful creative ability. The 3rd house is considered creativity, and the 5th house is also creativity as it is the 3rd house from the 3rd house.

Another important variable about the Moon here is that it is fully aspected by both Saturn and Mars. Mars' full Vedic aspect is 4 and 8 signs from its placement and Saturn's full

Vedic aspect is 3 and 10 placements from where it is located. In this case Saturn aspects by its 10th aspect and Mars by its 4th aspect. Therefore, the dark Moon is afflicted by two malefics and additionally with Mercury his thinking mind is affected in a very cruel way. He was reported to have suffered from severe mental illness, reportedly bipolar disorder, and was arrested in 1972 for threatening to shoot President Richard Nixon.

Chapter 4

Debilitated Planets

There is so much written about debilitated planets in Vedic astrology, and so many ways that the planet's debilitation can be canceled. A debilitated planet is the sign that the planet does not prosper, and it is considered that this planet is weak and cannot produce the results it is known to rule. It seems that these rules work sometimes but not all the time, very confusing. What is the answer to this? And how do you know what the debilitation's effects are, can its debilitation be canceled?

First of all, a debilitated planet's effects are never completely canceled regardless of the neecha banga raja yoga. In other words, a debilitated planet always indicates there is a problem with that planet. The problem this planet presents has to be worked on, and can become an asset as one is focused on the problems by working on them. Neecha banga are the ways a debilitated planet can be canceled. Neecha means debilitated and banga means reversal.

Here are the most powerful ways I find that work the best for strengthening a debilitated planet. There are many more ways, but these are the ones I find work.

1) If the ruler of the debilitated planet is exalted or in its own sign of rulership, example: Jupiter is in Capricorn (debilitated) and Saturn Ruler of Capricorn is in Libra (exalted).

2) If the debilitated planet is exalted in the Navamsha example: Sun in Libra (debilitated) and in Aries (exalted) in the navamsha

3) If the debilitated planet is in parivartana (mutual reception) with the planet that rules its sign. This

means the debilitated planet operates like it is in the sign of the ruler it is in exchange: for example if Mars is in Cancer and the Moon is in Scorpio, this gives the effects of Mars in Scorpio and the Moon in Cancer reversing the debilitation of both planets.

4) If the debilitated planet is in its own sign of rulership in the navamsha, Example: Jupiter in Capricorn (debilitated) and in Pisces or Sagittarius in Navamsha

5) Debilitated planet in an angle/kendra from the ascendant or the Moon

6) If the ruler of the debilitated planet is in a kendra from the ascendant or the Moon

7) If the debilitated planet sits with an exalted planet, example: debilitated Venus with exalted Mercury in Virgo

8) Debilitated planet retrograde, this can reverse the effects and can act like an exalted planet

All these are ways to strengthen the debilitated planet.

9th h.	10th h.	11th h.	12th h.
♓	♈ ☊ 00:19 Ash ☽ 21:14 Bha	♉ ♂ 15:40 Roh ☿ 17:08 Roh	♊ ☉ 07:34 Ard ♅ 07:35 Ard ♀ 25:16 Pun
8th h. ♒	Meryl Streep Wed 06-22-1949 08:05:00 Summit, NJ, New Jersey USA Timezone: 5 DST: 1 Latitude: 40N43'00 Longitude: 74W22'00 Ayanamsha: -23:08:58 Lahiri		♋ 1st h. Asc 09:35 Pus ♀ 21:42 Asl
7th h. ♑ ♃℞ 07:22 USh			♌ 2nd h. ♄ 08:25 Mag
6th h. ♐	5th h. ♍ ☋ 00:19 Cht	4th h. ♎ ♆℞ 19:14 Has	3rd h. ♍

45

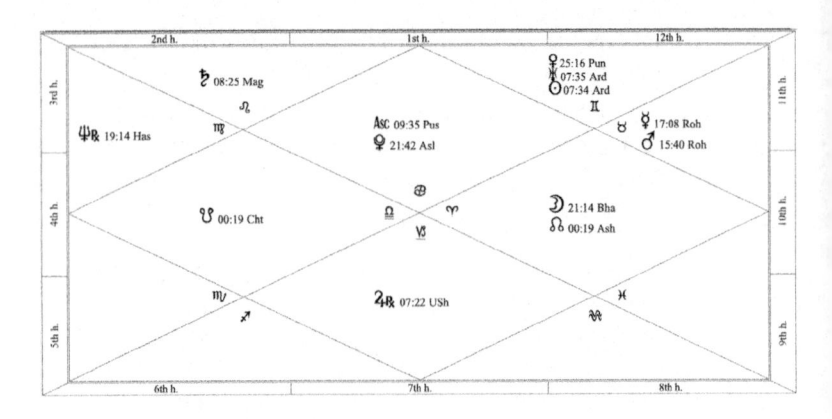

My best Tools and Techniques

Astrologer's Secrets

	2nd h.	1st h.	12th h.	
3rd h.	♄ 08:25 Mag ♆ᴿ 19:14 Has	Asc 09:35 Pus ♀ 21:42 Asl	♀ 25:16 Pun ♇ 07:35 Ard ☉ 07:34 Ard Ⅱ ☿ 17:08 Roh ♂ 15:40 Roh	11th h.
4th h.	☋ 00:19 Cht	⊕ ☊ ♑	☽ 21:14 Bha ☊ 00:19 Ash	10th h.
5th h.		♃ᴿ 07:22 USh		9th h.
	6th h.	7th h.	8th h.	

D9 Navamsha (spouse)

♓ ♃ᴿ 06:26	♈ ☊ 02:54	♉ ♀ 17:25 ♂ 21:08	Ⅱ ☿ 04:14 ♄ 15:46 ♆ᴿ 23:13
♒			⊕
♑ ♀ 15:18			♌
♐ ♇ 08:16 ☉ 08:06	♏ ☋ 02:54 ☽ 11:11	♎ Asc 26:17	♍

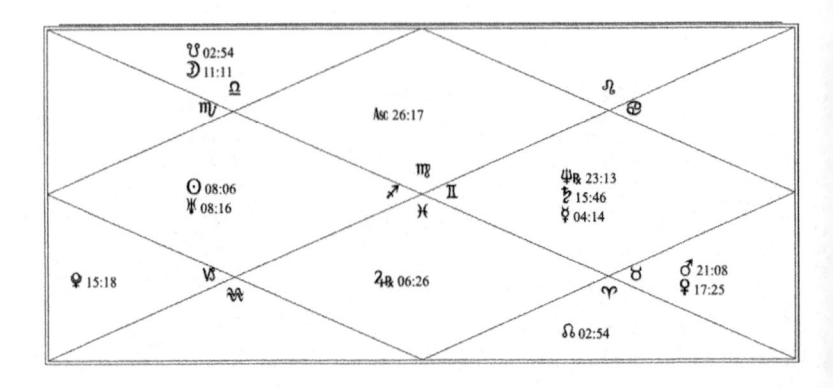

	☋ 02:54 ☽ 11:11 ♏		☊ ⊕	
		Asc 26:17		
	☉ 08:06 ♇ 08:16	♍ Ⅱ ♐ ♓	♆ᴿ 23:13 ♄ 15:46 ☿ 04:14	
♀ 15:18	♑ ♒	♃ᴿ 06:26	♈	♂ 21:08 ♀ 17:25
		☊ 02:54		

46

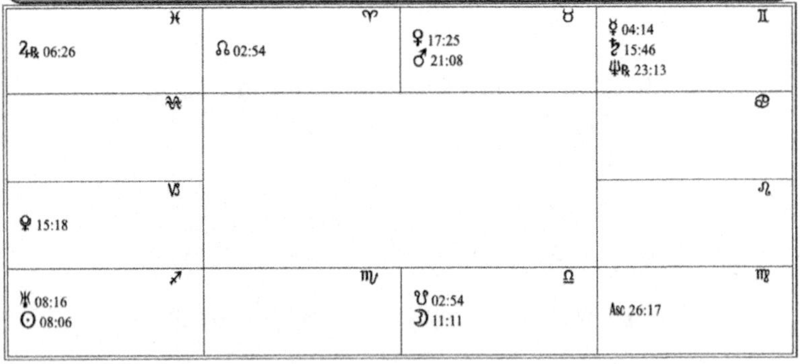

Jupiter Debilitated

We looked at Meryl Streep's chart in terms of her great success and fame through her powerful Moon and Rahu in her 10th house. But as Jupiter is the planet of luck, fortune and sits in the 10th house (career) from the Moon, how can it be debilitated with one of the most successful female actors of all time?

As I said before there will always be an issue to work out karmically, no matter how it is canceled, but it can be overcome and when worked on and become an asset.

The debilitated Jupiter is in her 7th house, and many don't know that Streep lost her first love to cancer. She lived with actor John Cazale for three years until he died of lung cancer in March 1978. Streep said of his death:

"I didn't get over it. I don't want to get over it. No matter what you do, the pain is always there in some recess of your mind, and it affects everything that happens afterwards. I think you can assimilate the pain and go on without making an obsession of it."

Streep married sculptor Don Gummer six months after Cazale's death and has remained married till today. They have four children.

Her debilitated Jupiter in the 7th house of relationships indicated the deep loss experienced early on. Jupiter is the planet in a woman's chart that gives indications for the partner, and it rules children. It seems after the loss of the partner she turned this debilitation around.

The most important variable that seems to indicate the reversal of this debilitation is that Jupiter is retrograde, indicating a reversal of the debilitation. It is believed that when a debilitated planet is retrograde it makes it like an exalted planet but when it exalted and retrograde it can become like a debilitated planet. I have seen this to work most of the time.

Another powerful way planets are strengthened is by being in an angle/kendra and Jupiter is in a kendra from the ascendant and from the Moon. Another important variable is that Jupiter is in Pisces its sign of rulership in the navamsha, plus it also sits in the 7th house in the navamsha proving a reversal in marriage and relationship in the second part of life.

She does have the Moon conjunct Rahu which always puts Ketu in the 7th house of the Moon, meaning difficulty with marriage, and her initial serious relationship was full of sadness and loss. The debilitation in the 7th house retrograde and in its sign of rulership in the 7th house of the navamsha and in an angle/kendra from the Moon and ascendant proved out her final results from this debilitation.

Another note as to the results of her Jupiter producing stellar results instead of difficult results is that in her Jupiter maha dasha she rose to the highest level of success in her acting career, from age 49–65.

Debilitated Mars

Another dilemma about debilitated planets can be seen in these three athletes with debilitated Mars. Mars is the planet of sports and competition; how can it be debilitated in the charts of some of the world's most outstanding athletes of all time?

10th h.	11th h.	12th h.	1st h.
♓	♈	♉	♊ ASC 19:44 Ard
♒ 9th h. ♃ 25:45 PBh ☉ 05:02 Dha	Michael Jordon Sun 02-17-1963 13:40:00 Brooklyn Heights, New York USA Timezone: 5 DST: 0 Latitude: 40N41'43 Longitude: 73W59'38 Ayanamsha : -23:20:17 Lahiri		♋ ☊ 05:57 Pus ♂℞ 16:37 Pus 2nd h.
♑ 8th h. ♄ 22:11 Shr ☿ 09:18 USh ☋ 05:57 USh			♌ ♅℞ 10:07 Mag ♀℞ 17:51 PPh 3rd h.
♐ ♀ 19:51 PSh	♏ ☽ 16:40 Jye	♎ ♆℞ 22:19 Vis	♍
7th h.	6th h.	5th h.	4th h.

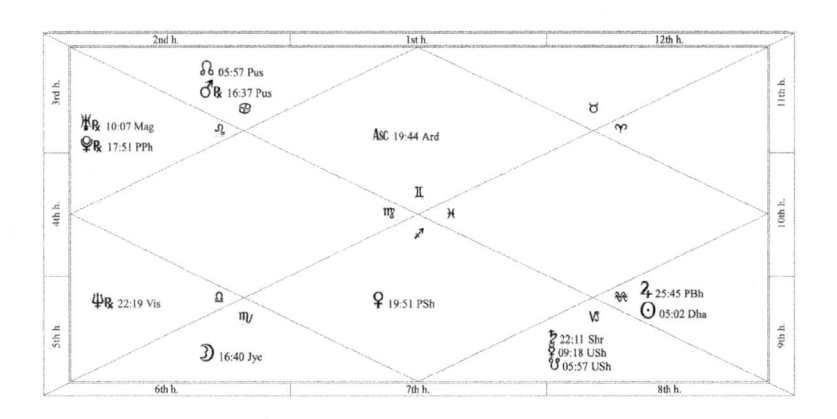

Debilitated Planets

Chapter 4

2nd h.	1st h.	12th h.
☊ 05:57 Pus ♂℞ 16:37 Pus		
♅℞ 10:07 Mag ♀℞ 17:51 PPh	Asc 19:44 Ard	♉
	♊ ♍ ♅ ♐	
♆℞ 22:19 Vis	♀ 19:51 PSh	♒ ♃ 25:45 PBh ○ 05:02 Dha
♎ ♏ ☽ 16:40 Jye		♑ ☿ 22:11 Shr ☿ 09:18 USh ☋ 05:57 USh
6th h.	7th h.	8th h.

D9 Navamsha (spouse)

♓ Asc 27:43 ☿ 23:49	♈ ♆℞ 20:56	♉ ♃ 21:49	♊
♒ ☋ 23:36			♋ ♅℞ 01:09 ♄ 19:43
♑			♌ ☊ 23:36
♐ ☽ 00:02	♏ ○ 15:23 ♂℞ 29:34	♎	♍ ♀℞ 10:42 ♀ 28:41

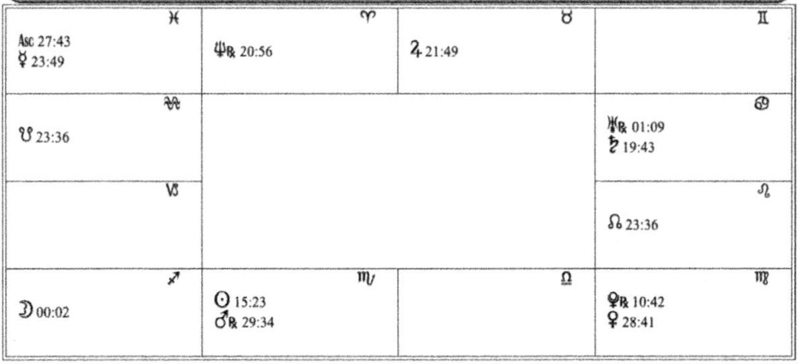

D9 Navamsha (spouse)

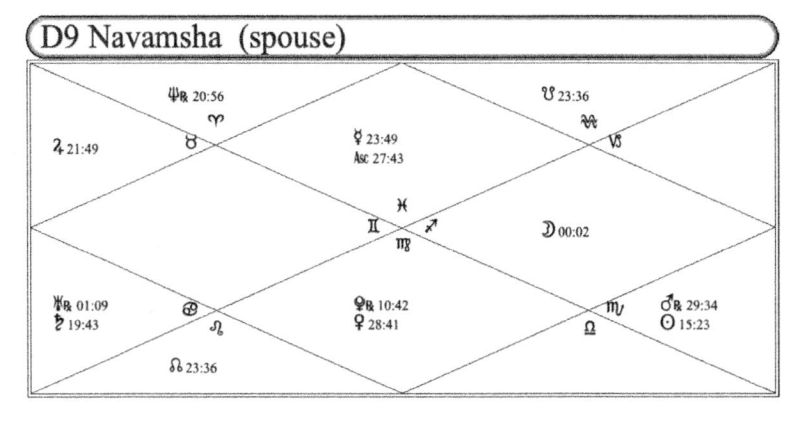

	♆℞ 20:56 ♈		☋ 23:36 ♒	
♃ 21:49	♉	☿ 23:49 Asc 27:43	♑	
		♓ ♊ ♍ ♐		☽ 00:02
♅℞ 01:09 ♄ 19:43	♋ ♌	♀℞ 10:42 ♀ 28:41	♏ ♎	♂℞ 29:34 ○ 15:23
	☊ 23:36			

Michael Jordan is a businessman and former professional basketball player. His biography on the official NBA website states: "By acclamation, Michael Jordan is the greatest basketball player of all time." He played fifteen seasons in the National Basketball Association (NBA), winning six NBA championships with the Chicago Bulls. Jordan is the principal owner and chairman of the Charlotte Hornets of the NBA and of 23XI Racing in the NASCAR Cup Series. He was integral in popularizing the NBA around the world in the 1980s and 1990s, becoming a global cultural icon in the process.

In the case of Jordan there must be a reversal of this debilitated Mars or none of this makes sense or is possible. Probably the most important variable that causes this debilitation to be reversed is the parivartana between Mars and the Moon. Mars is in Cancer ruled by the Moon and the Moon is in Scorpio ruled by Mars. This means Mars expresses itself as Mars in Scorpio and the Moon in Cancer changing the debilitation of both Mars and the Moon.

Another biggie is Mars is retrograde reversing the energy of a debilitated planet to an exalted planet, and to make the effects even more grand Mars is conjunct Rahu. Rahu will magnify the effect of the planets it is conjunct.

Lastly, his debilitated Mars picks up great strength by its placement in Scorpio, its sign of rulership in the navamsha.

11th h.	12th h.	1st h.	2nd h.
♓	♈	♉	♊
	♅℞ 16:35 Bha	ASC 03:15 Kri	☋ 08:39 Ard
10th h. ♒	Wilt Chamberland Fri 08-21-1936 23:27:00 Philadelphia, Pennsylvania USA		3rd h. ♋
♄℞ 27:41 PBh		♀ 04:51 Pus ♂ 14:34 Pus	
9th h. ♑	Timezone: 5 DST: 1 Latitude: 39N57'08 Longitude: 75W09'50 Ayanamsha : -22:58:38 Lahiri		4th h. ♌
		☉ 05:52 Mag ♀ 20:39 PPh ♇ 22:51 PPh ☿ 29:33 UPh	
♐	♏	♎	♍
☊ 08:39 Mul	♃ 21:46 Jye	☽ 02:00 Cht	
8th h.	7th h.	6th h.	5th h.

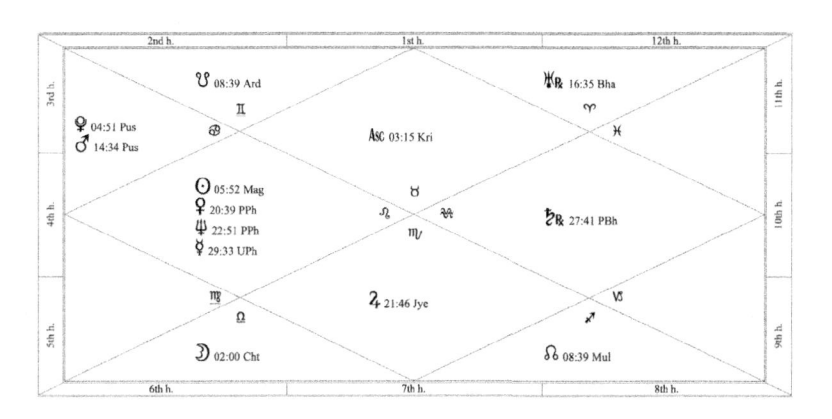

Debilitated Planets

Chapter 4

Rasi Chart

1st h. (Kri/Aries)	Asc 03:15 Kri
2nd h. (Tau)	☊ 08:39 Ard; ♂ (note: II = Gemini)
3rd h. (Gem)	♀ 04:51 Pus; ♂ 14:34 Pus
4th h. (Can)	☉ 05:52 Mag; ♀ 20:39 PPh; ♇ 22:51 PPh; ☿ 29:33 UPh
5th h. (Leo)	—
6th h. (Vir)	☽ 02:00 Cht
7th h. (Lib)	—
8th h. (Sco)	♃ 21:46 Jye
9th h. (Sag)	☋ 08:39 Mul
10th h. (Cap)	—
11th h. (Aqu)	♄R 27:41 PBh
12th h. (Pis)	⛢R 16:35 Bha

D9 Navamsha (spouse)

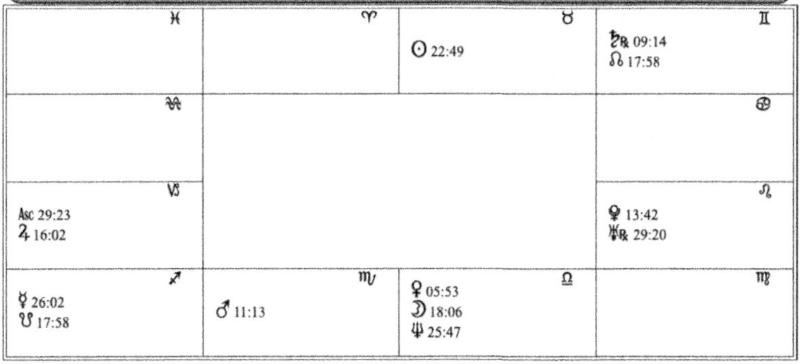

Pis	Ari	Tau	Gem
		☉ 22:49	♄R 09:14; ☋ 17:58

Aqu			Can

Cap			Leo
Asc 29:23; ♃ 16:02			♀ 13:42; ⛢R 29:20

Sag	Sco	Lib	Vir
☿ 26:02; ☊ 17:58	♂ 11:13	♀ 05:53; ☽ 18:06; ♇ 25:47	

D9 Navamsha (spouse)

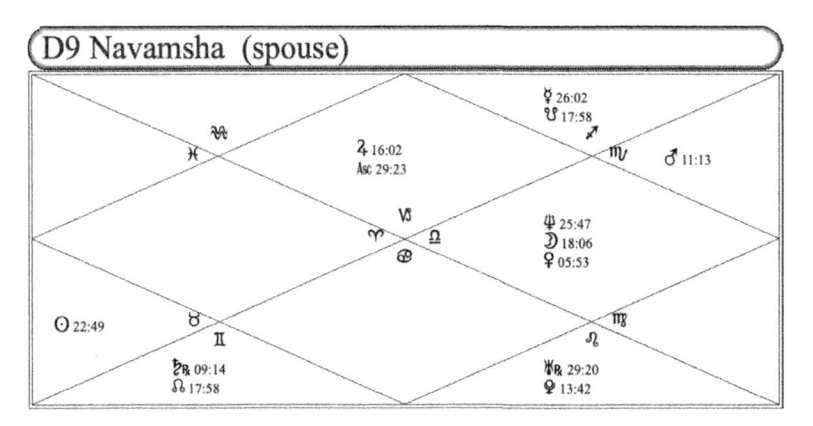

North Indian style chart:
- ♃ 16:02, Asc 29:23 (center/Cap)
- ☿ 26:02, ☊ 17:58 (Sag)
- ♂ 11:13 (Sco)
- ♇ 25:47, ☽ 18:06, ♀ 05:53 (Lib)
- ⛢R 29:20, ♀ 13:42 (Leo)
- ♄R 09:14, ☋ 17:58 (Gem)
- ☉ 22:49 (Tau)

51

Wilt Chamberlain was a professional basketball player. Standing at 7' ft 1" tall, he played in the National Basketball Association (NBA) for 14 years and is widely regarded as one of the greatest players in the sport's history. Several publications have argued that Chamberlain is the greatest NBA player of all time. He holds numerous NBA regular season records in scoring, rebounding, and durability categories; most notably he is the only player to score 100 points in a single NBA game, and average more than 40 and 50 points in a season.

Wilt's debilitated Mars is not as easily spotted as a powerful placement since it is debilitated and the dispositor of the Moon does not prove strong but notice that Mars is in an angle/kendra 10th from the Moon.

The next powerful situation is the sign Mars sits in the navamsha, which again is Scorpio like Jordan. Mars is in an Upachaya house in both the birth chart (3rd house) and the navamsha (11th house). Upachaya houses are houses 3, 6, 10 and 11. These are the houses of improvement over time, and they are all associated with drive and ambition. It is said that natural malefic planets are best in Upachaya houses because they give drive for improvement. The 3rd house, where Mars is in the birth chart, is the house of courage and can pertain to the dexterity of the arms and hands in which this house rules. It is a house of talent and can most definitely indicate talent with sports.

In both Jordan and Chamberland's charts the dispositor of Mars, the Moon sits in the 6th house, which is an Upachaya house that indicates ambition and drive. The areas of health and fitness are of great importance too.

Another variable that cannot be overlooked is that Pluto is conjunct Mars indicating a vast powerful drive with sports and sexuality. Chamberlain was also a lifelong bachelor and became notorious for his statement of having had sexual relations with as many as 20,000 women.

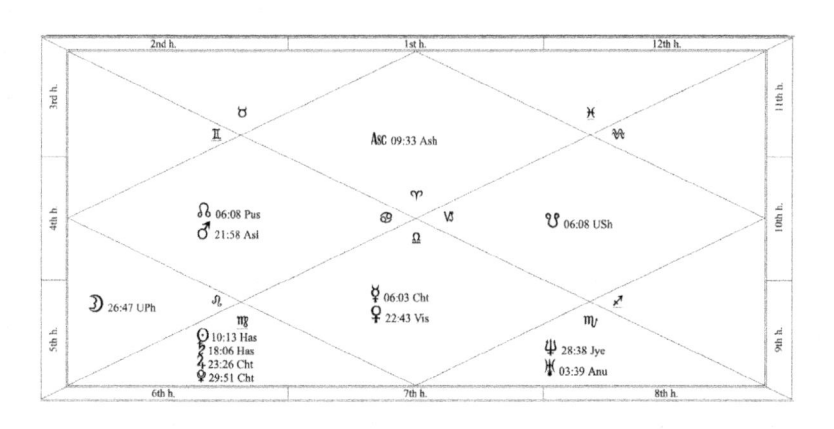

Debilitated Planets

Chapter 4

12th h.	1st h.	2nd h.	3rd h.
♓	♈ Asc 09:33 Ash	♉	♊

11th h.	♒	Serena Williams Sat 09-26-1981 20:28:00 Saginaw, Michigan USA Timezone: 5 DST: 1 Latitude: 43N25'10 Longitude: 83W57'03 Ayanamsha : -23:35:52 Lahiri	⊕ ☊ 06:08 Pus ♂ 21:58 Asl	4th h.
10th h.	♑ ☋ 06:08 USh		♌ ☽ 26:47 UPh	5th h.

9th h.	8th h.	7th h.	6th h.
♐	♍ ♅ 03:39 Anu ♆ 28:38 Jye	♎ ☿ 06:03 Cht ♀ 22:43 Vis	♏ ☉ 10:13 Has ♄ 18:06 Has ♃ 23:26 Cht ♀ 29:51 Cht

2nd h.	1st h.	12th h.
♉ ♊	Asc 09:33 Ash ♈	♓ ♒
☊ 06:08 Pus ♂ 21:58 Asl	⊕ ♑	☋ 06:08 USh
☽ 26:47 UPh ♌ ♍ ☉ 10:13 Has ♄ 18:06 Has ♃ 23:26 Cht ♀ 29:51 Cht	☿ 06:03 Cht ♀ 22:43 Vis	♎ ♏ ♆ 28:38 Jye ♅ 03:39 Anu

D9 Navamsha (spouse)

♓	♈	♉	♊
♆ 17:45	☉ 01:56 ♀ 24:33	♄ 13:00	Asc 26:05
♒ ☋ 25:20			⊕
♑ ♂ 17:50			♌ ♃ 00:59 ♅ 02:51 ☊ 25:20
♐ ☽ 01:10	♍ ☿ 24:29	♎	♍ ♀ 28:42

53

D9 Navamsha (spouse)

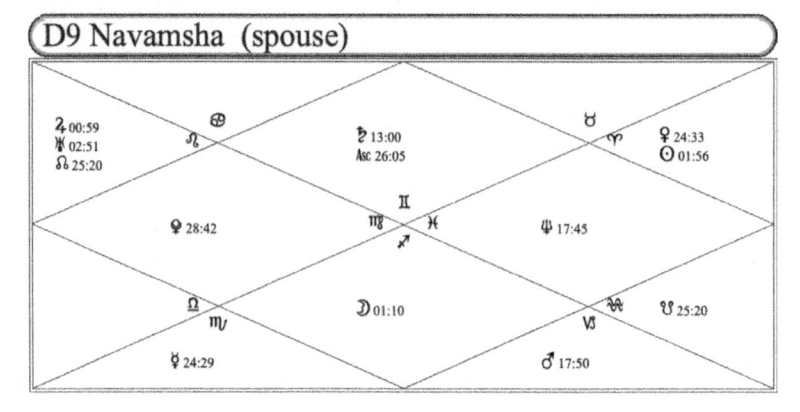

```
♃ 00:59        ⊕                    ♄ 13:00              ♉
℞ 02:51              ♌                Asc 26:05                  ♈    ♀ 24:33
☊ 25:20                                                                ☉ 01:56

                                    Ⅱ
         ♀ 28:42        ♍  ♓                        ♆ 17:45
                            ♐

              ♎
                ♏        ☽ 01:10            ♒      ☋ 25:20
                                      ♑
         ☿ 24:29                    ♂ 17:50
```

Serena Williams is considered among the greatest tennis players of all time, she was ranked world No. 1 in singles by the Women's Tennis Association (WTA) for 319 weeks, including a joint-record 186 consecutive weeks, and finished as the year-end No. 1 five times. She won 23 Grand Slam singles titles, the most by any player in the Open Era, and the second-most of all time.

Again, we have a debilitated Mars, but Mars is in an angle/kendra from the ascendant, and it seems the common denominator in all the athlete's charts is the fact that Mars goes to an extremely strong placement in the navamsha. I have always said if you use the navamsha chart for anything, it must be to see how the planets pick up or lose strength by the sign placements in the navamsha. Realize the sign placements in the navamsha will be correct for most of the entire day, so you don't have to worry if the time of birth is correct, if the time is questionable the houses may not be accurate but the signs you can count on. As you can see the navamsha will give planets strength or weakness by the sign they are in.

Another powerful indicator in William's chart is that Rahu is conjunct Mars which gives Mars more power. Rahu accentuates and empowers the planets it is conjunct, and both Jordan and Williams have Mars conjunct Rahu.

Debilitated Planets

Chapter 4

Debilitated Venus neecha banga
Debilitated Mars NO neecha banga

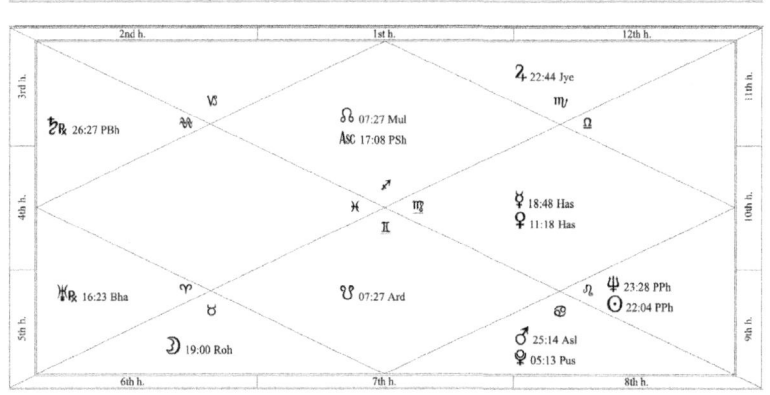

4th h.	5th h.	6th h.	7th h.
♓	♈	♉	♊
♅℞ 16:23 Bha	☽ 19:00 Roh	☊ 07:27 Ard	

♒ ♄℞ 26:27 PBh	Buddy Holly Mon 09-07-1936 15:30:00 Lubbock, Texas USA Timezone: 6 DST: 0 Latitude: 33N35'00 Longitude: 101W51'00 Ayanamsha : -22:58:39 Lahiri	♋ ♀ 05:13 Pus ♂ 25:14 Asl
♑		♌ ☉ 22:04 PPh ♆ 23:28 PPh

1st h.	12th h.	11th h.	10th h.
♐ Asc 17:08 PSh ☋ 07:27 Mul	♏ ♃ 22:44 Jye	♎	♍ ☿ 11:18 Has ☿ 18:48 Has

---

North Indian chart:

- 3rd h.: ♑, ♄℞ 26:27 PBh
- 4th h.: ♒
- 5th h.: ♓ / ♈, ♅℞ 16:23 Bha, ☽ 19:00 Roh
- 6th h.: ♉
- 2nd h.: ♒ / ♓, ☋ 07:27 Mul, Asc 17:08 PSh
- 1st h.: ♐
- 12th h.: ♏, ♃ 22:44 Jye
- 11th h.: ♎
- 7th h.: ♊, ☊ 07:27 Ard
- 8th h.: ♋
- 9th h.: ♌, ♆ 23:28 PPh, ☉ 22:04 PPh
- 10th h.: ♍, ☿ 18:48 Has, ♀ 11:18 Has
- ♂ 25:14 Asl, ♀ 05:13 Pus

D9 Navamsha (spouse)

♓	♈	♉	♊
	♀ 11:46	♄℞ 28:11	☋ 07:09 ☿ 19:11 ☽ 21:05
♒ ♂ 17:14			♋
♑ ♃ 24:39			♌ ♀ 17:02 ♅℞ 27:27
♐ ☊ 07:09	♏ ♆ 01:18	♎ ☉ 18:37	♍ Asc 04:13

55

D9 Navamsha (spouse)

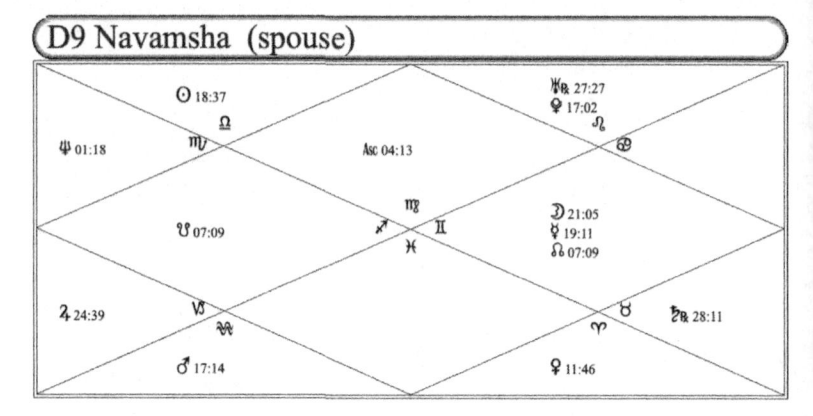

```
                    ☉ 18:37              ♅℞ 27:27
                       ☊                 ♀ 17:02
                                         ♌
    Ψ 01:18          ♍      Asc 04:13      ⊕

                              ♍
                    ☋ 07:09  ♐  ♊    ☽ 21:05
                                ♓    ☿ 19:11
                                     ☊℞ 07:09

    ♃ 24:39       ♑                   ♉   ♄℞ 28:11
                  ♒                   ♈

                  ♂ 17:14        ♀ 11:46
```

Buddy Holly, was a singer and songwriter who was a central and pioneering figure of mid-1950s rock and roll. He was born to a musical family in Lubbock, Texas during the Great Depression, and learned to play guitar and sing alongside his siblings. His style was influenced by gospel music, country music, and rhythm and blues acts, which he performed in Lubbock with his friends from high school.

During his short career, Holly wrote and recorded many songs. He is often regarded as the artist who defined the traditional rock-and-roll lineup of two guitars, bass, and drums. He was a major influence on later popular music artists, including Bob Dylan, The Beatles, The Rolling Stones, Eric Clapton, The Hollies (who named themselves in his honor), Elvis Costello, Dave Edmunds, Marshall Crenshaw, and Elton John. He was among the first artists inducted into the Rock and Roll Hall of Fame, in 1986.

The day the music died was referring to the death of Buddy Holly. Shortly after 12:55 am on February 3, 1959, Holly, Valens, Richardson, and Peterson were killed when the aircraft crashed into a cornfield five miles northwest of Mason City shortly after takeoff. Holly was 22 years old.

Holly has debilitated Mars in the 8th house, this seems to be the indicator of his untimely death as it is conjunct Pluto. Pluto can have a deep connection to death and sex, as it is related to the 8th sign Scorpio. Mars in Vedic astrology is the ruler of Scorpio which is uncanny how many indicators this has to death. Chamberland has Mars conjunct Pluto which has to be relative to his sexual obsession.

Mars' dispositor of the Moon is in the 6th house and Mars is in the 3rd house from the Moon. There is no uplifting power relative to the angles/kendras with this debilitation. It is not retrograde, nor does it go to a powerful sign in the navamsha. His Mars is truly weak and may have caused his early death.

His Venus is debilitated too. Venus rules creativity, the arts therefore his musical ability. But in this instance, it is neecha banga as it sits with exalted Mercury, and Mercury is the dispositor of Venus and it is in a kendra. In his 10th house he became a star overnight because he was so revolutionary and talented.

Another unrelated issue here is that his Sun sits exactly with Neptune which can be considered a higher octave if Venus represents his amazing talent, but it does cause problems and that he will be remembered after his death. Saturn in the 3rd house opposing Neptune and Sun in the 9th house of travel can represent death through travel, but truly debilitated Mars is the most difficult planet in his chart.

11th h.	12th h.	1st h.	2nd h.
☊ 04:56 UBh		ASC 21:24 Roh	⛢ ℞ 16:19 Ard
♃ ℞ 04:28 Dha	Barbara Wilson Tue 10-17-1950 19:57:00 Long Beach, California USA Timezone: 8 DST: 0 Latitude: 33N46'01 Longitude: 118W11'21 Ayanamsha : -23:10:11 Lahiri	♀ 26:24 Asl	
☽ 00:51 USh			
	♂ 22:42 Jye	☉ 01:02 Cht	♄ 03:24 UPh ♆ 04:38 UPh ♀ 21:02 Has ♂ 24:11 Cht ♀ 24:13 Cht
8th h.	7th h.	6th h.	5th h.

57

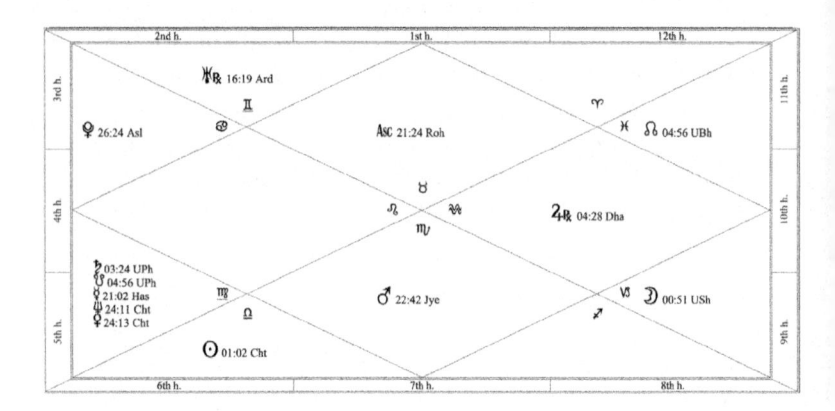

Astrologer's Secrets — My best Tools and Techniques

Birth Chart (North Indian style)

1st h. (Taurus)	ASC 21:24 Roh
2nd h. (Gemini)	♅ ℞ 16:19 Ard
3rd h. (Cancer)	♀ 26:24 Asl
5th h. (Virgo)	♄ 03:24 UPh; ☊ 04:56 UPh; ☿ 21:02 Has; ♆ 24:11 Cht; ♀ 24:13 Cht
6th h. (Libra)	☉ 01:02 Cht
7th h. (Scorpio)	♂ 22:42 Jye
8th h. (Sagittarius/Capricorn)	☽ 00:51 USh
10th h. (Aquarius)	♃ ℞ 04:28 Dha
12th h. (Pisces)	☋ 04:56 UBh

D9 Navamsha (spouse) — South Indian style

Pisces	Aries	Taurus	Gemini
Aquarius ♀ 27:41 ♅ ℞ 26:51 ☋ 14:31 ♄ 00:44			**Cancer** ☿ 09:24 Asc 12:36
Capricorn ♂ 24:23 ☽ 07:41			**Leo** ♆ 07:43 ♀ 08:00 ☊ 14:31
Sagittarius	**Scorpio** ♃ ℞ 10:20	**Libra** ☉ 09:20	**Virgo**

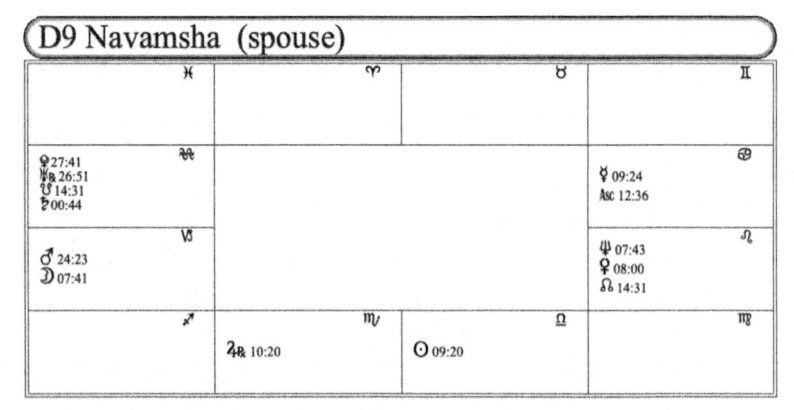

D9 Navamsha (spouse) — North Indian style

- Leo: ♆ 07:43, ♀ 08:00, ☊ 14:31
- Cancer: ☿ 09:24, Asc 12:36
- Gemini
- Libra: ☉ 09:20
- Scorpio: ♃ ℞ 10:20
- Capricorn/Sagittarius: ☽ 07:41, ♂ 24:23
- Aquarius/Pisces: ♀ 27:41, ♅ ℞ 26:51, ☋ 14:31, ♄ 00:44

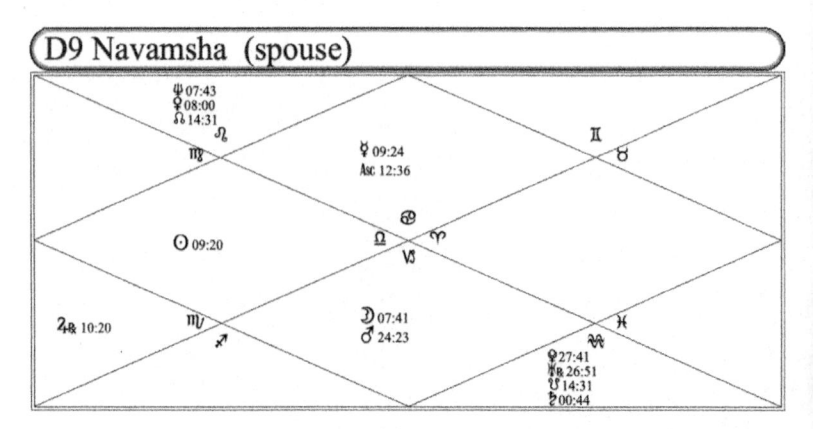

Many times, I am asked what can you see in a chart that can indicate gay tendencies? Because Venus is the planet of love and romance, I have found that many gay clients have a debilitated Venus.

Barbra Wilson is the founder of "Women in Transition", about women who are marginalized, and she gives support to gays adjusting to society. In Wilson's chart she has Venus debilitated exactly conjunct Neptune. This is a very difficult chart for relationships as Neptune can cause confusion regarding relationships. But exalted Mercury with Venus uplifts Venus' debilitation. She has turned her issue of confusion into a purpose to help herself as well as others. She has taken her difficulty and turned it into empowerment to help others.

Venus in its debilitation is further aggravated with Saturn conjunct Ketu, as this would indicate losses with love and loneliness. Venus is saved by the conjunction with exalted Mercury because it doesn't pick up strength in the navamsha.

It appears that debilitated and exalted planets are always a source of focus and must always be assessed accordingly. They are power points in a life and always tell an interesting story. Her problems became her strengths as she now helps others with the issues she grew up to overcome.

Planet's Houses and Rulers- 1st House

1st House: Death and Endings

An important aspect to learn from this chart is that the 1st house can represent death as it is the 8th house (death) from the 6th house (accidents). Christina Onassis, daughter of Aristotle Onassis is cited later about her inheritance of her father's shipping industry and at the time was one of the richest men in the world. She died suddenly from a heart attack and had major issues with drugs, diet pills and sleeping pills. Her heart was weakened from extreme weight loss and repeated weight gain. It was when transiting Jupiter was in her 1st house that she died as Jupiter rules her 8th house. Jupiter is the worst planet based on house rulership for Taurus ascendants. On the day she passed, transiting Neptune was 14–15 degrees Sagittarius which was right on Mercury in the 8th house and opposed Uranus, both planets were 15 degrees. Neptune rules drugs and death in the 8th house. Uranus, as the planet of sudden events is commonly found to indicate heart attacks.

11th h.	12th h.	1st h.	2nd h.
☊ 00:52 PBh		ASC 02:32 Kri	♅℞ 15:01 Ard
♃ 08:09 Sat	Christina Onassis Mon 12-11-1950 15:00:00 New York, New York USA Timezone: 5 DST: 0 Latitude: 40N42'51 Longitude: 74W00'22 Ayanamsha : -23:10:20 Lahiri		♀℞ 26:35 Asl
♂ 04:03 USh ☽ 00:24 USh			
☿ 15:57 PSh ♀ 02:51 Mul	☉ 26:02 Jye		☋ 00:52 UPh ♄ 08:19 UPh ♆ 25:54 Cht
8th h.	7th h.	6th h.	5th h.

Planet's Houses and Rulers - 1st House

Chapter 5

	2nd h.		1st h.		12th h.	
3rd h.	♅ ℞ 15:01 Ard ♊		Asc 02:32 Kri	♈	☊ 00:52 PBh ♓	11th h.
4th h.	♀℞ 26:35 Asl	⊕	♉ ☊ ♏		♃ 08:09 Sat	10th h.
5th h.	☋ 00:52 UPh ♄ 08:19 UPh ♆ 25:54 Cht	♍ ♎	☉ 26:02 Jye	♑ ♐	♂ 04:03 USh ☽ 00:24 USh ☿ 15:57 PSh ♀ 02:51 Mul	9th h.
	6th h.		7th h.		8th h.	

Death

Asc	08:26:44		Can
☉	04:20:57		Sco
☽	17:31:26		Pis
♂	09:24:08		Pis
☿	27:56:40	c	Lib
♃	07:44:53	R	Tau
♀	02:06:31		Lib
♄	07:05:43		Sag
☊	17:13:01		Aqu
☋	17:13:01		Leo
♅	05:35:56		Sag
♆	14:44:10		Sag
♀	19:25:40		Lib

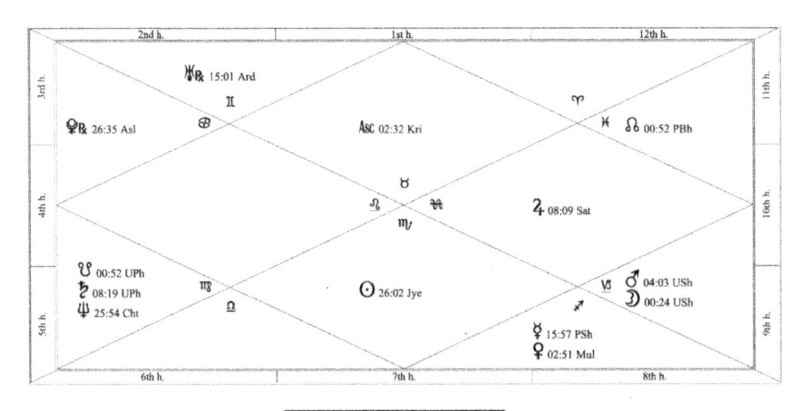

1st House: Death of pets

Another unusual meaning for the 1st house is that because it is the 8th from the 6th house, it can indicate the death of a pet, especially by accident since the 6th house is the house for pets and it is the 8th house (death) from the 6th house (pets).

Losing a pet is a very sad and emotional experience that we all go through deep within. No one really gives us the support that we get when a person dies. Our pets become a member of our family and when one dies, we seem to reminisce and grieve all the times that they were there during our lives. We feel the good and bad times that our pets were there, always with unconditional love. The loss of a pet is very sad and personal.

A friend who has gone through the tragic loss of her dog gives an indication as to the houses and area of life that are affected. The 6th house is the house that rules pets, but many do not realize the 1st house can indicate the death of a pet because it is the 8th house (death) from the 6th house (pets).

In her chart when she lost her beloved dog Sassy transiting Mars was aspecting her natal Rahu by opposition and Rahu is in the 1st house, but of course transiting Mars was in her 7th house conjunct natal Ketu indicating a feeling of deep loss. And her husband was just as close to the dog as her, so the 7th house also shows the heartache her spouse felt.

Transiting Saturn was exactly aspecting natal Rahu as well in the 1st house by its 3rd full aspect. Both Mars and Saturn were aspecting natal Rahu which sits in the 1st house indicating the death of a pet.

Death of pets

2nd h.	3rd h.	4th h.	5th h.
♓ ♃ 18:14 Rev	♈	♂ 29:29 Mrg ♉	☿ 04:48 Mrg ☉ 07:45 Ard ⛢ 15:57 Ard ♊
♒ ☊ 19:23 Sat ASC 09:16 Sat	Susie Patterson Fri 06-22-1951 23:05:00 Navasota, Texas USA Timezone: 6 DST: 0 Latitude: 30N23'16 Longitude: 96W05'15 Ayanamsha: -23:10:50 Lahiri		♀ 23:07 Asl ♀ 24:52 Asl ♋
♑ ☽ 29:19 Dha			☋ 19:23 PPh ♌
♐	♍	♎	♄ 02:53 UPh ♃℞ 23:34 Cht ♍
11th h.	10th h.	9th h.	8th h.

Planet's Houses and Rulers- 2nd House

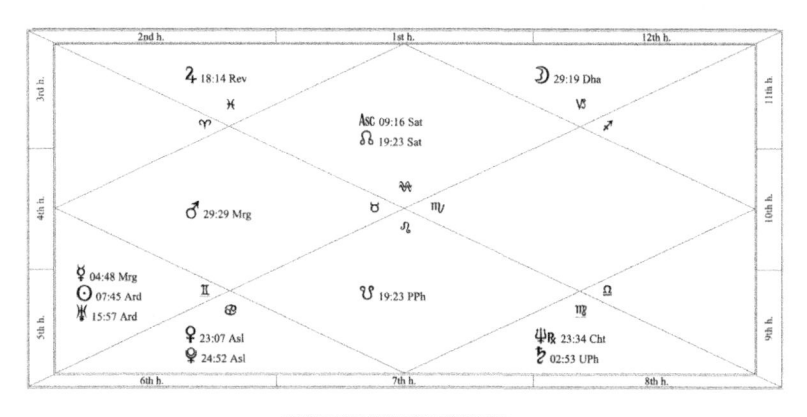

Chapter 5

Asc	19:30:59	Vir
☉	21:31:22	Leo
☽	20:11:56	Sag
♂	19:28:55 c	Leo
☿	25:40:00 c	Leo
♃	21:33:46	Sco
♀	28:27:29 c	Leo
♄	19:51:34 R	Sag
☊	21:50:46	Gem
☋	21:50:46	Sag
♅	12:11:05 R	Ari
♆	23:13:48 R	Aqu
♇	26:39:07 R	Sag

Sassy

Planet's Houses and Rulers- 2nd House

The first thing you must know is what planets rule each sign, because whichever sign sits on each house cusp is considered the ruling planet of that house. The Sun and Moon rule only one sign and the other planets rule two signs.

Sun: Leo

Moon: Cancer

Mercury: Gemini/Virgo

Venus: Taurus/Libra

Mars: Aries/Scorpio

Jupiter: Sagittarius/Pisces

Saturn: Capricorn/Aquarius

Let me repeat this most important understanding as we delve deeper into the meanings of the houses that I have observed.

The houses in astrology are the foundation of a chart, as they indicate all our life's experiences. They give planets meaning, strength or weakness depending on the houses they rule. Each planet has its array of meanings and things it rules. So, the planets are the energy, but they are also the transmitters of energy and carry the meanings of the houses to the house they reside in. Below are the planets and what they rule and represent individually, but their energetic properties will change as to the houses that they rule, transmitting or carrying with them the meanings of the houses they rule. This will make sense with all the examples of house rulers as they sit in different houses. In this section you will come to understand some of the discoveries I have made using this system.

2nd House: Money, earned income, early childhood, the mouth – as in your voice, and what you consume, and family

Many billionaires have the ruler of the 2nd house in the 11th house, or the ruler of the 11th house in the 2nd house. Any combination that connects these two houses produces great wealth.

The 2nd house is money earned, and the 11th house is the house of great gains or the wealth accumulated from the career, as it is the 2nd house (money) from the 10th house of purpose and career.

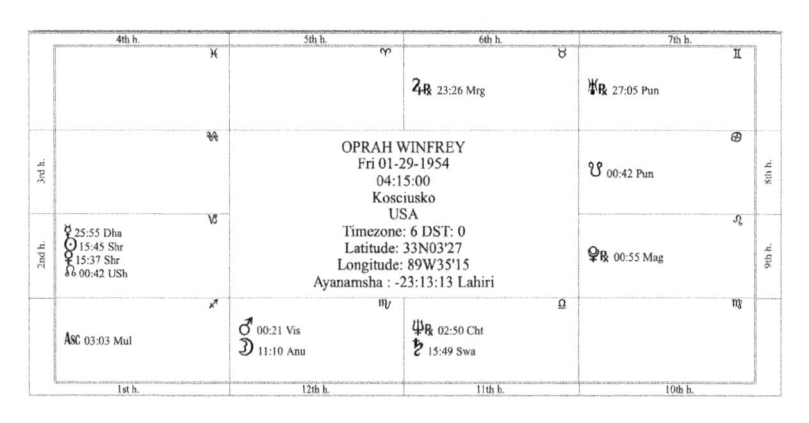

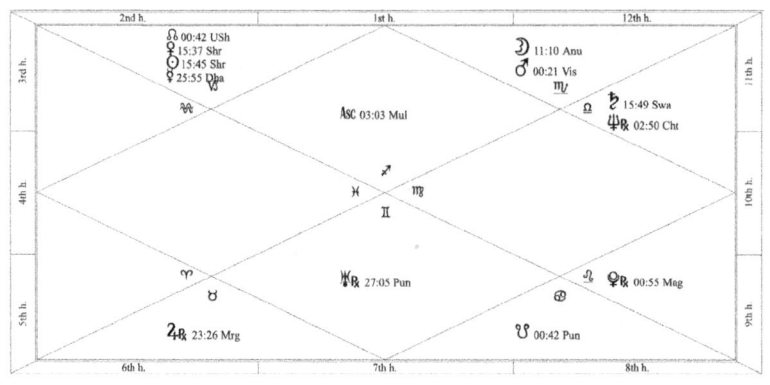

Ruler of 11ᵗʰ in 2ⁿᵈ or ruler of 2ⁿᵈ in 11ᵗʰ Great gains

Oprah Winfrey is a talk show host, television producer, actor, author, and philanthropist. She is best known for her talk show, *The Oprah Winfrey Show*, she is a billionaire, and one of the greatest philanthropist in U.S. history. She is ranked as one of the most influential women in the world. She was raised in poverty and her net worth today is about 3.5 billion.

Oprah has both the ruler of the 2ⁿᵈ house in the 11ᵗʰ house and the ruler of the 11ᵗʰ house in the 2ⁿᵈ house. Planets Saturn and Venus are in each other's sign of rulership, parivartana yoga, because they rule the two most powerful houses connected to money, these planets have brought her incredible great wealth. She is considered one of the richest and powerful women in the world today.

The 2nd house and 3rd house is ruled by Saturn, the 2nd house is our voice, and the 3rd house is communications and she made her fortune from using her voice in communication from her talk show. Saturn, ruler of these two houses sits in the 11th house of gains. Plus, not only is Saturn and Venus in parivartana but Saturn is exalted in Libra, its most powerful sign of exaltation, giving it enormous strength.

Another powerful variable is that Venus is ruler of the 11th house and is conjunct Rahu which always expands and empowers for more gains but can also represent fame. And even another very rare aspect is that Venus and the Sun are exactly conjunct. When the Sun is close to other planets it is usually considered combust, which can burn and weaken a planet's energy, but in this case because they are less than a degree from each other they are considered Cazimi. A Cazimi planet is one that is within a degree of the Sun and means that the planet becomes one with the Sun and enables the Sun to produce or emit the energy of the planet it is exactly conjunct through its rays. This means the Sun shines and puts out the energy of Venus. This is quite rare and Venus in the 2nd house of money and ruler of the 11th house of great grains enabled Oprah to go from poverty to a billionaire all on her own.

Planet's Houses and Rulers- 2nd House

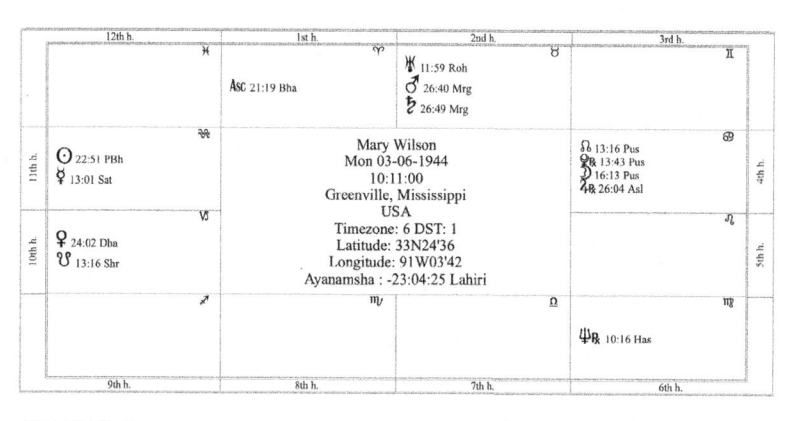

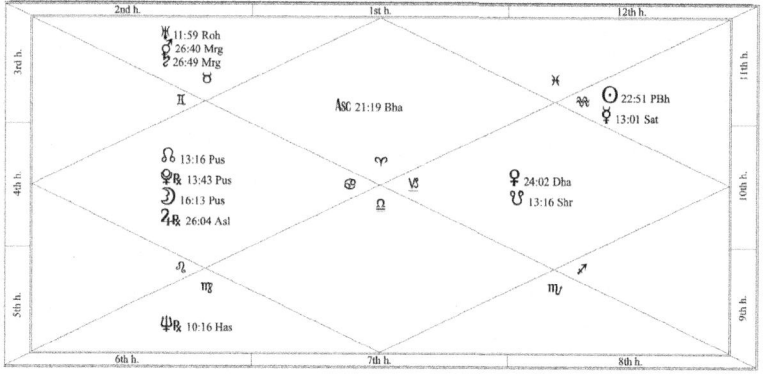

Chapter 5

12th h.	1st h.	2nd h.	3rd h.
♓	♈ ASC 21:19 Bha	♅ 11:59 Roh ♂ 26:40 Mrg ♄ 26:49 Mrg ♉	♊
♒ ☉ 22:51 PBh ☿ 13:01 Sat (11th h.)	Mary Wilson Mon 03-06-1944 10:11:00 Greenville, Mississippi USA Timezone: 6 DST: 1 Latitude: 33N24'36 Longitude: 91W03'42 Ayanamsha: -23:04:25 Lahiri		☊ 13:16 Pus ☿ℝ 13:43 Pus ☽ 16:13 Pus ♃ℝ 26:04 Aal (4th h.)
♑ ♀ 24:02 Dha ☋ 13:16 Shr (10th h.)			♌ (5th h.)
♐	♏	♎	♍ ♆ℝ 10:16 Has
9th h.	8th h.	7th h.	6th h.

2nd h.	1st h.	12th h.
♅ 11:59 Roh ♂ 26:40 Mrg ♄ 26:49 Mrg ♉ ♊ (3rd h.)	ASC 21:19 Bha ♓ ♈ (11th h.)	♒ ☉ 22:51 PBh ☿ 13:01 Sat
☊ 13:16 Pus ☿ℝ 13:43 Pus ☽ 16:13 Pus ♃ℝ 26:04 Aal (4th h.)	♋ ♑ ♎	♀ 24:02 Dha ☋ 13:16 Shr (10th h.)
♌ ♍ (5th h.) ♆ℝ 10:16 Has	♏ (6th h.) ♐	♐ (8th h.)

Malefics in 2nd house-very difficult childhood

Malefics in 4th house-no sense of security, difficult mother

Malefics in both 2nd and 4th houses have a bad childhood, no security.

Mary Wilson gained worldwide recognition as a founding member of The Supremes, the most successful Motown act of the 1960s and the best-charting female group in U.S. chart history, as well as one of the best-selling girl groups of all-time. The trio reached number one on *Billboard*'s Hot 100 with 12 of their singles, ten of which feature Wilson on backing vocals.

Wilson later became a *New York Times* best-selling author in 1986 with the release of her first autobiography, *Dreamgirl: My Life as a Supreme*, which set records for sales in its genre, and later for the autobiography *Supreme Faith: Someday We'll Be Together*.

Whenever difficult malefics are in the 2nd house it means the early childhood experiences were very difficult, with little security. Wilson has both Saturn and Mars tightly conjunct here. She grew up in the projects in Detroit. Her parents separated and she lived with her aunt who she came to believe was really her biological mother.

Since the ruler of the 2nd house is Venus and Venus is conjunct Ketu in the 10th house, she had a very unusual career as a singer (2nd house-voice). To further understand how the childhood and their security through family was, look also to the 4th house of family and mother. She has a very complex 4th house. Jupiter with the Moon in Cancer gives happiness and security, but Pluto and Rahu represent intensity and possibility of abuse. Her mother was not her real mother whom she believed to be growing up as a child.

7th h.	8th h.	9th h.	10th h.
	♆℞ 11:35 Ash		☋ 25:15 Pun
6th h. — ♄℞ 11:42 Sat	Julie Andrews Tue 10-01-1935 06:00:00 Walton Upon Thames United Kingdom Timezone: 0 DST: 1 Latitude: 51N23'00 Longitude: 00W26'00 Ayanamsha: -22:57:50 Lahiri	♀ 04:16 Pus	11th h.
5th h.		♀ 13:40 PPh ♆ 22:12 PPh	12th h.
☊ 25:15 PSh	♂ 17:07 Jye	☿ 08:32 Swa ☽ 22:44 Vis ♃ 29:02 Vis	ASC 02:29 UPh ☉ 14:07 Has
4th h.	3rd h.	2nd h.	1st h.

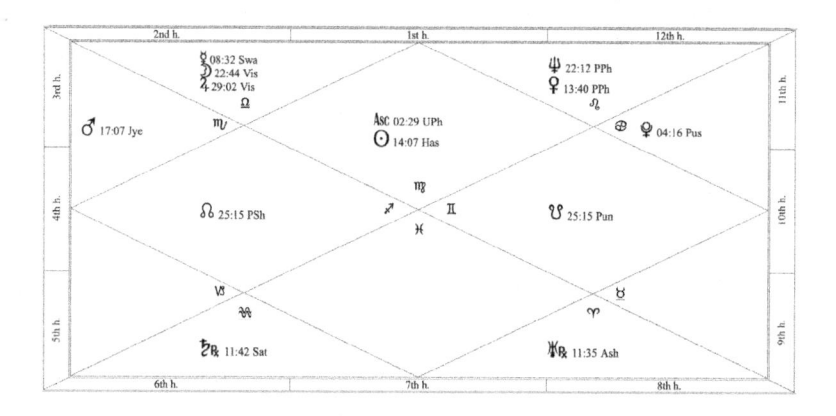

2nd House: The Voice

Julie Andrews is an English actor, singer, and author. She gained numerous accolades throughout her career spanning over seven decades, including an Academy Award. She is known for her beautiful voice. The range, accuracy and tone of Andrew's voice is a rare gift of absolute pitch and reach four octaves.

She has three benefics in the 2nd house of the voice. Jupiter, Moon and Mercury are a very interesting combination. Mercury rules the 10th house of career, and she made a career out of her voice-singing. Jupiter is a natural benefic and sits with the Moon, which is a Gaja Kesari yoga (Jupiter in an angle/kendra from the Moon). This denotes greatness and leadership, which gave an amazing voice and brought wealth and money being placed in this house, but the Moon also rules the 11th house. Ruler of the 11th in the 2nd house gives great wealth like with Oprah.

You would be led to believe from this that she had a good childhood experience, but this is not true. Andrews was conceived as a result of an affair her mother had with a family friend. She discovered her true parentage from her mother in 1950. She was raised during World War II and after her parents divorced, her new stepfather was alcoholic and abused her. The ruler of the 2nd house is Venus and Venus is placed in the 12th house of loss and endings, so this really changes the situation concerning her early life. Remember to always look to where the rulers of the houses sit, not only the houses the planets occupy. They are transmitters of the planets and house energies.

The problems are seen by looking at Rahu in her 4th house of home, mother and family. But also, to be able to understand this you must always look at a chart not only from the ascendant but also from the Moon as the ascendant (Chandra Lagna). This reflects the feeling and emotions as well. From the Moon, Mars sits in the 2nd house of childhood experiences explaining why she had a difficult time growing up.

2nd House: Eating Disorders

10th h. Pis	11th h. Ari	12th h. Tau	1st h. Gem
☊ 14:27 UBh			ASC 07:25 Ard ♅ ℞ 07:48 Ard
9th h. Aqu ☉ 18:22 Sat	Karen Carpenter Thu 03-02-1950 11:45:00 New Haven, CT, Connecticut USA		♀ ℞ 23:16 Asl ☽ 25:16 Asl	2nd h. Can
8th h. Cap ☿ 28:35 Dha ♃ 27:36 Dha ♀ 11:47 Shr	Timezone: 5 DST: 0 Latitude: 41N18'00 Longitude: 72W54'00 Ayanamsha : -23:09:38 Lahiri		♄ ℞ 23:14 PPh	3rd h. Leo
			☋ 14:27 Has ♂ ℞ 15:41 Has ♆ ℞ 23:42 Cht	
7th h. Sag	6th h. Sco	5th h. Lib	4th h. Vir

Planet's Houses and Rulers- 2nd House

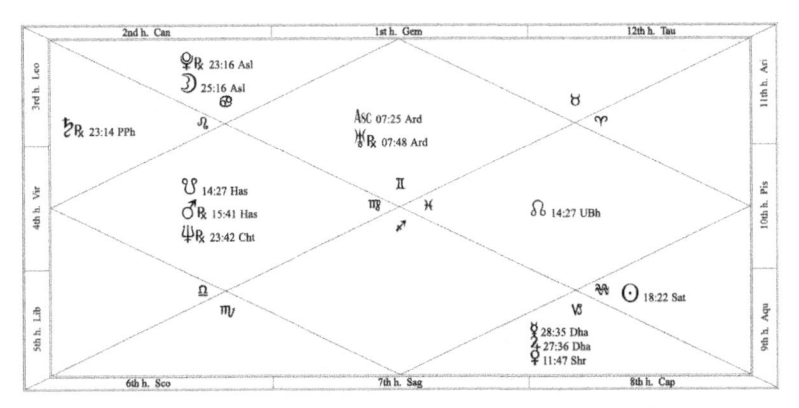

Chapter 5

```
| 2nd h. Can              | 1st h. Gem          | 12th h. Tau       |
| ♀℞ 23:16 Asl            |                     |                   |
| ☽ 25:16 Asl             | ASC 07:25 Ard       | ♉                 |
| ⊕                       | ♅℞ 07:48 Ard        | ♈                 |
| ♄℞ 23:14 PPh            |                     |                   |
|                         | ♊                   |                   |
| ☋ 14:27 Has             | ♍    ♓              | ☊ 14:27 UBh       |
| ♂℞ 15:41 Has            | ♐                   |                   |
| ♆℞ 23:42 Cht            |                     |                   |
|                         |                     | ♒ ☉ 18:22 Sat     |
| ♎                       |                     | ♑                 |
| ♏                       |                     | ☿ 28:35 Dha       |
|                         |                     | ♃ 27:36 Dha       |
|                         |                     | ♀ 11:47 Shr       |
| 6th h. Sco              | 7th h. Sag          | 8th h. Cap        |
```

Karen Carpenter was an American singer and drummer who, along with her older brother Richard, were part of the duo the Carpenters. She was praised for her 3-octave contralto vocal range. Her drumming abilities were viewed positively by other musicians and critics. Her struggles with eating disorders would later raise awareness of anorexia and body dysmorphia.

Briefly married in the early 1980s, she suffered from anorexia nervosa, which was little-known at the time. Her death from heart failure at age 32, related to complications of her illness, led to increased visibility and awareness of eating disorders. Her work continues to attract praise, including being listed among Rolling Stone's 100 greatest singers of all time.

Her mother was known among her musical acquaintances as the dragon lady. At Karen's worst, her family insisted she had no emotional problems and that her 'over dieting' was something they could sort out by themselves.

Emotional problems were the cause of her eating disorder, her mother's inability to show love and affection was paramount. She was adored by millions, but it was her mother's love she never received. Her mother was intensely overbearing and controlling as can be seen with Pluto conjunct the Moon in the 2nd house. The Moon is not only closely conjunct Pluto but it is intensified by being in Cancer which rules the Moon. I find that the Moon in Cancer drastically magnifies the areas it rules.

Interestingly the 2nd house rules early family life as well as the mouth. This means it rules what goes into the mouth, as well as what comes out of the mouth. So it rules our voice and the foods we eat. All these variables are affected profoundly with Pluto conjunct the Moon in the 2nd house. She had a magnificent voice and which made her great wealth as the 2nd house is our ability to make money. Additionally her family life was very controlled as her stage mother pushed her to success.

Her mother's problems are also seen with Mars in the 4th house with Ketu and Neptune. This indicates a problematic home life with many secrets that are ignored. Mars and Ketu point to a difficult mother, and the lack of security from both home and mother. Furthermore, Mars and Ketu are in the sign of Virgo which can be unusually concerned with perfection and diet and weight issues.

Chapter 6

Planets in Houses and ruling houses: 3rd house

The number three is the number of creativity and talent and the same goes for the 3rd house. It pertains to communication and the media but never forget it is the house of creative talents. This is known as the house of performers and entertainers. The 5th house in which we first think of as the house of creativity gets its meaning because it is the 3rd house counting from the 3rd house. So, both houses pertain to creativity and the performing arts. When there is a connection between one of these two houses 3 and 5 a star is born.

The 3rd house is probably, in my opinion the most underrated house in a chart. I have many examples proving the power of this house, especially when it is connected to the 5th house for talent and entertainment.

3rd House: Entertainers

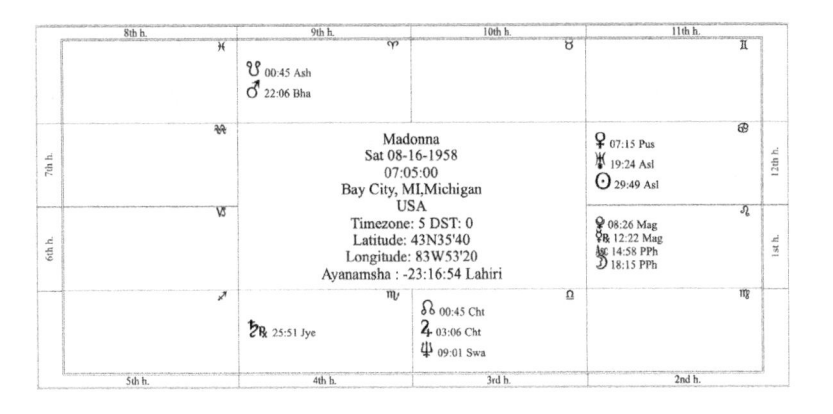

8th h.	9th h.	10th h.	11th h.
♓	♈ ☊ 00:45 Ash ♂ 22:06 Bha	♉	♊
♒ (7th h.)	Madonna Sat 08-16-1958 07:05:00 Bay City, MI, Michigan USA Timezone: 5 DST: 0 Latitude: 43N35'40 Longitude: 83W53'20 Ayanamsha : -23:16:54 Lahiri	♀ 07:15 Pus ⛢ 19:24 Asl ☉ 29:49 Asl	⊕ (12th h.)
♑ (6th h.)		☿ 08:26 Mag ♀R 12:22 Mag Asc 14:58 PPh ☽ 18:15 PPh	♌ (1st h.)
♐	♏ ♄R 25:51 Jye	☋ 00:45 Cht ♃ 03:06 Cht ♆ 09:01 Swa	♎	♍
5th h.	4th h.	3rd h.	2nd h.

73

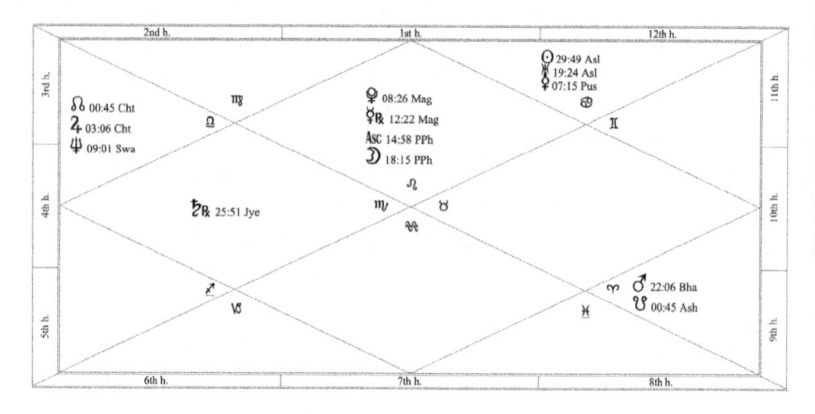

```
                2nd h.              1st h.                 12th h.

   ☊ 00:45 Cht         ♏          ♀ 08:26 Mag       ☉ 29:49 Asl
   ♃ 03:06 Cht         ♎          ☿℞ 12:22 Mag      ♅ 19:24 Asl
   ♆ 09:01 Swa                    Asc 14:58 PPh     ☿ 07:15 Pus
                                  ☽ 18:15 PPh       ♋

                                        ♌
                       ♏                          ♉
                   ♄℞ 25:51 Jye        ♍
                                       ♒

                       ♐                             ♈   ♂ 22:06 Bha
                       ♑                             ♓   ☋ 00:45 Ash

                6th h.              7th h.              8th h.
```

Referred to as the "Queen of Pop", Madonna is noted for her continual reinvention and versatility in music production, songwriting, and visual presentation. She has pushed the boundaries of artistic expression in mainstream music, while maintaining control over every aspect of her career. Her works, which incorporate social, political, sexual, and religious themes, have generated both controversy and critical acclaim.

Madonna's chart totally explains her success within the entertainment field. She has Jupiter ruler of the 5th house in the 3rd house. The 5th house concerns a deep desire for self-expression and her Jupiter in the 3rd house sits with Rahu which always magnifies the planet it is next to, giving her an incredibly intense desire to be famous and perform. Additionally, this combo includes Neptune which rules photography, movies and film. She was in a number of films, but she also did very well with writing and books, which is also a 3rd house component. Madonna's book: "Sex" takes a provocative look at sexual fantasies in photographs and words, with the erotic imaginings highlighted by a series of innovative special effects. Now she writes children's books, as the 5th house rules children.

Planets in Houses and ruling houses: 3rd house

Chapter 6

Her Jupiter and Rahu are in the nakshatra Chitra which is a very colorful nakshatra said to be noticed in a crowd, standing out with brilliance. They love bright colors, and many performers have this nakshatra. Plus, she has her Moon and ascendant in Leo, the nakshatra Purva Phalguni which is said to be the nakshatra of very expressive and creative people in the performing arts.

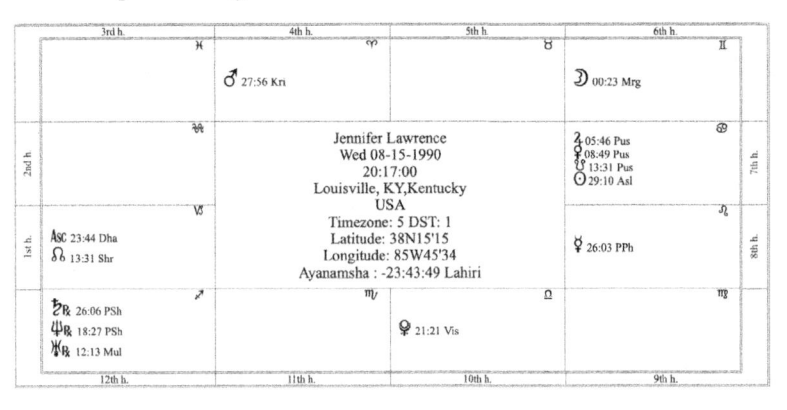

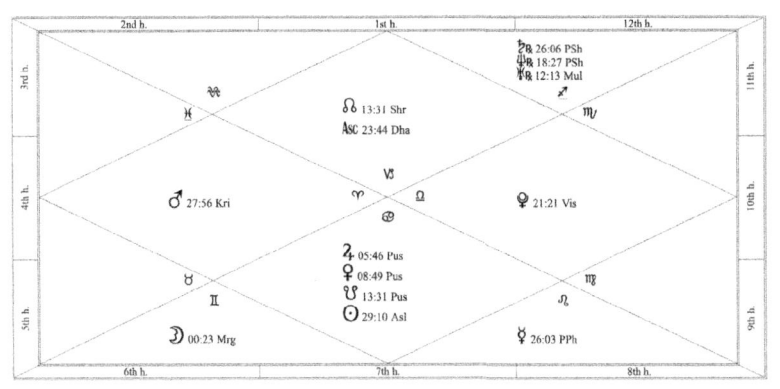

3rd h.	4th h.	5th h.	6th h.
♓	♈ ♂ 27:56 Kri	♉	♊ ☽ 00:23 Mrg
2nd h. ♒	Jennifer Lawrence Wed 08-15-1990 20:17:00 Louisville, KY, Kentucky USA Timezone: 5 DST: 1 Latitude: 38N15'15 Longitude: 85W45'34 Ayanamsha : -23:43:49 Lahiri		♋ ♃ 05:46 Pus ♀ 08:49 Pus ☋ 13:31 Pus ☉ 29:10 Asl	7th h.
1st h. ♑ Asc 23:44 Dha ☊ 13:31 Shr			♌ ☿ 26:03 PPh	8th h.
12th h. ♐ ♄℞ 26:06 PSh ⛢℞ 18:27 PSh ♆℞ 12:13 Mul	11th h. ♏	10th h. ♎ ♀ 21:21 Vis	9th h. ♍

2nd h.	1st h.	12th h.
	♄℞ 26:06 PSh ⛢℞ 18:27 PSh ♆℞ 12:13 Mul ♐	11th h.
♒ ♓	☊ 13:31 Shr Asc 23:44 Dha	♏
3rd h.	♑	
4th h. ♂ 27:56 Kri	♈ ♎ ⊕	♀ 21:21 Vis 10th h.
	♃ 05:46 Pus ♀ 08:49 Pus ☋ 13:31 Pus ☉ 29:10 Asl	
5th h. ♉ ☊ ☽ 00:23 Mrg	♊	♍ ♌ ☿ 26:03 PPh 9th h.
6th h.	7th h.	8th h.

Entertainer: 3rd house ruler exact degree of exaltation- Jupiter and aspects and rules 3rd house

Jennifer Lawrence was the world's highest-paid actress in 2015 and 2016, her films have grossed over $6 billion worldwide to date. She appeared in *Time*'s 100 most influential people in the world list in 2013 and the *Forbes* Celebrity 100 list from 2013 to 2016.

At first glance you may not see the performing capability in this chart till you take a closer look at her chart where the ruling planet of the 3rd house Jupiter is not only exalted but sits at its exact degree of exaltation. Not only are planets exalted in a certain sign but there is also a particular degree that the planets are most exalted in. Degrees that are close to this degree make the planet even stronger, especially a few degrees before the exact degree. Jupiter's highest degree of exaltation is 5 degrees Cancer. Remember the entire sign of Cancer Jupiter is exalted, but this degree is at its absolute peak making it astoundingly powerful. Plus, it sits in the 7th house an angle/kendra making it a maha purusha yoga, Hamsa yoga (when a planet is in its own sign or exalted in an angle/kendra). This profoundly empowers Jupiter and everything it rules becomes hugely empowered.

Venus rules Lawrence's 5th house of creativity, and it is closely conjunct Jupiter, bringing together the ruler of the 3rd house with the ruler of the 5th house. From the Moon, Venus again rules the 5th house and is with the Sun ruler of the 3rd house. She was born to be a performer.

Also, the opposite degrees of the exalted degrees are the weakest therefore, 5 degrees of Capricorn is Jupiter's exact debilitation degree, these degrees are powerful one way or another.

Exalted and Debilitation degrees of the planets

Sun: 10 degrees Aries Exalted / 10 degrees Libra Debilitated

Moon: 3 degrees Taurus Exalted / 3 degrees Libra Debilitated

Planets in Houses and ruling houses: 3rd house

Mercury: 15 Degrees Virgo Exalted / 15 degrees Pisces Debilitated

Venus: 27 degrees Pisces Exalted / 27 degrees Virgo Debilitated

Mars: 28 degrees Capricorn Exalted / 28 degrees Cancer Debilitated

Jupiter: 5 degrees Cancer Exalted / 5 degrees Capricorn Debilitated

Saturn: 20 degrees Libra Exalted / 20 degrees Aries Debilitated

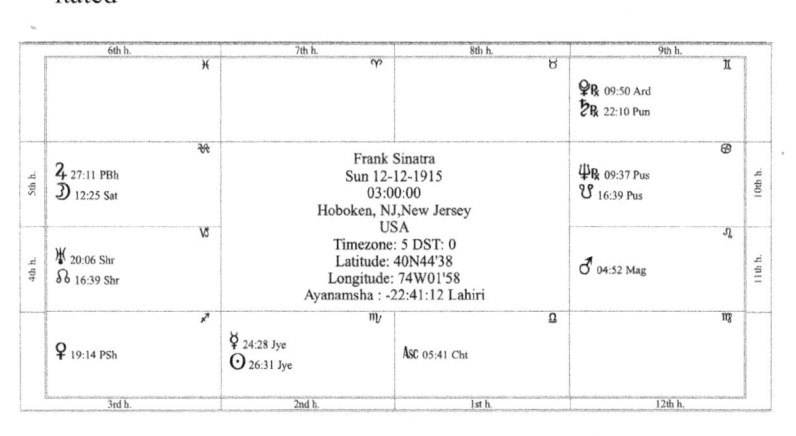

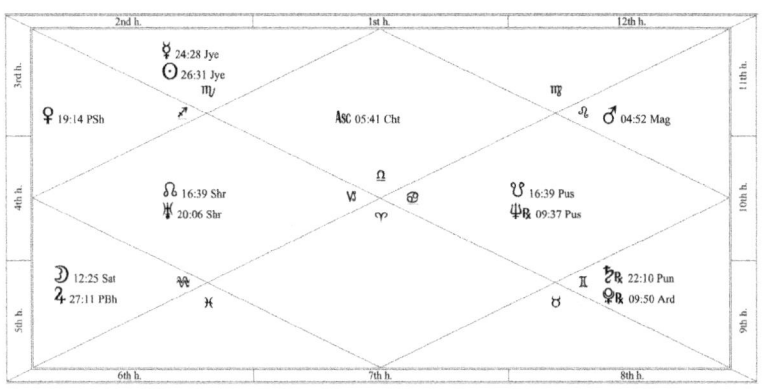

When I think of some of the greatest performers throughout history Frank Sinatra is one of the greats! He spent his entire life performing with a voice smooth as silk. His records transcend time. I thought there must be 3rd and 5th house connections here, and of course there is!

Sinatra has the ruler of the 3rd house Jupiter in the 5th house and it conjuncts the Moon (Gaja Kesari yoga, Moon/ Jupiter), plus the Moon rules the 10th house of fame and career. Venus is in his 3rd house and is in Sagittarius ruled by Jupiter in the 5th house.

Since he is a singer, he must have a powerful 2nd house ruling the voice. Looking to his 2nd house he has Mercury with the Sun in Scorpio. Mars is the ruler of the 2nd house and sits in the 11th house of gains through the voice, but his Sun and Mars are in parivartana connecting these two planets intrinsically. He became very wealthy through his voice just as Oprah became extremely wealthy through her voice even though she was a talk show host, with her parivartana with the 2nd and 11th houses.

1st h.	2nd h.	3rd h.	4th h.
ASC 14:15 UBh		♃ 04:45 Kri ♂ 09:41 Kri ♀ 11:29 Roh ☽ 18:31 Roh	☉ 03:41 Mrg ☿ 11:01 Ard ♀ 17:50 Ard ☋ 18:00 Ard
♅℞ 00:51 Dha	Dean Martin Sun 06-17-1917 23:55:00 Steubenville, OH, Ohio USA Timezone: 6 DST: 0 Latitude: 40N22'00 Longitude: 80W37'00 Ayanamsha: -22:42:32 Lahiri		♄ 06:32 Pus ♆ 10:29 Pus
☊ 18:00 PSh			
10th h.	9th h.	8th h.	7th h.

Planets in Houses and ruling houses: 3rd house

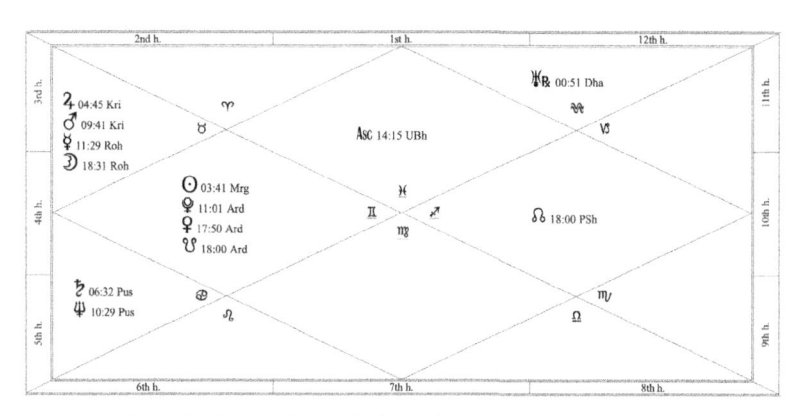

Chapter 6

2nd h.	1st h.	12th h.
♃ 04:45 Kri ♂ 09:41 Kri ☿ 11:29 Roh ☾ 18:31 Roh	♈ ♉ ASC 14:15 UBh	♅ ℞ 00:51 Dha ♒ ♑
☉ 03:41 Mrg ♆ 11:01 Ard ♀ 17:50 Ard ☊ 18:00 Ard	♓ ♊ ♐ ♍	☋ 18:00 PSh
♄ 06:32 Pus ♇ 10:29 Pus	⊕ ♌	♏ ♎
6th h.	7th h.	8th h.

Dean Martin is another all-time favorite voice of the past. Another silky-smooth voice like Sinatra. Martin and Frank Sinatra were great friends in the entertainment business. They were part of an iconic Hollywood group called the "Rat Pack", doing performances together in Las Vegas.

Martin has the ruler of the 5th house, the Moon in the 3rd house. The Moon is very powerful as it is in its sign of exaltation, Taurus. In the 3rd house he has four powerful planets, Moon, Mercury, Mars and Jupiter.

The 2nd house of the voice is ruled by Mars, and his Mars sits with Moon, Mercury and Jupiter creating Raja Yoga (kingship power yoga) and Dhana yogas (wealth producing). A Dhana yoga is when there is any combination of the rulers of the wealth/money producing house rulers. It is when the rulers of the trikona houses (1, 5 and 9) are combined with the two money houses (2 and 11). This is when the rulers of these houses in any combination are connected. Mars and Jupiter in conjunction is a Dhana yoga since Jupiter rules the 1st (trikona) and Mars rules the 2nd (money). The Moon is also the ruler of a trikona (5th house) adding another Dhana yoga. These planets in the 3rd house of performing and entertaining mean that he made his wealth and money through the performing arts.

The ruler of the 3rd house is Venus, and it is in a mutual exchange with Mercury in the 3rd house. This chart is easily spotted as a performer with great talent. Even from Chandra lagna Venus is in parivartana with Mercury in the 2nd house explaining his beautiful voice that made him famous and unforgettable.

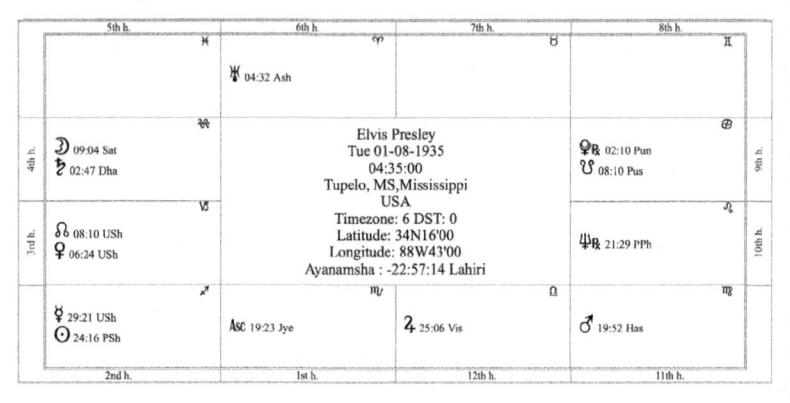

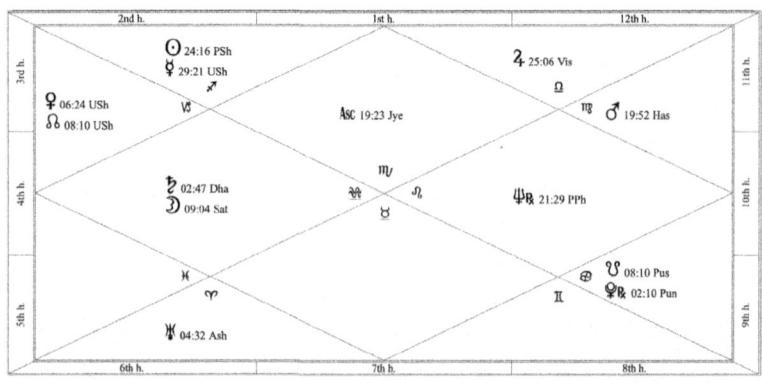

	5th h.	6th h.	7th h.	8th h.
4th h.		♅ 04:32 Ash	Elvis Presley Tue 01-08-1935 04:35:00 Tupelo, MS, Mississippi USA Timezone: 6 DST: 0 Latitude: 34N16'00 Longitude: 88W43'00 Ayanamsha : -22:57:14 Lahiri	♀℞ 02:10 Pun ☋ 08:10 Pus	9th h.
3rd h.	☽ 09:04 Sat ♄ 02:47 Dha			
	☊ 08:10 USh ♀ 06:24 USh			♆℞ 21:29 PPh	10th h.
	☿ 29:21 USh ☉ 24:16 PSh	Asc 19:23 Jye	♃ 25:06 Vis	♂ 19:52 Has
	2nd h.	1st h.	12th h.	11th h.

	2nd h.	1st h.	12th h.	
3rd h.	☉ 24:16 PSh ☿ 29:21 USh ♀ 06:24 USh ☊ 08:10 USh	Asc 19:23 Jye	♃ 25:06 Vis ♂ 19:52 Has	11th h.
4th h.	♄ 02:47 Dha ☽ 09:04 Sat		♆℞ 21:29 PPh	12th h.
5th h.	♅ 04:32 Ash		☋ 08:10 Pus ♀℞ 02:10 Pun	9th h.
	6th h.	7th h.	8th h.	

Elvis Presley is still a household name and is called the "King of Rock and Roll". Everyone knows Elvis Presley!

Entertainers that are singers usually have the 3rd'd and 2nd houses connected as well as the 5th house. Also, the 2nd house connects the 11th house to the performers using their voice

Elvis has Venus in the 3rd house conjunct Rahu, Rahu gave him fame and charisma. In his 2nd house of the voice, he has a Sun and Mercury conjunction and Mercury rules his 11th house of great gains.

The interesting aspect in his chart is that Jupiter is in the 12th house ruler of the 2nd house and 5th indicated imprisonment and losses. When someone is as famous as Elvis, he was certainly a prisoner as one can never go out into the public without getting mobbed. Furthermore, it has since come out that his manager Colonel Tom Parker imprisoned him as he told Elvis he owed him millions and that he could not leave the country due to contract agreements, so Elvis was imprisoned in more than one way.

Turns out the Colonel was a fraud, not actually a Colonel and defrauded Elvis by gambling his money and the reason they could never leave the country was that Parker was not a U.S. citizen and never could get a passport.

2nd h.	3rd h.	4th h.	5th h.
♓	♈	♅ 08:53 Kri ♄ 12:05 Roh ☿℞ 25:31 Mrg ♉	☉ 03:04 Mrg ♃ 08:40 Ard ♊
♀ 25:21 Bha			

1st h.		6th h.
♒ ASC 17:56 Sat ☋ 13:37 Sat	Paul McCartney Thu 06-18-1942 02:00:00 Liverpool England Timezone: 0 DST: 2 Latitude: 53N25'00 Longitude: 03W00'00 Ayanamsha : -23:03:06 Lahiri	⊕ ♂ 09:19 Pus ♀ 11:12 Pus ☽ 18:19 Asl ♋
♑ 12th h.		♌ ☊ 13:37 PPh 7th h.

11th h.	10th h.	9th h.	8th h.
♐	♏	♎ ♇ 04:03 UPh	♍

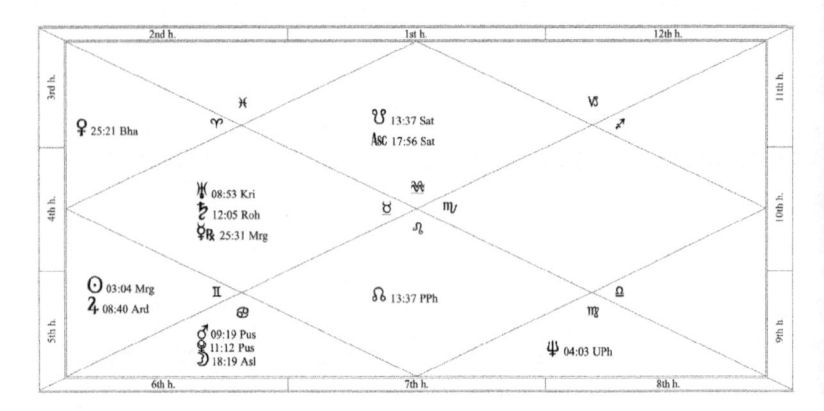

Paul McCartney, one of the legendary Beatles must have 2nd, 3rd and 5th house influences from all his performing, singing and writing. McCartney was the driving force of the Beatles as both Ringo and John said he forced them go to the recording studio when they both were too busy getting high. Song writers will have a connection between the 2nd house of the voice as in singing and the 3rd house of talent but also writing. Paul has Jupiter ruler of the 2nd house in the 5th house of creativity conjunct the Sun. The Sun is close though to Jupiter and weakens it to a certain degree.

Venus overturns these effects as it is in the 3rd house of talent and entertainers and rules the 9th and 4th house giving it yoga karaka status (rules a trikona and kendra). His 2nd, 3rd and 5th houses are empowered for an entertainer, singer and wealth.

The wealth through singing is seen through Jupiter as it rules the 11th house of great gains and the 2nd house of money and singing. McCartney is the highest grossing entertainer of all time at 1.2 billion today.

Planets in Houses and ruling houses: 3rd house

Chapter 6

7th h.	8th h.	9th h.	10th h.
♓	♈	♉	♊
		☊ 29:33 Pun	

6th h. / ♒ / Brittany Spears / Wed 12-02-1981 / 01:30:00 / Mahon, MS, Mississippi / USA / Timezone: 6 DST: 0 / Latitude: 34N48'53 / Longitude: 89W30'55 / Ayanamsha: -23:36:00 Lahiri / 11th h.

5th h. / ♑ / ☽ 18:47 Shr / ♀ 01:30 USh / ♂ 29:40 UPh / 12th h.

4th h.	3rd h.	2nd h.	1st h.
♐	♏	♎	♍
☋ 29:33 USh	♅ 07:22 Anu	♀ 02:21 Cht	ASC 09:47 UPh
♆ 00:26 Mul	☿ 11:49 Anu	♃ 07:24 Swa	♄ 25:40 Cht
	☉ 16:26 Anu		

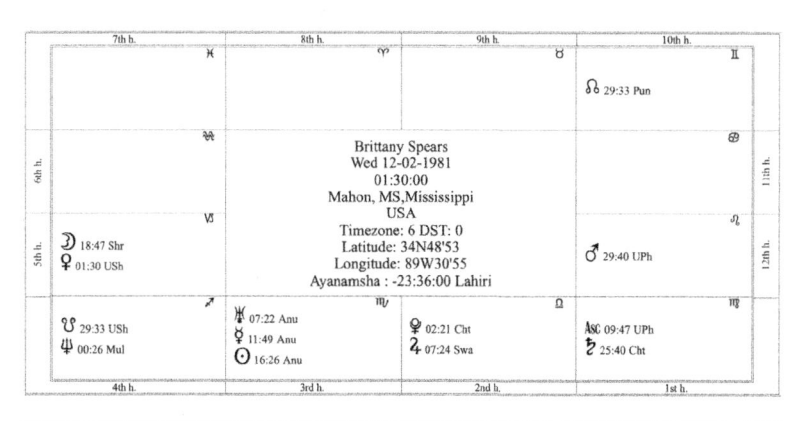

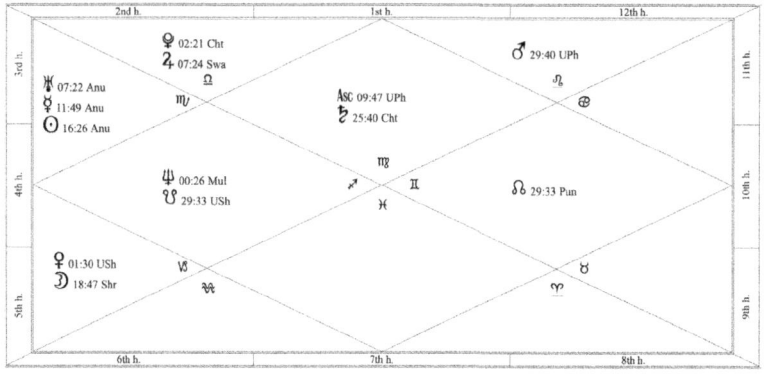

2nd h.	1st h.	12th h.
♀ 02:21 Cht ♃ 07:24 Swa ♎	ASC 09:47 UPh ♄ 25:40 Cht	♂ 29:40 UPh
3rd h. ♅ 07:22 Anu ☿ 11:49 Anu ☉ 16:26 Anu ♏	♍	11th h.
4th h. ♆ 00:26 Mul ☋ 29:33 USh ♐	♊ ♓	10th h. ☊ 29:33 Pun
5th h. ♀ 01:30 USh ☽ 18:47 Shr ♑ ♒	7th h. ♈	9th h. ♉

A younger singer, performer and entertainer that must be mentioned as she was a household name in the 1990s is Brittany Spears. She shot to such extreme stardom that she lost her mind with all the demands and control put on her life.

Her chart displays all the classic indications of a talented entertainer, with extremely strong 3rd and 5th house influences. The 2nd house of the voice and singing has Jupiter in Libra ruled by Venus which goes to the 5th house of creativity and the performing arts. Venus in the 5th house is conjunct the Moon which these two planets together are always auspicious.

In the 3rd house sits the Sun with Mercury, as Mercury is the planet of versatility and adaptability and it rules the 10th

83

house of the career, indicating a career as an entertainer but also Mercury tightly conjunct Uranus gave her the ability to be ingenious and do things in a new unique way.

The Sun and Mars are in Parivartana exchanging between the 12th and 3rd houses which seems to be a common factor with the stars that become so famous they don't have a normal life due to the problems fame brings, no privacy and being hunted by the paparazzi. This is what the 12th house brings, loneliness and imprisonment. It is very lonely at the top and although many believe fame is great, most hate it once they get there.

Ruler of 3rd in 5th house: Entertainers!

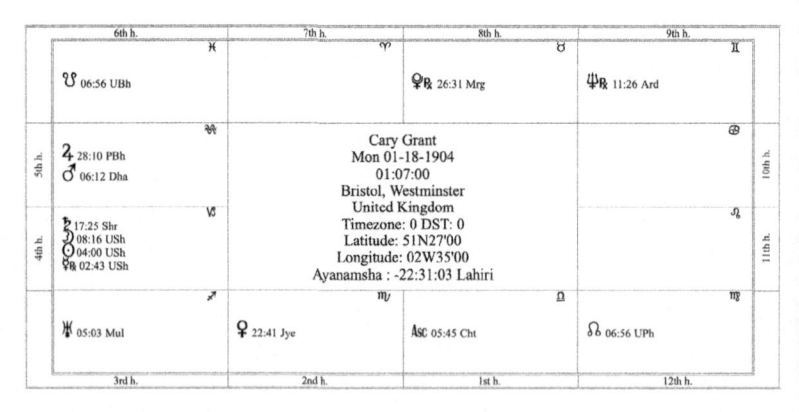

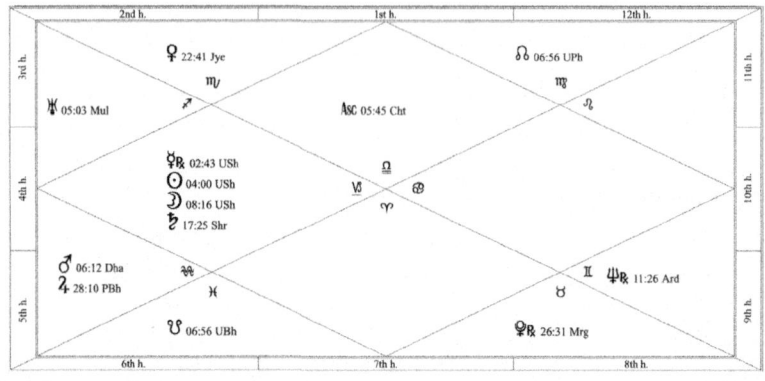

6th h.	7th h.	8th h.	9th h.
☊ 06:56 UBh		♀℞ 26:31 Mrg	♆℞ 11:26 Ard
♃ 28:10 PBh ♂ 06:12 Dha	Cary Grant Mon 01-18-1904 01:07:00 Bristol, Westminster United Kingdom		
♄ 17:25 Shr ☽ 08:16 USh ☉ 04:00 USh ☿℞ 02:43 USh	Timezone: 0 DST: 0 Latitude: 51N27'00 Longitude: 02W35'00 Ayanamsha : -22:31:03 Lahiri		
♅ 05:03 Mul	♀ 22:41 Jye	ASC 05:45 Cht	☋ 06:56 UPh
3rd h.	2nd h.	1st h.	12th h.

Cary Grant is one of my all-time legendary favorite actors, especially in Alfred Hitchcock's movies. He was handsome, suave, debonair, and a lady's man. I just had to see if he had the 3rd house and 5th house connections. He has the ruler of the 3rd house, Jupiter in the 5th house conjunct Mars. His Venus in the 2nd house in Scorpio gives charisma with a very interesting voice or accent, as it is ruled by Mars in the 5th house of creativity and conjunct the ruler of the 3rd house, Jupiter.

3rd House: Technology

Mars/Venus Parivartana

Sun/Rahu in 10th house (Raja Yoga)

Again, I have always said the 3rd House is the most underrated house in the chart as it has many meanings and indications. Aside from entertainers, creativity, and talent, it also rules writing, media, and technology. Maybe it makes an entertainer more popular because it can deal with mass media and attention.

As mentioned before, the 3rd house also pertains to communications and media. Therefore, it rules the Internet and anything that concerns ways that people are connected through communications. Understanding this, it makes sense that individuals who work with mass media and communications will have a very strong 3rd house.

Technology used to connect with others through communications will be represented in the 3rd house. Mark Zuckerberg, creator of Facebook explains this principle very well. Zuckerberg became a multibillionaire with his Facebook platform. In his third house he has Mars, Moon Saturn and Pluto in Libra. Mars is the planet that pertains to engineering and mechanics. What adds benefit to this chart, is the aspects of Venus and Mercury in opposition in the 9th house. Notice that Venus and Mars are in parivartana, exchanging of signs. Venus in its rulership of the 3rd and 10th houses directs his career and the mechanics of Mars in the 3rd House of communications. Mercury as his money planet rules both the 2nd and 11th houses, Bringing him great wealth through the mechanics of communications.

Zuckerberg's Moon is afflicted due to its position between two malefic planets, both Mars and Saturn. This means emotionally he is disconnected from other people.

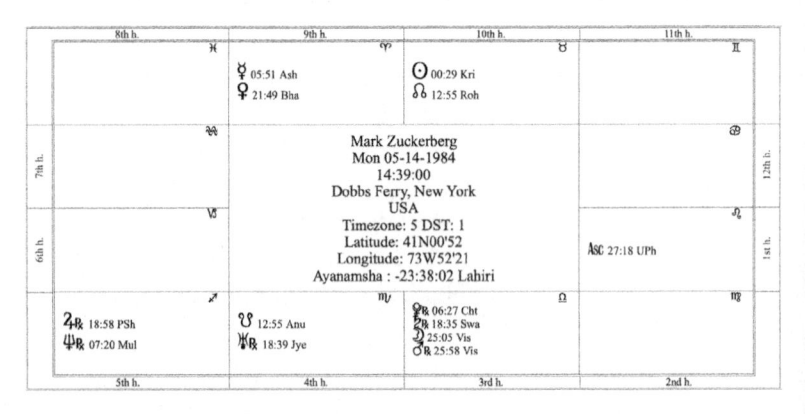

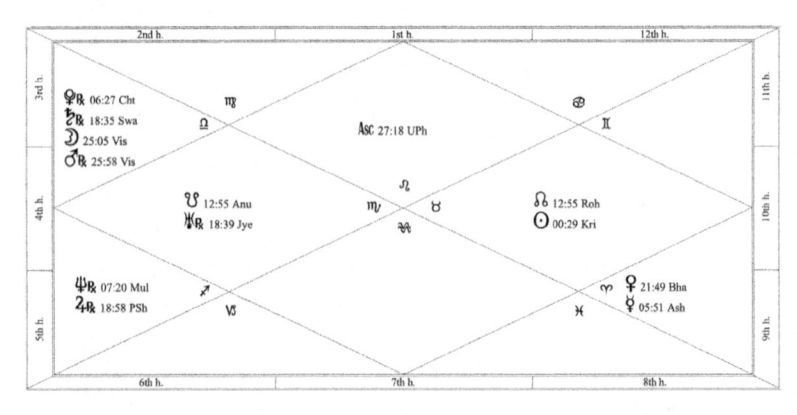

8th h.	9th h.	10th h.	11th h.
	☿ 05:51 Ash ♀ 21:49 Bha	☉ 00:29 Kri ☊ 12:55 Roh	
7th h.	Mark Zuckerberg Mon 05-14-1984 14:39:00 Dobbs Ferry, New York USA Timezone: 5 DST: 1 Latitude: 41N00'52 Longitude: 73W52'21 Ayanamsha: -23:38:02 Lahiri		12th h.
6th h.			ASC 27:18 UPh — 1st h.
♃℞ 18:58 PSh ♆℞ 07:20 Mul	☋ 12:55 Anu ♅℞ 18:39 Jye	☿℞ 06:27 Cht ♄℞ 18:35 Swa ☽ 25:05 Vis ♂℞ 25:58 Vis	
5th h.	4th h.	3rd h.	2nd h.

3rd and 5th house: Creativity, Expression, Writing

Exalted Mercury conjunct Neptune

Stephen King is an author of horror, supernatural fiction, suspense, crime, science-fiction, and fantasy novels. His books have sold more than 350 million copies, and many have been adapted into films, television series, miniseries, and comic books. King has published 64 novels.

Since The 3rd house pertains to creativity and talent then King's chart has a powerful 3rd house. Mercury is in its exaltation sign, ruler of the 3rd house, in the 3rd house. Mercury is the planet that rules writing skills all by itself. Neptune is the planet of fantasy and imagination being conjunct Mercury, this gives him a mind that can invent great imaginative stories. Furthermore, Neptune sits between both Mercury and debilitated Venus, adding a vast creative edge to planet Venus. Venus seems to be problematic due to its debilitation and combust the Sun. But as seen before when a debilitated planet is conjunct an exalted planet (Mercury in Virgo) the debilitation seems to be lifted.

Going to the 5th House of authorship, there sits Jupiter, Ketu, and the Moon. Both Jupiter and the Moon create a Raja yoga (kingship), and the Moon and Ketu also create a Raja yoga as the Moon rules an angle/kendra house and sits in a trikona house. This empowers the 5th house for authorship, creativity and intelligence.

Kings chart is a great example of talent with writing creativity and authorship.

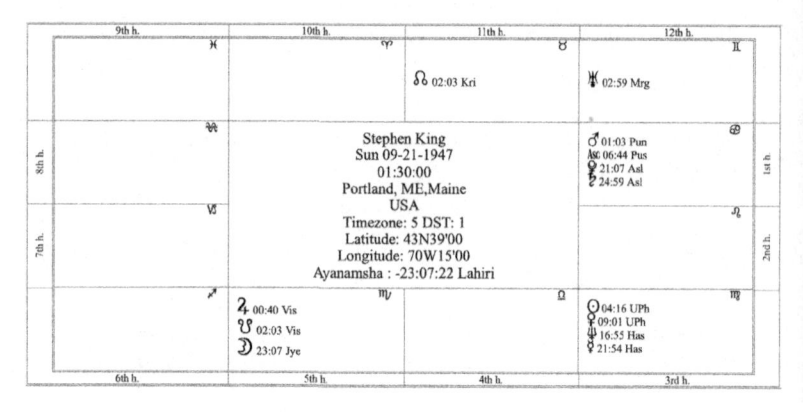

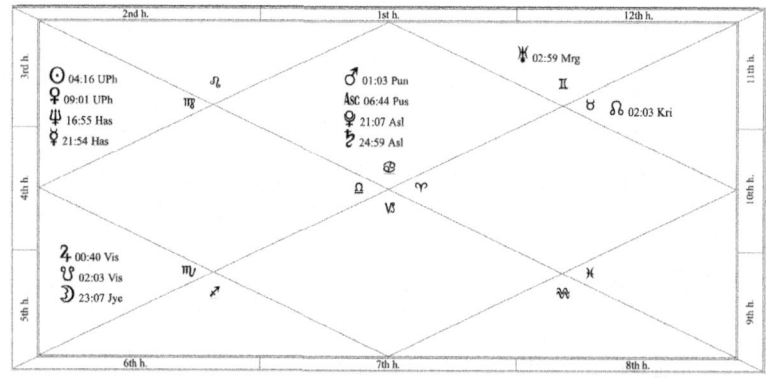

9th h.	10th h.	11th h.	12th h.
♓	♈	♉	♊
	☊ 02:03 Kri	♅ 02:59 Mrg	
♒	Stephen King		⊕
	Sun 09-21-1947		♂ 01:03 Pun
	01:30:00		Asc 06:44 Pus
	Portland, ME, Maine		♀ 21:07 Asl
	USA		☿ 24:59 Asl
♑	Timezone: 5 DST: 1		♌
	Latitude: 43N39'00		
	Longitude: 70W15'00		
	Ayanamsha: -23:07:22 Lahiri		
♐	♏	♎	♍
	♃ 00:40 Vis		☉ 04:16 UPh
	☋ 02:03 Vis		♀ 09:01 UPh
	☽ 23:07 Jye		♆ 16:55 Has
			☿ 21:54 Has
6th h.	5th h.	4th h.	3rd h.

2nd h.	1st h.	12th h.
	♅ 02:59 Mrg	
☉ 04:16 UPh	♂ 01:03 Pun	
♀ 09:01 UPh ♍	Asc 06:44 Pus	♉ ☊ 02:03 Kri
♆ 16:55 Has	♀ 21:07 Asl ♊	
☿ 21:54 Has	☿ 24:59 Asl	
	⊕ ♎ ♈ ♑	
♃ 00:40 Vis		♓
☋ 02:03 Vis ♏ ♐		♒
☽ 23:07 Jye		
5th h.	6th h. 7th h.	8th h.

Another indication of the 3rd house is siblings. Whenever Mars sits in the 3rd house of siblings there is competition and difficulty through a sibling.

Warren Beatty was an actor and filmmaker, whose career spans over six decades, and best known from the movie Bonnie and Clyde. His sister Shirley MacLaine was just as famous, a major movie star, singer, dancer, and writer, she wrote the metaphysical book *"Out on a Limb"*, which was controversial at the time but opened the minds of many spiritual seekers.

It is well known that MacLaine and Beatty never got along. They never worked together on any movies. And when Beatty had the debacle during the Academy Awards in 2017 where he announced the wrong winner, McLean tried to contact her brother to give him solace but he would never answer any of her calls.

Mars is the karaka meaning indicator of siblings, and whenever the karaka is in a house that it represents concerning people it produces great difficulty with what it is karaka for. Mars in the 3rd house for siblings causes great problems with the relationship or the life of a sibling. Just as Jupiter is the karaka for children and when Jupiter is placed in the 5th House of children it can create problems with children.

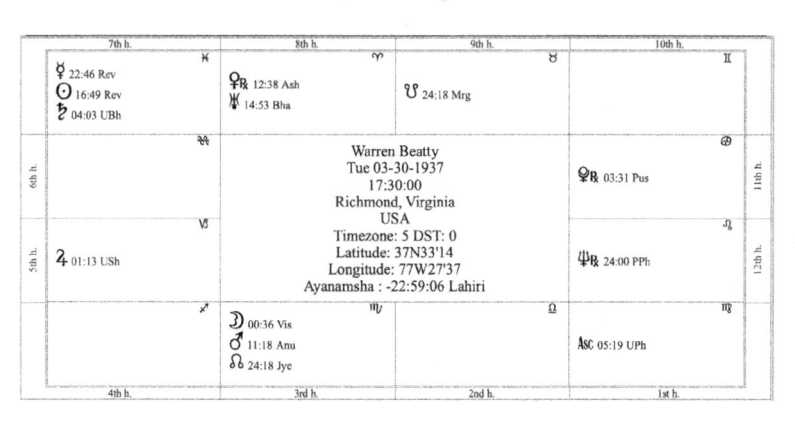

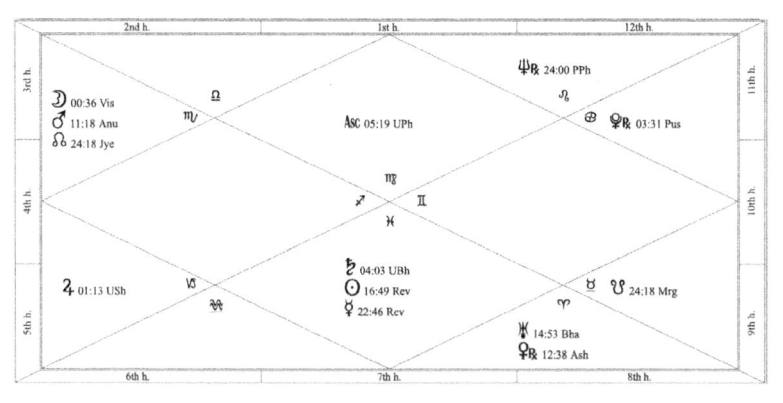

Planet's Houses and Rulers: 4th house Chapter
4th House: Ruler of 4th in 12th or ruler of 12th in 4th – Live in foreign country

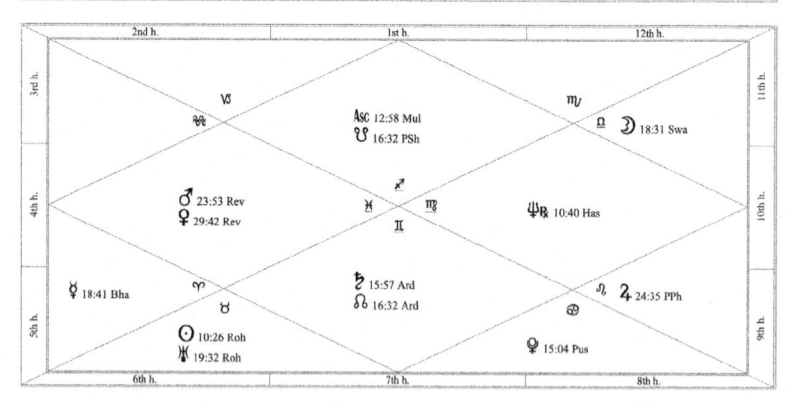

The 4th house rules your home, family, mother and specifically real estate. Whenever the ruler of the 4th house, of the home, is in the 12th House of foreign lands and countries these individuals will live in a foreign country. Another combination can be when the ruler of the 12th house is in the 4th house.

Priscilla Presley, ex-wife of Elvis Presley was living in Germany when she met Elvis while he was stationed in the service. This is an example of someone who has the ruler of the 12th in the 4th house. She was born and lived in Germany but later lived back in the United States.

Chapter 7

Planet's Houses and Rulers: 5ʰ house

5ᵗʰ House – Final Dispositor in the 5ᵗʰ – Creativity

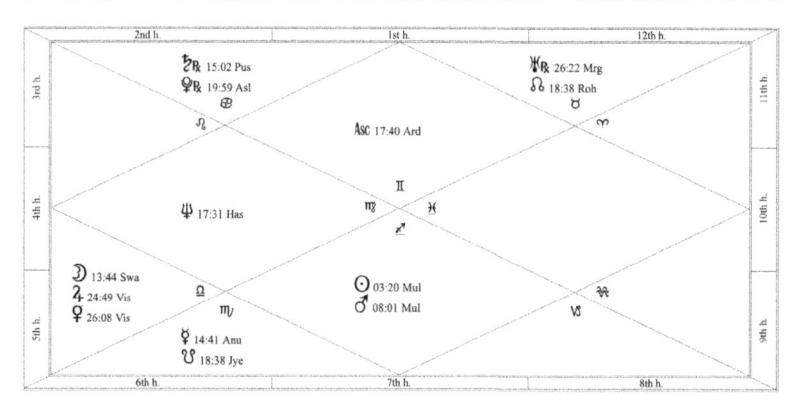

10th h.	11th h.	12th h.	1st h.
♓	♈	☊ 18:38 Roh ♅ ℞ 26:22 Mrg ♉	ASC 17:40 Ard ♊
♒ (9th h.)	Steven Spielberg Wed 12-18-1946 18:16:00 Cincinnati, OH,Ohio USA Timezone: 5 DST: 0 Latitude: 39N09'00 Longitude: 84W27'00 Ayanamsha : -23:06:42 Lahiri	♄℞ 15:02 Pus ♀℞ 19:59 Asl ⊕ (2nd h.)
♑ (8th h.)			♌ (3rd h.)
♂ 08:01 Mul ☉ 03:20 Mul ♐	☿ 14:41 Anu ☋ 18:38 Jye ♏	☽ 13:44 Swa ♃ 24:49 Vis ♀ 26:08 Vis ♎	♆ 17:31 Has ♍
7th h.	6th h.	5th h.	4th h.

Benefics and final dispositor Venus in 5ᵗʰ house

Steven Spielberg is one of the greatest film directors, producer, and screenwriter of all time. His vast creativity can be seen in his chart with the Moon, Jupiter and Venus in the 5ᵗʰ house in Libra. His powerful 5ᵗʰ house explains his incredible talent and creativity. His Natal Jupiter in the 5ᵗʰ house rules the 10ᵗʰ House of his work and career. And his

Jupiter and Venus conjunction creates a Raja yoga – yoga of leadership in kings.

But what truly explains his creative powers is due to his Venus' powerful placement, planet of creativity sits in the 5th house in its own sign of rulership and most of all it is the final dispositor planet of the entire chart.

When a planet sits in its own sign of rulership, it is the ruler of the house that it sits in. A dispositor is the planet that rules the sign a planet is in. For example, In Steven Spielberg's chart all the planets when following their dispositors all point to the final dispositor being Venus in his chart. Looking at any planets they always follow back to Venus. Such as, Saturn in Cancer which is ruled by the Moon and the Moon is in Libra ruled by Venus and Venus is the final dispositor.

The final dispositor in any chart will be the subject of focus throughout an individual's life. In order to have a final dispositor a planet must be in its own sign of rulership. Many charts do not have a final dispositor but when they do this planet takes precedence over all the other planets in the chart.

Chapter 8

Planet's Houses and Rulers: 6ʰ house

The 6ᵗʰ house -Health and stomach issues – Moon in 6ᵗʰ house

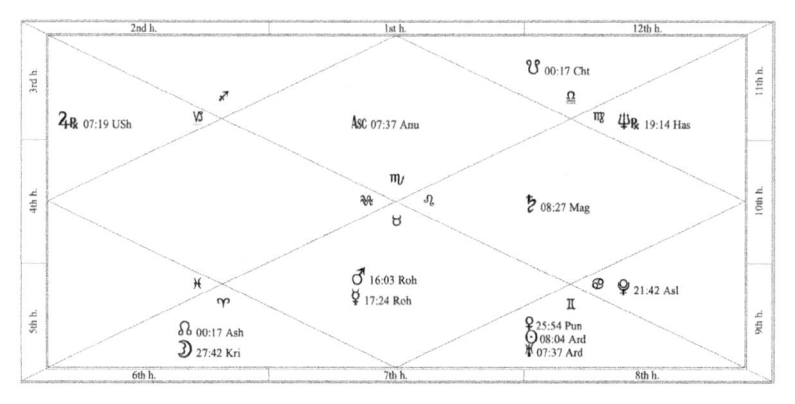

5th h.	6th h.	7th h.	8th h.
⟨H⟩	♈ ☊ 00:17 Ash / ☽ 27:42 Kri	♉ ♂ 16:03 Roh / ☿ 17:24 Roh	♊ ♅ 07:37 Ard / ☉ 08:04 Ard / ♀ 25:54 Pun
♒ (4th h)	Lindsay Wagner Wed 06-22-1949 16:42:00 Los Angeles, California USA Timezone: 8 DST: 0 Latitude: 34N03'08 Longitude: 118W14'37 Ayanamsha : -23:08:58 Lahiri		⊕ (9th h) ♀ 21:42 Asl
♑ (3rd h) ♃℞ 07:19 USh			♌ (10th h) ♄ 08:27 Mag
♐ (2nd h) ASC 07:37 Anu	♏ (1st h) ☋ 00:17 Cht	♎ (12th h)	♍ (11th h) ♇℞ 19:14 Has

Moon in the 6ᵗʰ house causes stomach and digestive disorders

Played bionic woman, Ulcers at early age

Lindsay Wagner was an actor who played the bionic woman in a popular television series in the 70s. It is well documented that she suffered from stomach ulcers and digestive disorders. The 6ᵗʰ house is the house of our health in healing.

I have come to find out through vast experience that when the Moon, which rules the stomach, is in the 6th house, these individuals suffer from digestive problems with the stomach. In Wagner's case, Rahu sits with the Moon in the 6th house magnifying the problems she experienced with her health dealing with stomach issues. Always look at the Moon whenever it's in the 6th house to represent problems with the stomach in the digestion in the body.

Chandra lagna gives confluence as the ruler of the 6th house with the Moon in Aries is Mercury and it is in the 2nd house of eating with Mars. Mars as ruler of the 8th house gives severe health issues from eating and digestion.

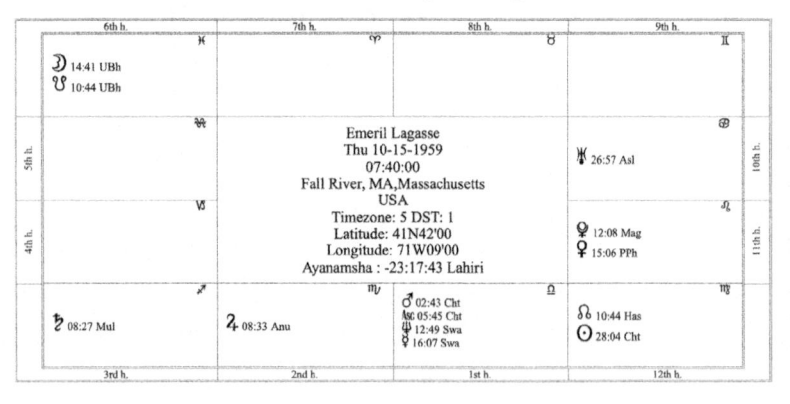

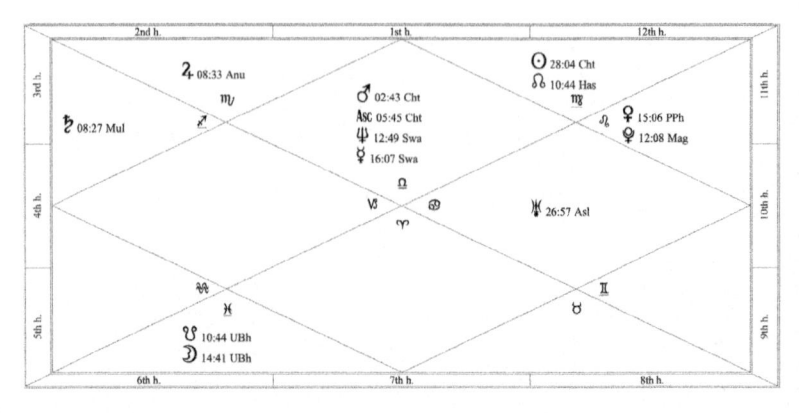

6th h.	7th h.	8th h.	9th h.
☽ 14:41 UBh ☋ 10:44 UBh			
(5th h.)	Emeril Lagasse Thu 10-15-1959 07:40:00 Fall River, MA, Massachusetts USA Timezone: 5 DST: 1 Latitude: 41N42'00 Longitude: 71W09'00 Ayanamsha: -23:17:43 Lahiri	♅ 26:57 Asl	(10th h.)
(4th h.)		♀ 12:08 Mag ♀ 15:06 PPh	(11th h.)
♄ 08:27 Mul	♃ 08:33 Anu	♂ 02:43 Cht Asc 05:45 Cht ♆ 12:49 Swa ☿ 16:07 Swa	☊ 10:44 Has ☉ 28:04 Cht
3rd h.	2nd h.	1st h.	12th h.

Ruler of 2nd and 6th houses associated with food or drink

Whenever there is a connection between the 2nd and the 6th houses, there will be a connection to work with food or drink. Since the 2nd house rules the mouth in terms of what we eat, when it sits in the 6th house of health and healing it will deal with a career or job where we work with food or drink. This applies to the reverse combination of the ruler of the 6th house in the 2nd house.

Emeril Lagasse is a celebrity chef who has many successful restaurants, been on many television shows and sold the rights to all his products to Martha Stewart for over $50 million in 2008.

The 6th house is the house of health, but it's also known to be the house of the service industries such as restaurants and the hospitality business. Lagassie has the ruler of the 6th in the 2nd house, making him a wonderful chef. Since the 2nd house deals with the food we eat when it is connected to the 6th house it can deal with those that could cook or be a chef. Lagassie has the Moon in his 6th house and the Moon rules the 10th House of his career.

He was born during a lunar eclipse, which places the Sun and the Moon in opposition. The Sun is the ruler of his 11th House of great gains and aspects the Moon ruler of the 10th House of career. I have noticed that the 12th house can refer to a job behind the scenes, working in the kitchen of a restaurant is a 12th house matter behind the scenes.

Jupiter, as the ruler of the 6th being placed in the 2nd house of money represents his ability to be extremely successful and make his fortune from food and cooking.

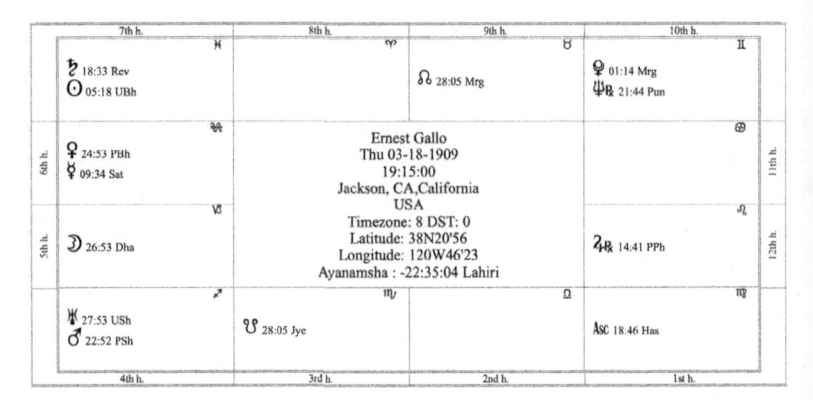

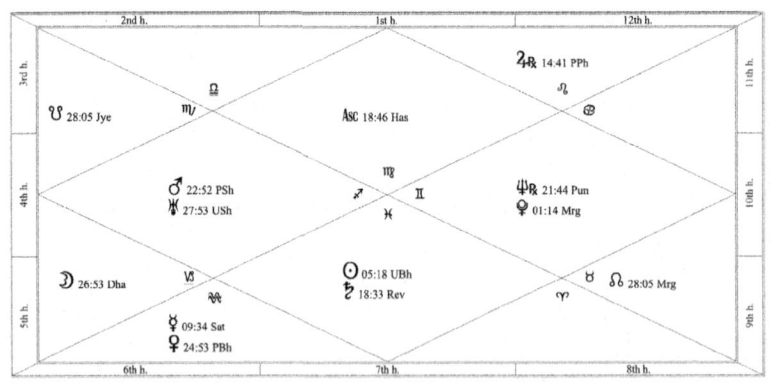

7th h.	8th h.	9th h.	10th h.
♄ 18:33 Rev ☉ 05:18 UBh	☊ 28:05 Mrg	♀ 01:14 Mrg ♆℞ 21:44 Pun	
♀ 24:53 PBh ☿ 09:34 Sat	Ernest Gallo Thu 03-18-1909 19:15:00 Jackson, CA, California USA Timezone: 8 DST: 0 Latitude: 38N20'56 Longitude: 120W46'23 Ayanamsha: -22:35:04 Lahiri		
☽ 26:53 Dha			♃℞ 14:41 PPh
♅ 27:53 USh ♂ 22:52 PSh	☋ 28:05 Jye		ASC 18:46 Has
4th h.	3rd h.	2nd h.	1st h.

Ruler of 2nd and 6th houses associated with food or drink

Another example of the 6th house pertaining to a business that concerns food or drink is the chart of Ernest Gallo of Gallo Wines. Ernest and Julio Gallo are two brothers that made a wine business into a huge successful company.

Ernest Gallo is the brother that was known to deal more with the wine sales. But it was both brothers working together that made Gallo wines such a household name. In Ernest's chart he has the ruler of the 2nd house in the 6th house conjunct Mercury. Both Mercury and Venus together in the 6th house form both a Raja yoga and a Dhana yoga. Because

Mercury rules the 10th house angle/kendra, and Venus rules the 9th house trikona, this forms the Raja yoga of kingship and power. While Venus rules the 2nd house of money and Mercury rules the 10th house and the first house this forms Dhana yoga which is a wealth producing yoga in the 6th House of the service industry. The two yogas formed by Venus and Mercury in the 6th house represent great wealth and fortune through the service industry and because Venus rules the 2nd house of food and drink that we ingest this is how they gave rise to a great wine dynasty.

Chapter 9

Planet's Houses and Rulers: 7^h house

7th- house grandmother (4th from the 4th)

Grandmother died right before election: Transiting Ketu on his Sun

The 7th house's main feature that it rules is marriage, relationship and partners. But there is something that must always be remembered about the 7th house, it is the 4th house from the 4th house meaning it rules your mother's mother, in essence it rules the grandmother.

This was a lesson to be learned when Barack Obama who won the presidential election in 2008 lost his grandmother who had a major effect on his morals and personality died November 3rd right before the elections. What I learned out of this was to never forget that the 7th house also rules the grandmother because at the time of her death and the elections transiting Ketu exactly conjoined his natal Sun in the 7th House of the grandmother.

Believing that the 7th house pertains to partners, I thought this may be a loss with the elections as the Sun is the spirit of the individual and the 7th house could mean his running mate in the election. Ketu is known to bring losses into an individual's life and since he was running for the president of the United States, I thought Ketu conjunct his Natal Sun could indicate a loss, but instead it represented the loss of the grandmother.

Planet's Houses and Rulers: 7h house

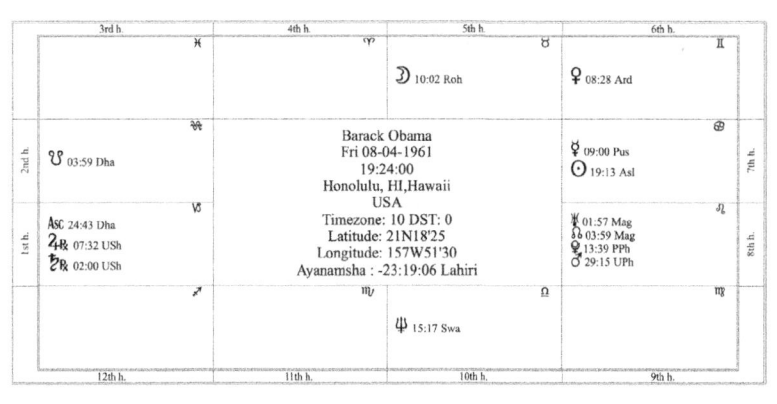

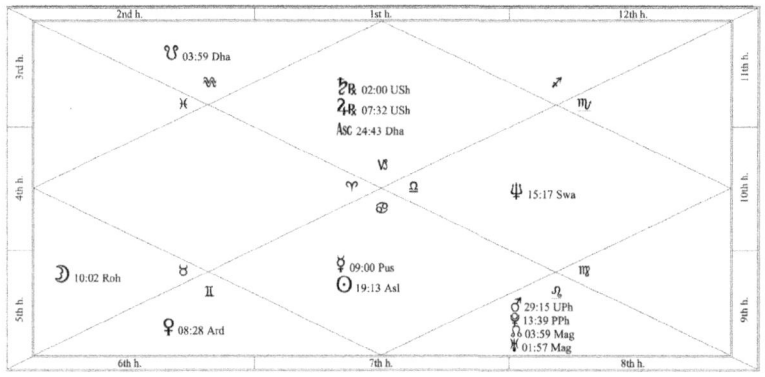

Chapter 9

	3rd h.	4th h.	5th h.	6th h.	
	♓	♈	☉ 10:02 Roh ♉	♀ 08:28 Ard Ⅱ	
2nd h.	♒ ☊ 03:59 Dha	Barack Obama Fri 08-04-1961 19:24:00 Honolulu, HI,Hawaii USA Timezone: 10 DST: 0 Latitude: 21N18'25 Longitude: 157W51'30 Ayanamsha : -23:19:06 Lahiri		☿ 09:00 Pus ☉ 19:13 Asl ♋	7th h.
1st h.	♑ Asc 24:43 Dha ♃℞ 07:32 USh ♄℞ 02:00 USh			♅ 01:57 Mag ☊ 03:59 Mag ♀ 13:39 PPh ♂ 29:15 UPh ♌	8th h.
	♐	♏ ♆ 15:17 Swa	10th h.	♎ ♍	
	12th h.	11th h.		9th h.	

Client Chart – parivartana with ruler of the 7th house with 8th house

Parivartana: Mutual Exchange: Ruler of 8th in 7th and Ruler of 7th in 8th house: Death of two husbands

The 8th house and the ruler of the 8th house can create problems for whatever houses it is connected to since the 8th house is the most difficult house of the chart. The 8th house concerns difficulties such as disgrace, humiliation and death. It also rules money through other people such as inheritances, psychic ability transformation, and metaphysics.

When the ruler of the 8th house is in the 7th house, or the ruler of the 7th house is in the 8th house this is not good for marriage. This is the chart of one of my clients, who has the ruler of the 7th house, Venus in the 8th house, and the ruler of the 8th house Mars in the 7th house. She had two husbands die. Venus and Mars exchange each other's signs in a parivartana yoga, connecting both the 7th and the 8th houses directly. This is a very difficult combination for marriage as can be seen in the effects that occurred in my private client's life.

Private Client Chart

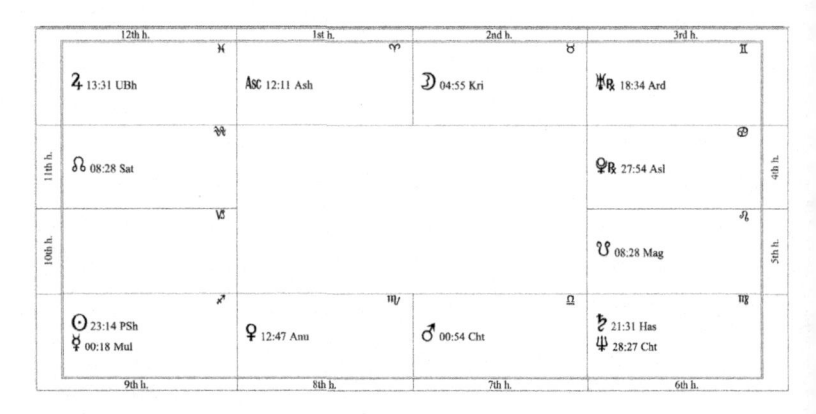

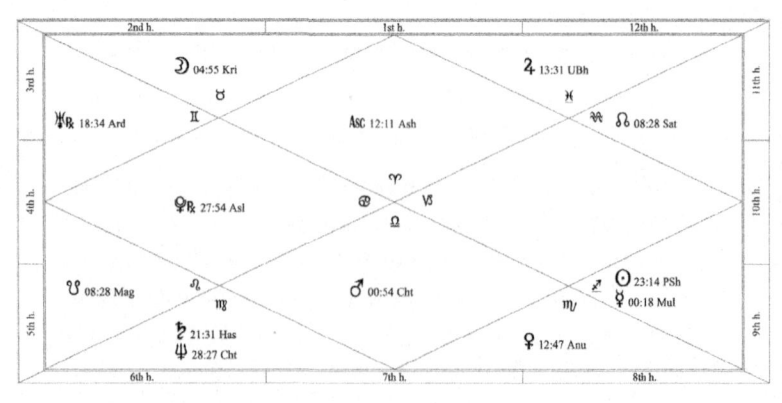

12th h.	1st h.	2nd h.	3rd h.
♓ ♃ 13:31 UBh	♈ ASC 12:11 Ash	♉ ☽ 04:55 Kri	♊ ♅℞ 18:34 Ard
♒ ☊ 08:28 Sat (11th h.)			♋ ♀℞ 27:54 Asl (4th h.)
♑ (10th h.)			♌ ☋ 08:28 Mag (5th h.)
♐ ☉ 23:14 PSh ☿ 00:18 Mul	♏ ♀ 12:47 Anu	♎ ♂ 00:54 Cht	♍ ♄ 21:31 Has ♆ 28:27 Cht
9th h.	8th h.	7th h.	6th h.

North Indian chart:
- 2nd h.: ☽ 04:55 Kri (♉)
- 3rd h.: ♅℞ 18:34 Ard (♊)
- 1st h.: ASC 12:11 Ash (♈)
- 12th h.: ♃ 13:31 UBh (♓)
- 11th h.: ☊ 08:28 Sat (♒)
- 4th h.: ♀℞ 27:54 Asl (♋)
- 10th h.: (♑)
- 5th h.: ☋ 08:28 Mag (♌)
- 7th h.: ♂ 00:54 Cht (♎)
- 6th h.: ♄ 21:31 Has, ♆ 28:27 Cht (♍)
- 9th h.: ☉ 23:14 PSh, ☿ 00:18 Mul (♐)
- 8th h.: ♀ 12:47 Anu (♏)

Chapter 10

Planet's Houses and Rulers: 8th house

The 8th House
8th House: Scandals, Disgrace, Charisma

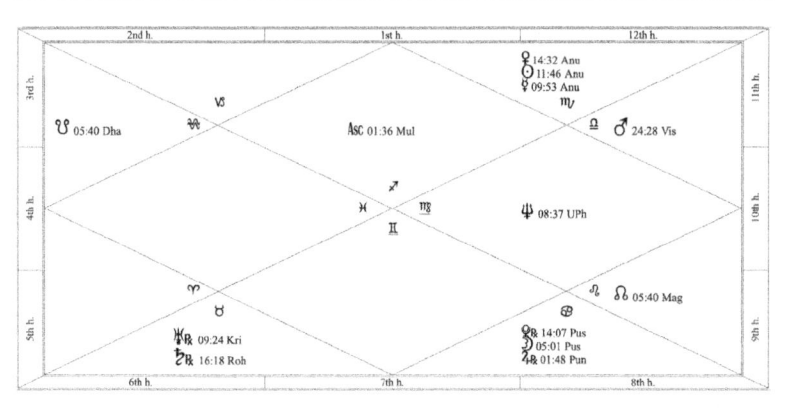

4th h.	5th h.	6th h.	7th h.
♓	♈ ♅℞ 09:24 Kri ♄℞ 16:18 Roh	♉	♊
♒ ☊ 05:40 Dha	Jimi Hendrix Fri 11-27-1942 10:15:00 Seattle, WA, Washington USA Timezone: 8 DST: 1 Latitude: 47N36'23 Longitude: 122W19'51 Ayanamsha: -23:03:25 Lahiri		♋ ♃℞ 01:48 Pun ☽ 05:01 Pus ♀℞ 14:07 Pus ☋ 05:40 Mag (♌ 9th h.)
♑ ASC 01:36 Mul	♐ ☿ 09:53 Anu ☉ 11:46 Anu ♀ 14:32 Anu	♏ ♂ 24:28 Vis	♎ ♇ 08:37 UPh (♍ 10th h.)
1st h.	12th h.	11th h.	10th h.

Jimi Hendrix, rock and roll legend is considered one of the best guitarists of all time, but his life had many extremes dealing with scandals around his death. The 8th house is the house of death, scandals, obsessions, addictions, and sexual charisma. Looking at Hendrick's 8th house he has the Moon, Jupiter, and Pluto. The Moon is highly sensitive here because it is the ruler of the 8th house in the 8th house accentuating all the definitions attributed to the 8th house. Jupiter rules the 1st house which is who we are, conjuncts the Moon in Cancer – Jupiter's exaltation sign.

Another variable that intensifies this more is Pluto is conjunct the Moon and Jupiter. Pluto can deal with obsessions and the dark side of life. This combination of these three planets indicates a deep dark loss through addictions which became a big scandal after his death.

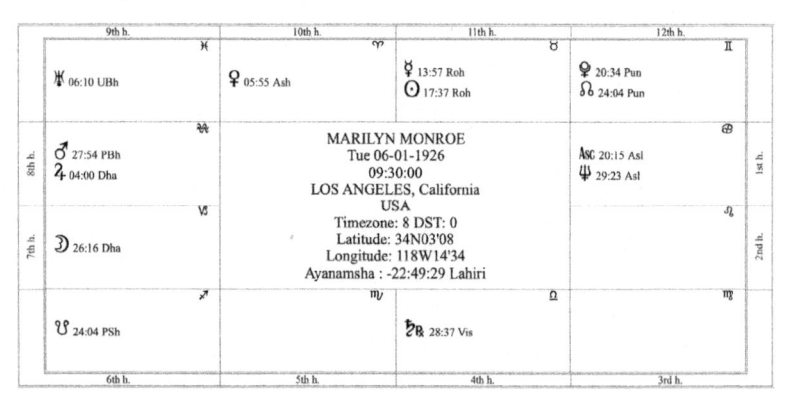

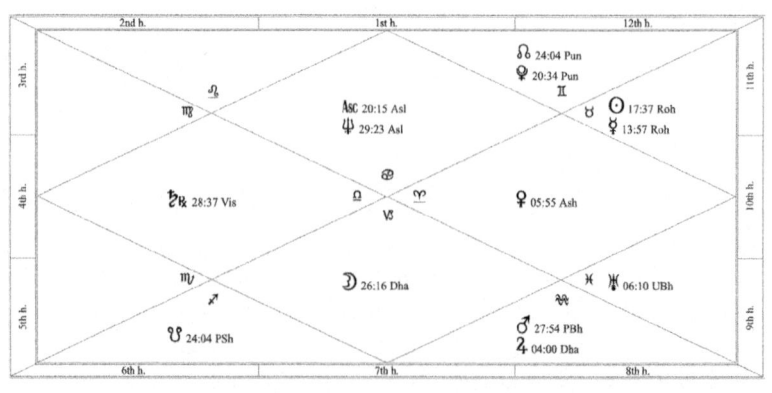

9th h.	10th h.	11th h.	12th h.
♓	♈	♉	♊
⛢ 06:10 UBh	♀ 05:55 Ash	☿ 13:57 Roh ☉ 17:37 Roh	♀ 20:34 Pun ☊ 24:04 Pun
♒	MARILYN MONROE		♋
♂ 27:54 PBh ♃ 04:00 Dha	Tue 06-01-1926 09:30:00 LOS ANGELES, California USA		Asc 20:15 Asl ♆ 29:23 Asl
♑	Timezone: 8 DST: 0 Latitude: 34N03'08 Longitude: 118W14'34		♌
☽ 26:16 Dha	Ayanamsha : -22:49:29 Lahiri		
♐	♍	♎	♍
☋ 24:04 PSh		♄℞ 28:37 Vis	
6th h.	5th h.	4th h.	3rd h.

Marilyn Monroe is the most recognized name to this day for sexual charisma and attraction. She has been a fascination since her death in 1962. Her death is still a mystery and has many conspiracy theories connected with it. But one thing that can never be denied is her sexual charisma and this can be seen by analyzing the 8th house in her chart.

Monroe has Jupiter and Mars in her 8th house, Jupiter rules her 9th house (trikona) and Mars rules her 10th house (kendra) creating a very powerful Raja yoga in the 8th house. This brings to light the many aspects of the 8th house including scandals. At the time of her death she was in the Jupiter maha dasha and Mars bhukti, indicating the timing of her death with both planets in the 8th house and the activation of the many scandals that surrounded her death.

Monroe's association with the Kennedys, President John F Kennedy and his brother Robert Kennedy have been linked to her death for many years because of her scandalous affair with the President. Her charisma and sexual attraction is still brought out in many movies and write ups even today.

8th House
Scandals, Disgrace and humiliation

4th h.	5th h.	6th h.	7th h.
♅ 23:55 Rev ♀ 18:39 Rev ☊ 03:20 UBh			♀R 27:22 Pun
☉ 09:37 Sat ☿ 05:53 Dha ♂ 04:55 Dha	Ted Kennedy Mon 02-22-1932 03:58:00 Dorchester, MA, Massachusetts USA Timezone: 5 DST: 0 Latitude: 42N17'00 Longitude: 71W04'00 Ayanamsha: -22:54:36 Lahiri		♃R 22:49 Asl
♄ 06:54 USh			☽ 13:30 PPh ♆R 13:49 PPh
Asc 17:55 PSh			☋ 03:20 UPh
1st h.	12th h.	11th h.	10th h.

103

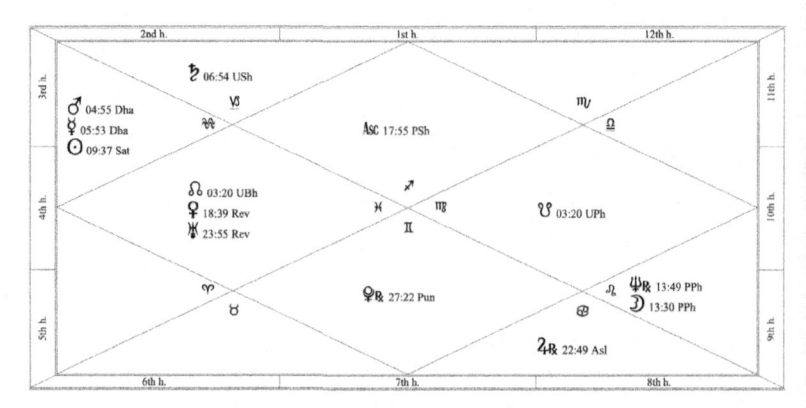

2nd h.	1st h.	12th h.
♄ 06:54 USh ♂ 04:55 Dha ♑ ☿ 05:53 Dha ♒ ☉ 09:37 Sat	Asc 17:55 PSh	♍ ♎
☊ 03:20 UBh ♀ 18:39 Rev ♅ 23:55 Rev	♐ ♓ ♍ ♊	☋ 03:20 UPh
♈ ♉	⚷ ℞ 27:22 Pun ⊕	♌ ♆℞ 13:49 PPh ☽ 13:30 PPh ♃ ℞ 22:49 Asl
6th h.	7th h.	8th h.

Edward (Ted) Kennedy Was a hopeful for the presidency of the United States until one late night leaving a party at Chappaquiddick Island on Martha's Vineyard while driving drunk Kennedy crashed into a pond. Kennedy escaped from the overturned vehicle, and Mary Jo Kopechne was still trapped inside the vehicle. Kennedy did not report the accident to authorities until the next morning, by which time Kopechne's body had already been discovered.

A week after the incident, Kennedy pleaded guilty to leaving the scene of an accident and was given a suspended sentence of two months in jail. Destroying any hopes for the Presidency.

Kennedy has the ruler of the chart Jupiter (ascendant ruler) in the 8th house, in exalted Cancer. The 8th house and all its indications are maxed out with this Jupiter in Cancer bringing everything the 8th house means into life; death, disgrace, humiliation, addictions, and most of all in his case scandals.

Most importantly the Moon as it rules the 8th house sits in the 9th house of truth and the law, but it is exactly conjunct Neptune, which is the planet of deception, illusions, alcohol, and lies. His chart is a very sad story that caused his downfall from this infamous disgraceful incident. He could

Planet's Houses and Rulers: 8h house

never be trusted after the wrongful death of the young girl he denied for years.

Kennedy's father played a huge role in his feelings of disgrace since his father was ashamed and would never talk to his son since the incident, not because of his wrongdoing, but for him losing the chance to be President.

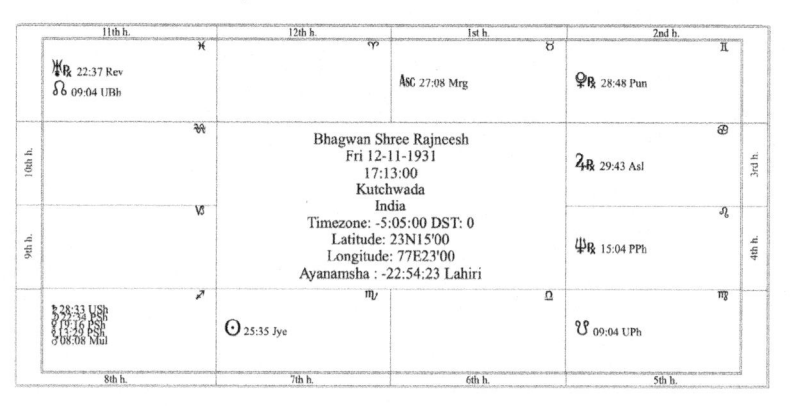

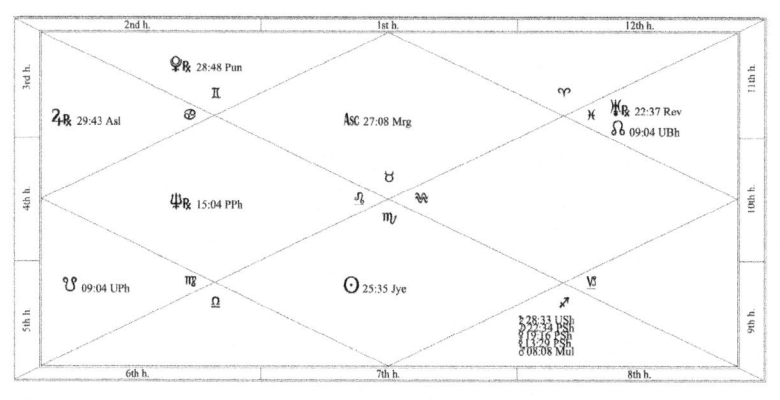

	11th h.	12th h.	1st h.	2nd h.
	♓	♈	♉	♊
	♅℞ 22:37 Rev ☋ 09:04 UBh		ASC 27:08 Mrg	♀℞ 28:48 Pun
10th h. ♒		Bhagwan Shree Rajneesh Fri 12-11-1931 17:13:00 Kutchwada India Timezone: -5:05:00 DST: 0 Latitude: 23N15'00 Longitude: 77E23'00 Ayanamsha: -22:54:23 Lahiri		♃℞ 29:43 Asl · 3rd h.
9th h. ♑				♆℞ 15:04 PPh · 4th h.
	♐	♏	♎	♍
	☽ 28:33 USh ☿℞ 22:34 PSh ♄ 17:16 PSh ♂ 08:08 Mul	☉ 25:35 Jye		☊ 09:04 UPh
	8th h.	7th h.	6th h.	5th h.

Bhagwan Shree Rajneesh was an Indian mystic, and founder of the Rajneesh movement. During his lifetime, he was viewed as a controversial new religious movement leader and a mystic guru. He rejected institutional religions. Rajneesh emphasized the importance of freethought, meditation, mindfulness, love, celebration, courage, creativity, and humor, qualities that he viewed as being suppressed by adherence to static belief systems, religious dogmas and traditions, and socialization. In advocating a more open attitude to human sexuality he caused controversy in India during the late 1960s and became known as "the sex guru".

In 1981, the Rajneesh movement's focused activities in the United States and Rajneesh relocated to a facility known as Rajneeshpuram in Wasco County, Oregon. Almost immediately the movement ran into conflict with county residents and the state government, and a succession of legal battles concerning the ashram's construction and continued development curtailed its success. In 1985, in the wake of a series of serious crimes by his followers, including a mass food-poisoning attack with *Salmonella* bacteria and an aborted assassination plot on U.S. attorney Charles H. Turner, Rajneesh alleged that his personal secretary and her close supporters had been responsible. He was later deported from the United States.

After his deportation, 21 countries denied him entry. He ultimately returned to Mumbai, India, in 1986. After staying in the house of a disciple where he resumed his discourses for six months, he returned to Pune in January 1987 and revived his ashram, where he died in 1990.

Rajneesh has five planets in the 8th house, Mars, Mercury, Venus, Moon, and Saturn in Sagittarius, and Jupiter the dispositor is even in the 8th house from the Moon and all these planets. Everything concerning the 8th house is who he is, a mystic, consumed with scandals, disgrace and humiliation. He was even called the sex guru which is another indication of the 8th house.

Jupiter is in Cancer (exalted) ruled by the Moon in the 3rd house of his teachings, and the Moon is in Jupiter's sign

Sagittarius. This is a parivartana yoga connecting the 3rd house with the 8th house, his teachings were metaphysical and controversial. His life is a lesson for understanding the 8th house.

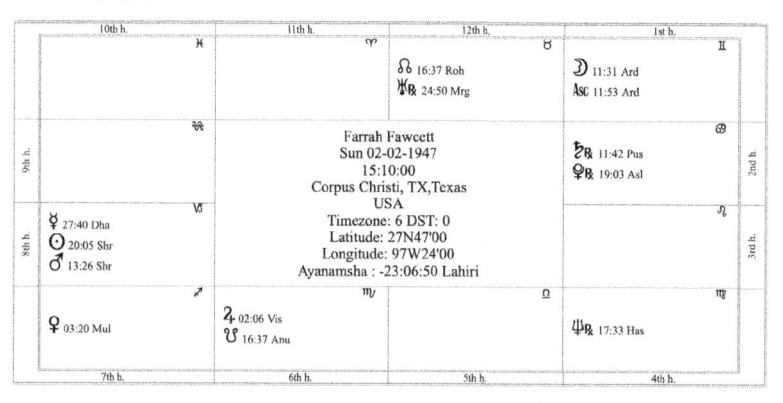

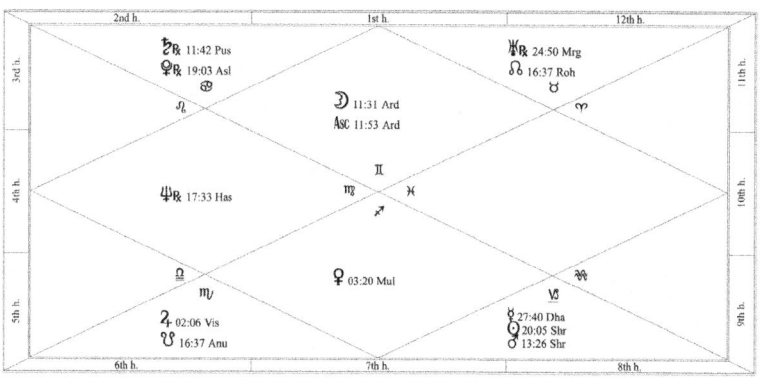

10th h.	11th h.	12th h.	1st h.
♓	♈	☊ 16:37 Roh ♅℞ 24:50 Mrg ♉	☽ 11:31 Ard ASC 11:53 Ard ♊
♒ 9th h.	Farrah Fawcett Sun 02-02-1947 15:10:00 Corpus Christi, TX, Texas USA Timezone: 6 DST: 0 Latitude: 27N47'00 Longitude: 97W24'00 Ayanamsha: -23:06:50 Lahiri		♄℞ 11:42 Pus ♀℞ 19:03 Asl 2nd h.
♑ ☿ 27:40 Dha 8th h. ☉ 20:05 Shr ♂ 13:26 Shr			♌ 3rd h.
♐ ♀ 03:20 Mul	♃ 02:06 Vis ☋ 16:37 Anu ♏	♎	♍
7th h.	6th h.	5th h.	4th h.

2nd h.	1st h.	12th h.
♄℞ 11:42 Pus ♀℞ 19:03 Asl ⊕ ♌ 3rd h.	☽ 11:31 Ard ASC 11:53 Ard ♊	♅℞ 24:50 Mrg ☊ 16:37 Roh ♉ 11th h.
4th h. ♆℞ 17:33 Has	♍ ♓ ♐	10th h.
♎ ♏ 5th h. ♃ 02:06 Vis ☋ 16:37 Anu	♀ 03:20 Mul	♒ ♑ ☿ 27:40 Dha 9th h. ☉ 20:05 Shr ♂ 13:26 Shr
6th h.	7th h.	8th h.

Farrah Fawcett was a supermodel and actress known for her beautiful hair that created a new style that has never ended. She was an icon of the 1970s as she appeared in the television series called Charlie's Angels. One thing about her was her massive charisma, she lit up the stage when she appeared back in her prime.

The ruler of her chart (ascendant) is Mercury, and it is in the 8th house with both malefic Sun and Mars. Her life was full of controversy and scandals. She left the show Charlie's Angels before her contract ended and was said to be blackballed by those in Hollywood never receiving any great movie opportunities.

She was married to popular TV star Lee Majors, star of The Big Valley and the 6 Million Dollar Man, Majors asked his best friend Ryan O'Neal to watch over Farrah when he was gone and the two fell in love abandoning her marriage to Majors. This scandalous and problematic affair lasted till she died in 2009 from anal cancer.

As to the cause of her death Anal cancer, the colon and elimination system is ruled by the 8th house as well. The malefics with her chart ruler is not good for her health and manifested from this area of the body.

Her death from cancer was unusual too, as she died the same day as Michael Jackson, whose death overruled any media attention about her death. Remember the 8th house is the house of death. Her life was an example of the extremes of charisma, scandals and problems associated with the 8th house.

8th house Research and Investigation

10th h.	11th h.	12th h.	1st h.
♀ 24:48 Rev ☿ 12:00 UBh ♀ 10:58 UBh ☉ 01:20 PBh	♆ 15:41 Bha	♀ 02:33 Kri	ASC 19:28 Ard
9th h. ♃ 05:18 Dha	Albert Einstein Fri 03-14-1879 11:30:00 Ulm, Baden-Wurttemberg Germany Timezone: -0:40:00 DST: 0 Latitude: 48N24'00 Longitude: 10E00'00 Ayanamsha : -22:10:27 Lahiri		☊ 10:33 Pus — 2nd h.
8th h. ☋ 10:33 Shr ♂ 04:44 USh			♅ 09:06 Mag — 3rd h.
7th h.	☽ 22:21 Jye 6th h.	5th h.	4th h.

Planet's Houses and Rulers: 8h house

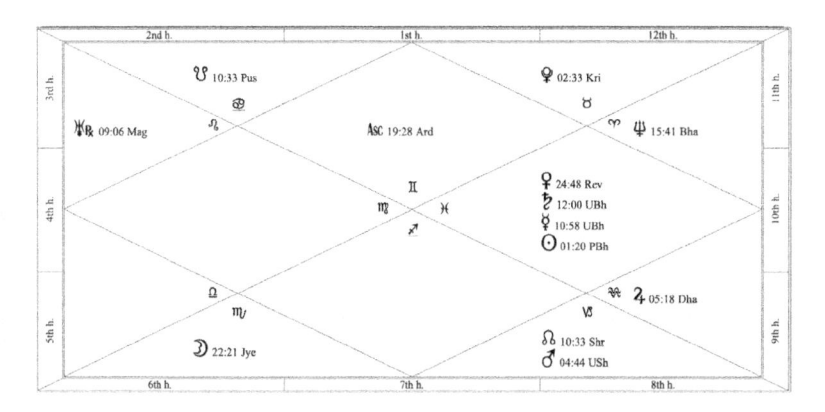

Chapter 10

2nd h.	1st h.	12th b.

☊ 10:33 Pus
♋
♅℞ 09:06 Mag ♌
ASC 19:28 Ard
♀ 02:33 Kri
♉
♈ ♆ 15:41 Bha

Ⅱ
♍ ♓
♐
♀ 24:48 Rev
♄ 12:00 UBh
☿ 10:58 UBh
☉ 01:20 PBh

♎
♏
☽ 22:21 Jye

♒ ♃ 05:18 Dha
♑
☋ 10:33 Shr
♂ 04:44 USh

6th h.	7th h.	8th h.

Albert Einstein was widely acknowledged to be one of the greatest and most influential physicists of all time. Einstein is best known for developing the theory of relativity, but he also made important contributions to the development of the theory of quantum mechanics.

He worked with the Manhattan project to develop nuclear weapons to end World War II. But when the bomb was dropped on Japan he was horrified at the destruction, suffering, and death his developments created.

Einstein has exalted Mars and Rahu in the 8th house, indicating his deep profound intellect that is beyond the normal confines of this world. The 8th house can pertain to the spirit world as in awareness beyond this world. This could be why it deals with psychics and metaphysics.

As to the issue of disgrace and humiliation Einstein felt incredible remorse over the destruction his discovery created. His Mars in Capricorn was not only exalted, increasing the strength, but Rahu is the magnifier of any planet's force and energy and what it represents. This combination is attributed to his deep mental discoveries and the pain he felt as to the suffering his discovery brought to the world.

The 8th house is the house of research, investigation, and detective work. Those with powerful planets in the 8th house love research and discovering the secrets of the Universe. If there is something hidden to uncover, Einstein will find it with this most powerful conjunction in the 8th house. And his discoveries opened the door to a new era of science.

Chapter 11

Planet's Houses and Rulers: 9th house

Religious Beliefs: 9th House
Jupiter Ruler of 9th house in 9th house

The 9th house is the house of law, and this entails all laws, such as spiritual and man-made laws to create order in the world. It is the house of truth and spirituality; this is the Divine law of the Universe. Jupiter is the natural ruler of this house as it rules the 9th sign Sagittarius and Jupiter is the spiritual teacher- Guru.

It is said to be the luckiest house, the house of luck and fortune. The house the ruler of the 9th house sits in brings fortune and luck. Such as, when the ruler of the 9th house sits in the 2nd house, it always brings luck through money.

The most important aspect I want to bring out is the issue of beliefs. This may be the house of the truth, but what it truly represents is an individual's beliefs. This may not always be the actual truth, but it is what someone believes to be the truth, and therefore this is the house of religion. Consider that the sign Sagittarius is focused on very strong opinions, which deal with their steadfast beliefs.

The chart of Pope Francis represents this strong religious belief with four planets in the 9th house. Jupiter, as the planet of spirituality and truth sits in its own sign Sagittarius ruler of the 9th house in the 9th house. Jupiter expands whatever it is next to also Rahu magnifies any planets it sits in the same sign with. Jupiter, Sun, Rahu, and Mercury all in the sign Sagittarius in the 9th house represent a powerful strong belief in his truth which is his religious beliefs. His chart is a powerful representation of the 9th house ruling religious beliefs.

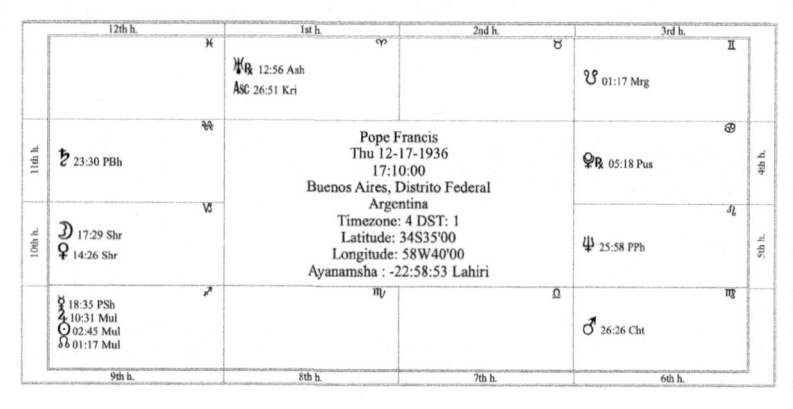

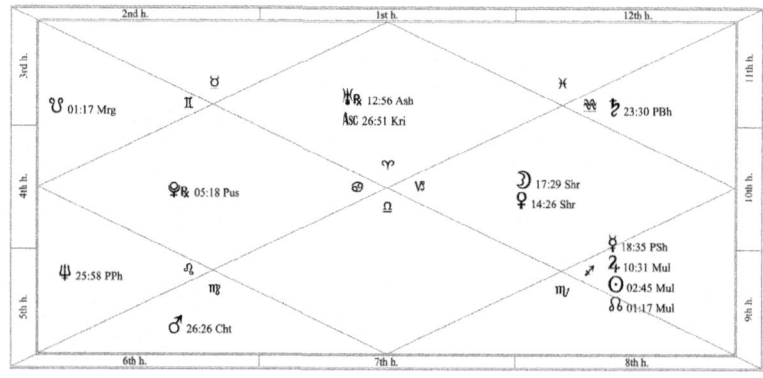

Religious Beliefs change with transiting Saturn in Sagittarius

This is the chart of a client who went through an incredible shift in her religious beliefs around the time that transiting Saturn was in Sagittarius. With six planets in Sagittarius in the 9th house she questioned all her previous beliefs, as Saturn the planet of doubt crossed over all of her planets in the 9th house.

It is very difficult when someone's belief systems are threatened and the truth is revealed, because everything that they base their truth on changes. Initially, there is confusion, but an awakening will change their entire outlook on their life. Many people cannot handle the understanding that everything they grew up with is wrong, therefore they revert to denial. For others, this represents a great freedom, but this means their family and friends with the old belief become ostracized from the individual. This is what happened to my client with this chart.

Private Client

12th h. ♓	1st h. ♈	2nd h. ♉	3rd h. ♊
♃ 16:27 UBh	ASC 12:11 Ash		☊ 17:48 Ard

| 11th h. ♒ | | | 4th h. ♌ ⊕ |

| 10th h. ♑ ♄ 25:44 Dha | | | 5th h. ♅℞ 16:43 PPh / ♀℞ 20:52 PPh |

| 9th h. ♐ ☿ 29:17 USh / ♀ 22:03 PSh / ☽ 21:15 PSh / ☋ 17:48 PSh / ♂ 16:09 PSh / ☉ 01:49 Mul | 8th h. ♏ | 7th h. ♎ ♆ 23:25 Vis | 6th h. ♍ |

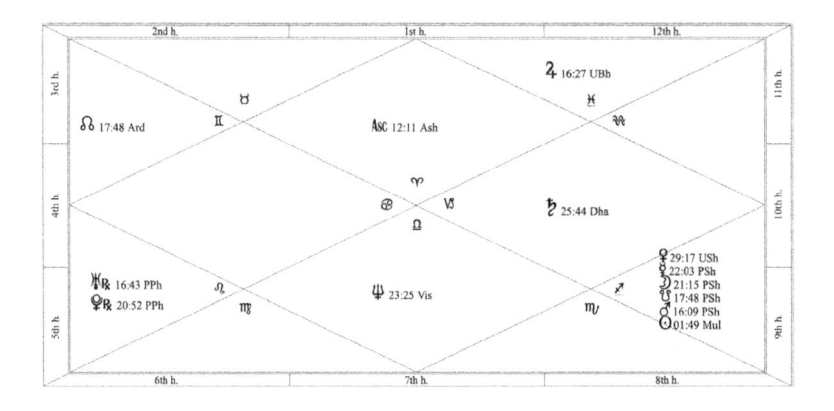

113

Chapter 12

Planet's Houses and Rulers: 10th house

The 10th house is the 2nd house from the 9th house this indicates the father's wealth.

Christina Onassis was the daughter and heir to her father's shipping industry, Her father was the Greek shipping magnate Aristotle Onassis, who amassed the world's largest privately-owned shipping fleet and was one of the world's richest and most famous men.

Within a 29-month period, Christina lost her entire immediate family. Her brother Alexander died in a plane crash in Athens in 1973 at 24, which devastated the family. Her mother died of a suspected drug overdose in 1974, leaving Christina her $77 million estate. Her father's health deteriorated after Alexander's death, and he died in March 1975.

In Christina's natal chart she has Jupiter in the 10th house representing her father's wealth. Also, Mars and Moon are in conjunction forming a Chandra Mangala yoga, which indicates business success in the 9th house of the father. This is when both the Moon and Mars are in conjunction or opposition, additionally Mars is exalted in Capricorn. This yoga represents the father's great success in the 9th house, but Jupiter in the 2nd house from the 9th house indicates the great wealth her father accumulated.

From 1973–1975 when Christina lost all her immediate family, she was in Rahu's maha dasha and Rahu bhukti and extended to Rahu maha dasha and Jupiter bhukti. During this dasha she came into power to run her father's business and she acquired great wealth herself as natal Rahu is in the 11th house of gains. But realize she lost her older brother (11th house) and her mother, the 11th house is the house of the mother's death.

Planet's Houses and Rulers: 10th house

Rahu's dasha was exceptionally difficult because it is connected to Saturn, as it is conjunct Ketu. Ketu conjunct Saturn is a very difficult aspect and can represent something very difficult in a lifetime. When individuals go into the dashas of Rahu and Ketu and Saturn is conjunct the nodes, difficult events usually occur.

When her mother died transiting Saturn was 25 degrees Gemini the same degree as Neptune, and within a degree of the Sun and Pluto. This is a lot occurring, I will train you to begin to start looking at degrees of the transiting planets to the natal planets connecting the planets and their meanings, regardless of the aspect and the houses they are in or rule. This technique is in a later section in this book.

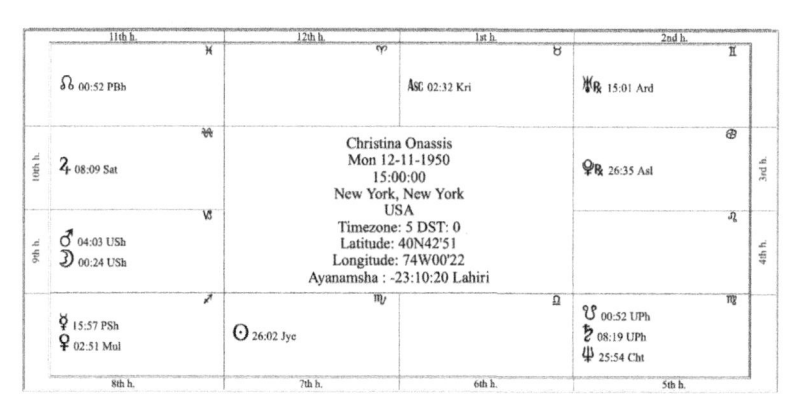

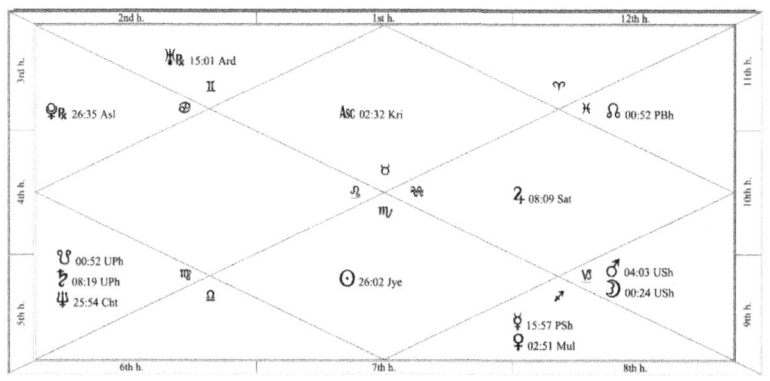

Dasha

☊ (18y)
From 21y3m to 39y3m

Antar	Beginning	Ending
☊	04-06-1972	12-18-1974
♃	12-18-1974	05-13-1977
♄	05-13-1977	03-18-1980
☿	03-18-1980	10-06-1982
☋	10-06-1982	10-24-1983
♀	10-24-1983	10-24-1986
☉	10-24-1986	09-18-1987
☽	09-18-1987	03-19-1989
♂	03-19-1989	04-06-1990

Transits

Death

Asc	08:26:44		Can
☉	04:20:57		Sco
☽	17:31:26		Pis
♂	09:24:08		Pis
☿	27:56:40	c	Lib
♃	07:44:53	R	Tau
♀	02:06:31		Lib
♄	07:05:43		Sag
☊	17:13:01		Aqu
☋	17:13:01		Leo
♅	05:35:56		Sag
♆	14:44:10		Sag
♇	19:25:40		Lib

Mother

Asc	20:49:53		Tau
☉	23:54:37		Vir
☽	24:24:54		Can
♂	25:01:29	c	Vir
☿	16:41:43		Lib
♃	15:23:23	R	Aqu
♀	17:07:48	c	Vir
♄	25:00:36		Gem
☊	18:19:23		Sco
☋	18:19:23		Tau
♅	03:57:13		Lib
♆	14:04:28		Sco
♇	13:36:14		Vir

Planet's Houses and Rulers: 11th house

Separation and loss of the mother: 11th house
8th from the 4th house

The 11th house is the house of friends, groups, and organizations as well as great gains because it is the second house from the 10th house, money from our career. But there is one meaning that many do not see that is very specific to the 8th house. This is based on the fact that the 11th house is the 8th house from the 4th house of the mother.

The 11th house being the 8th house from the 4th house can represent the mother's death and her deep psychology. Many times, natural malefics in the 11th house can represent a mother's mental condition. If there is mental illness for the mother, it can be seen through the 11th house.

Julio Gallo, brother of Ernest Gallo, both brothers experienced the tragic death of their mother when they were young. In an argument of passion and anger the father murdered the mother and committed suicide. In Julio's chart he has Mars and Rahu in the 11th house. This is an indication of great difficulty mentally for the mother and a violent death. Both Mars and Rahu are natural malefics, and Rahu magnifies the violent nature of Mars. I have seen many instances of mental disease, and the timing of the death of the mother with difficult planets in the 11th house.

Going back to his brother's chart, Ernest reflecting how the 2nd and the 6th house represent a business with food or drink, Julio has the ruler of the 6th house Jupiter aspecting the Sun by opposition ruler of the 2nd house, connecting the 6th and 2nd houses.

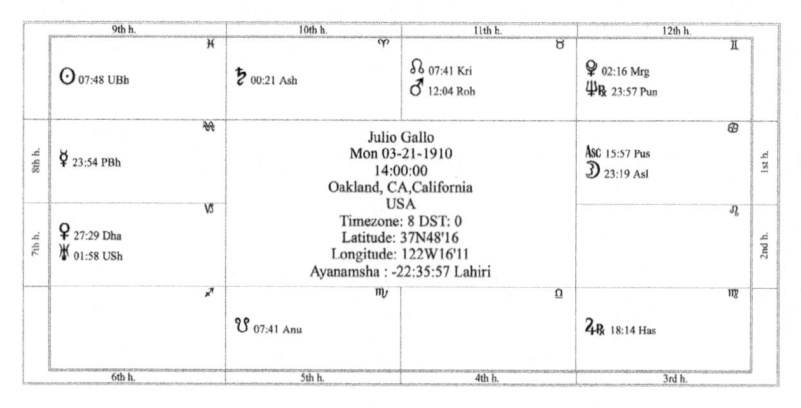

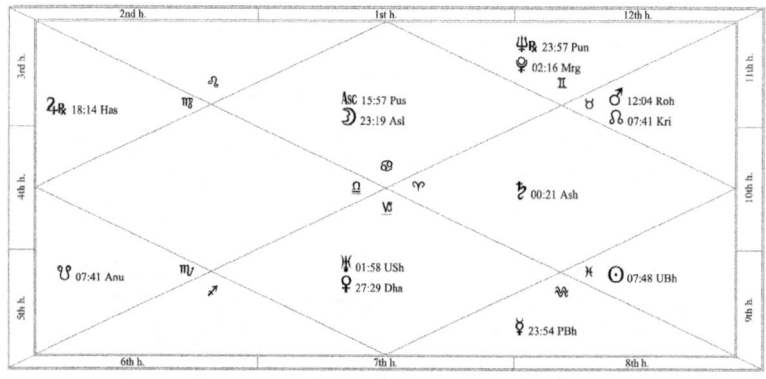

9th h.	10th h.	11th h.	12th h.
☉ 07:48 UBh	♄ 00:21 Ash	☊ 07:41 Kri ♂ 12:04 Roh	♀ 02:16 Mrg ♅℞ 23:57 Pun
☿ 23:54 PBh	Julio Gallo Mon 03-21-1910 14:00:00 Oakland, CA, California USA Timezone: 8 DST: 0 Latitude: 37N48'16 Longitude: 122W16'11 Ayanamsha: -22:35:57 Lahiri		Asc 15:57 Pus ☽ 23:19 Asl
♀ 27:29 Dha ♆ 01:58 USh			
	☋ 07:41 Anu		♃℞ 18:14 Has
6th h.	5th h.	4th h.	3rd h.

Problems with Mother: Moon conjunct debilitated Saturn in 11th house, Mars in Virgo in 4th house

Tonya Harding was an Olympic skater who was involved with hit men who injured Nancy Kerrigan, another competitor skater during the Olympics in 1994. Consequently, for hurting Kerrigan, she was barred from all skating competitions for the rest of her life. In a movie called "I Tonya" her mother was portrayed as a very destructive and hurtful mother.

In Tonya's 11th house, which is the 8th house from the 4th sits debilitated Saturn with the Moon in Aries. This is a very complicated 11th house depicting her mother's mind, and psychology. The dispositing planet of both Saturn and the Moon and

Planet's Houses and Rulers: 11th house

Chapter 12

ruler of the 11th house is Mars, which sits in the 4th House of the mother conjunct unpredictable Uranus. Mars with Uranus can represent explosive angry outbursts and Pluto can make it even more sinister.

Even the ruler of the 4th house which represents the mother is Mercury, sits exactly with Neptune which can represent deception, deceit and denial.

Saturn is the same degree as the Moon in the 11'h house, the mother's mind can be haunted with depression, and deep-rooted problems from the past. You can see from Tonya's chart that all of her issues originated in childhood from the care and mental attitude of her mother.

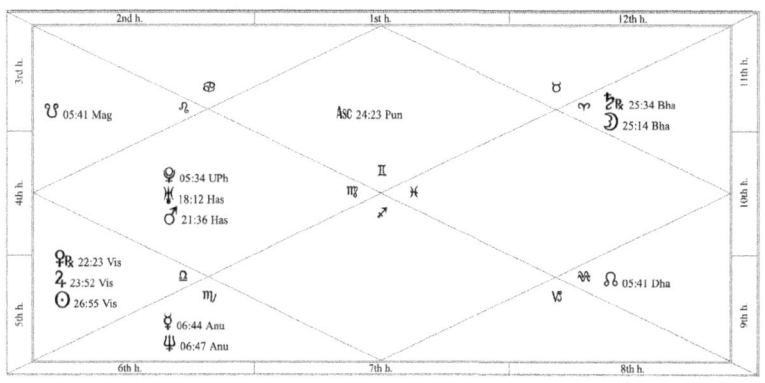

10th h.	11th h.	12th h.	1st h.
♓	♈	♉	♊
	☽ 25:14 Bha ♄℞ 25:34 Bha		ASC 24:23 Pun
♒	Tonya Harding Thu 11-12-1970 20:22:00 Portland, Oregon USA Timezone: 8 DST: 0 Latitude: 45N31'24 Longitude: 122W40'34 Ayanamsha : -23:27:07 Lahiri		⊕
9th h. ☊ 05:41 Dha			2nd h.
♑			♌
8th h.			☋ 05:41 Mag 3rd h.
♐	♍	♎	♍
	☿ 06:44 Anu ♇ 06:47 Anu	♀℞ 22:23 Vis ♃ 23:52 Vis ☉ 26:55 Vis	♀ 05:34 UPh ⛢ 18:12 Has ♂ 21:36 Has
7th h.	6th h.	5th h.	4th h.

2nd h.	1st h.		12th h.
3rd h.			11th h.
☋ 05:41 Mag ♌	ASC 24:23 Pun	♉	♈ ♄℞ 25:34 Bha ☽ 25:14 Bha
	♊ ♍ ♓ ♐		
4th h. ♀ 05:34 UPh ⛢ 18:12 Has ♂ 21:36 Has			10th h.
5th h. ♀℞ 22:23 Vis ♃ 23:52 Vis ☉ 26:55 Vis	♎ ♍	♒ ☊ 05:41 Dha ♑	9th h.
	☿ 06:44 Anu ♇ 06:47 Anu		
6th h.	7th h.	8th h.	

Chapter 13

Planet's Houses and Rulers: 12th house

Alienation, ostracized, exiled

The 12th house can deal with alienation and isolation. Because it deals with foreign lands and countries it can also mean having to leave a country or foreign land. Another variable of the 12th house pertains to prisons, as prisons isolate and take one out of the world.

Timothy Leary was an American psychologist and author known for his strong advocacy of psychedelic drugs. As a clinical psychologist at Harvard University, Leary founded the Harvard Psilocybin Project He led the Project from 1960 to 1962, testing the therapeutic effects of LSD, which were legal in the U.S. at the time. Harvard fired Leary and his colleague Richard Alpert (later known as Ram Dass) in May 1963. Many people only learned of psychedelics after the Harvard scandal.

Following the Harvard scandal, Leary was in prison many times for his use and belief of psychedelic drugs. At the time, President Nixon named him as the most dangerous man in America.

Leary has in his 12th house debilitated Sun with Rahu and Mercury in Libra. His Sun rules the 10th house of his career, in which he was fired for the scandal he created at Harvard. Furthermore, Mercury rules the 8th house bringing more problems to his incarceration so many times for his beliefs. In this case the 12th house represents imprisonment, isolation, loneliness and a withdrawal from society and the world. This indicates huge losses in the life of Timothy Leary.

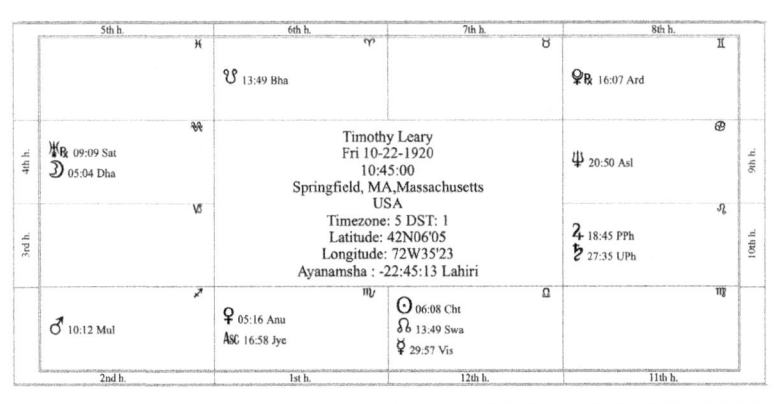

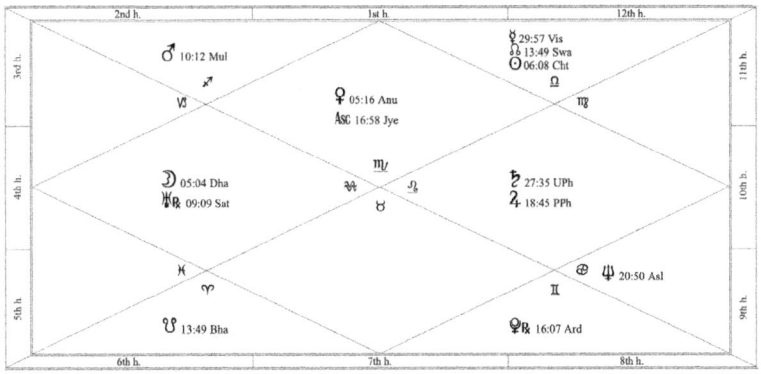

12th House – exiled

Roman Polanski is a film director, producer, screenwriter, and actor. During his career Polanski has received five Oscar nominations, winning the Best Director in 2003 for *The Pianist*.

The invasion of Poland by Nazi Germany started World War II, and his family found themselves trapped in the Kraków Ghetto. After his mother and father were taken in raids, Polanski spent his formative years in foster homes, surviving the Holocaust by adopting a false identity and concealing his Jewish heritage.

Polanski's life turned upside-down in 1969 when his pregnant wife, actress Sharon Tate, and four friends were murdered by members of the Manson Family. Polanski was later arrested and charged with drugging and raping a 13-year-old girl. As a result of a plea bargain, he pleaded guilty to the lesser offense of unlawful sex with a minor. In 1978, upon learning that the judge planned to reject his plea deal and impose a prison term instead of probation, he fled to Paris. As a result, Polanski is a fugitive from the U.S. criminal justice system.

In Polansky's 12th house sits the Sun tightly conjunct Ketu in the sign of Leo. Since the Sun rules Leo this strongly affects the 12th house as an indicator of great loss. Polanski had to leave Poland his country during World War II, and he was exiled from the United States for sexual relations with a minor. This chart represents great losses and an exile from more than one country.

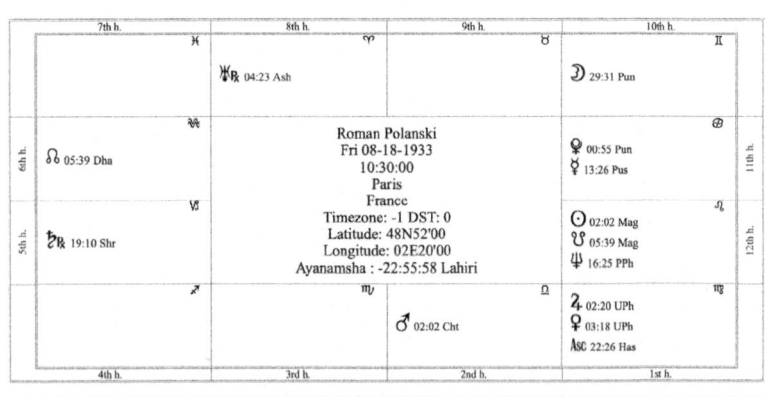

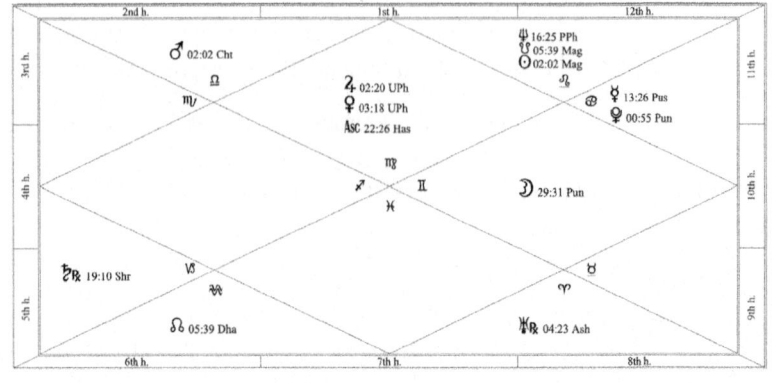

7th h.	8th h.	9th h.	10th h.
♓ ♅℞ 04:23 Ash	♈	♉	♊ ☽ 29:31 Pun
♒ ☊ 05:39 Dha (6th h.)	Roman Polanski Fri 08-18-1933 10:30:00 Paris France		♋ ♀ 00:55 Pun ☿ 13:26 Pus (11th h.)
♑ ♄℞ 19:10 Shr (5th h.)	Timezone: -1 DST: 0 Latitude: 48N52'00 Longitude: 02E20'00 Ayanamsha : -22:55:58 Lahiri		♌ ☉ 02:02 Mag ☋ 05:39 Mag ♆ 16:25 PPh (12th h.)
♐	♏ ♂ 02:02 Cht	♎	♍ ♃ 02:20 UPh ♀ 03:18 UPh Asc 22:26 Has
4th h.	3rd h.	2nd h.	1st h.

(South Indian style chart below with same planetary positions)

122

12th house – Loss or separation of children (8th from 5th)

Another very difficult loss that is represented by the 12th house is the loss of children, as it is the 8th house from the 5th House of children. Joseph Kennedy, the father of the Kennedy clan, must have a planetary combination that represents loss of children, as he lost four children violently in his lifetime. His oldest son Joseph and oldest daughter Kathleen both died in airplane crashes, then his sons President John F Kennedy and Robert Kennedy were assassinated. He also had a mentally challenged daughter that consequently died of a lobotomy later.

In Kennedy's 12th house sits both the Sun and the Moon in Leo. The Sun as the ruler of the 12th house, in the 12th house focuses on great losses, plus the Moon sits very close to the Sun representing a very dark Moon.

Since the 5th house is the house of children it goes to reason that Kennedy would have Ketu the indicator of losses in the 5th house of children. Saturn ruler of the 5th house sits opposed to the 5th house conjunct Rahu. All this combined represents great losses for children.

7th h.	8th h.	9th h.	10th h.
♓	♈ ♅℞ 10:01 Roh ♀℞ 13:40 Roh	♉	♊
6th h. ♒	Joseph Kennedy P. Sr. Thu 09-06-1888 07:06:00 Boston, MA, Massachusetts USA	☊ 07:25 Pus ♄ 22:13 Asl	11th h. ♋
5th h. ☋ 07:25 USh ♑	Timezone: 5 DST: 0 Latitude: 42N21'30 Longitude: 71W03'35 Ayanamsha: -22:17:54 Lahiri	☉ 21:58 PPh ☽ 25:54 PPh	12th h. ♌
♐	♂ 04:51 Anu ♃ 07:06 Anu ♍	♎	☿ 03:41 UPh ♀ 07:30 UPh Asc 12:44 Has ✶ 23:16 Has ♍
4th h.	3rd h.	2nd h.	1st h.

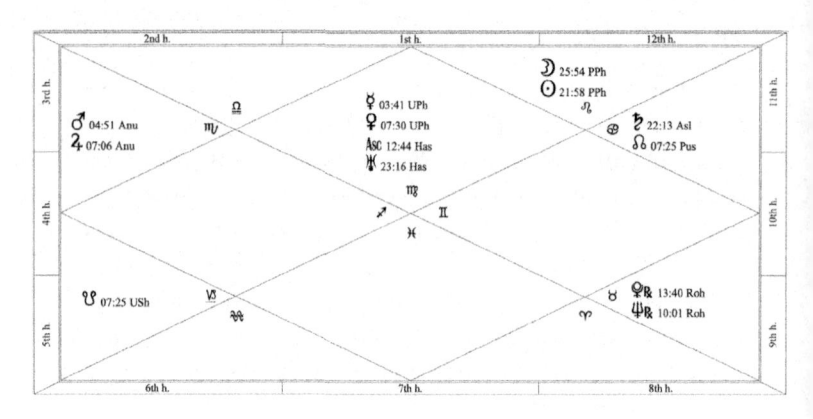

Astrologer's Secrets — My best Tools and Techniques

North Indian Chart (Rasi)

2nd h.	**1st h.**	**12th h.**	
♂ 04:51 Anu ♃ 07:06 Anu	☿ 03:41 UPh ♀ 07:30 UPh Asc 12:44 Has ♅ 23:16 Has	☽ 25:54 PPh ☉ 21:58 PPh ☊ ♄ 22:13 Asl ☋ 07:25 Pus	**11th h.**
3rd h.	♍ ♐ ♊ ♓		
4th h.			**10th h.**
☋ 07:25 USh	♑ ♒	♉ ♀℞ 13:40 Roh ♆℞ 10:01 Roh ♈	**9th h.**
5th h.	**6th h.**	**7th h.**	**8th h.**

South Indian Chart

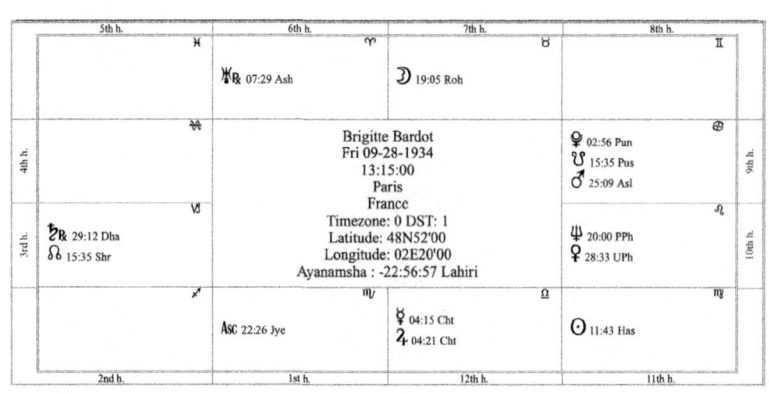 5th h.	6th h.	7th h.	8th h.
♓	♈ ♅℞ 07:29 Ash	♉ ☽ 19:05 Roh	♊
♒ (4th h.)	**Brigitte Bardot** Fri 09-28-1934 13:15:00 Paris France Timezone: 0 DST: 1 Latitude: 48N52'00 Longitude: 02E20'00 Ayanamsha: -22:56:57 Lahiri		♋ ♀ 02:56 Pun ☋ 15:35 Pus ♂ 25:09 Asl (9th h.)
♑ (3rd h.) ♄℞ 29:12 Dha ☊ 15:35 Shr			♌ ♆ 20:00 PPh ♀ 28:33 UPh (10th h.)
♐ (2nd h.) Asc 22:26 Jye	♏ (1st h.) ☿ 04:15 Cht ♃ 04:21 Cht	♎ (12th h.)	♍ (11th h.) ☉ 11:43 Has

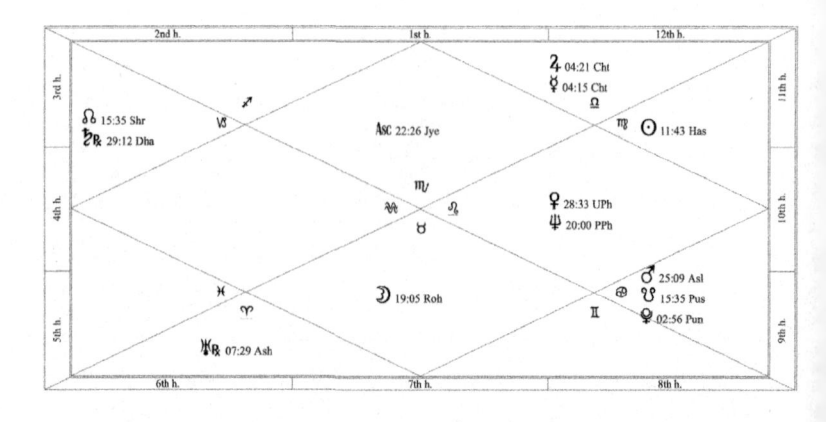

North Indian Chart (Navamsa / alternate)

2nd h.	**1st h.**	**12th h.**	
☊ 15:35 Shr ♄℞ 29:12 Dha	♐ Asc 22:26 Jye	♃ 04:21 Cht ☿ 04:15 Cht ♎ ♍ ☉ 11:43 Has	**11th h.**
3rd h.	♏ ♒ ♌ ♉	♀ 28:33 UPh ♆ 20:00 PPh	**10th h.**
4th h.		♂ 25:09 Asl ☋ 15:35 Pus ♀ 02:56 Pun	**9th h.**
5th h.	♓ ♈ ♅℞ 07:29 Ash	☽ 19:05 Roh ♉	♊
6th h.	**7th h.**	**8th h.**	

12th house: Problems with children

Brigitte Bardot is a former French actor, singer and model. Famous for portraying sexually emancipated characters with hedonistic lifestyles, she was one of the best known sex symbols of the 1950s and 1960s. Although she withdrew from the entertainment industry in 1973, she remains a major popular culture icon.

Throughout her life, Bardot had seventeen relationships with men and was married four times. Bardot said, "I have always looked for passion. That's why I was often unfaithful. And when the passion was coming to an end, I was packing my suitcase".

As soon as Bardot found out she was pregnant, she immediately tried to find a doctor to perform a termination. But in France, such operations were banned, so no one dared to do so. Actor Jacques Charrier was the father of the child, and persuaded the actress to quit termination and marry him.

Immediately after giving birth, she said "I started screaming, begging them to take him away from me. I never wanted to see him again."

Her only son Nicolas was raised by relatives, and attempted suicide 6 times. He did overcome his difficulties and become a successful family man but has held great resentment towards his mother.

Her problems with children can easily be seen by looking at her 12th house. In her 12th house sits Jupiter exactly conjunct Mercury, and Jupiter (indicator of children), plus Jupiter is the ruler of the 5th house and sits in the 12th house with Mercury ruler of the difficult 8th house. This combination in the 12th house being the 8th house from the 5th describes her difficulty with wanting and sustaining a relationship with her children.

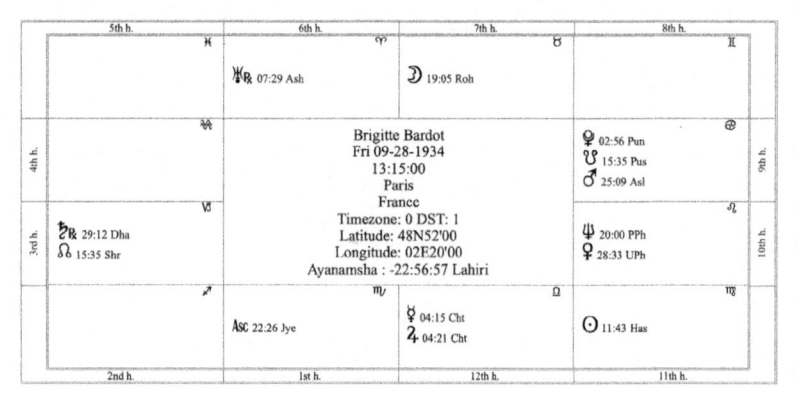

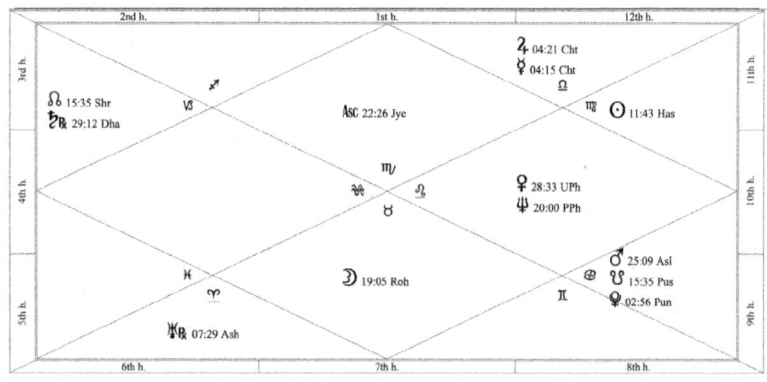

Venus in 12th – Wealth

Gloria Vanderbilt was an artist, author, actor, fashion designer, heiress, and socialite.

During the 1930s, she was the subject of a high-profile child custody trial in which her mother, Gloria Morgan Vanderbilt, and her paternal aunt, Gertrude Vanderbilt Whitney, each sought custody of her and control over her trust fund. Called the "trial of the century" by the press, the court proceedings were the subject of wide and sensational press coverage due to the wealth and prominence of the involved parties, and the scandalous evidence presented to support Whitney's claim that Gloria Morgan Vanderbilt was an unfit parent.

Upon their father's death from cirrhosis when Vanderbilt was 18 months old, she and her half-sister became heiresses to a half share each in a $5 million trust fund, equivalent to $77 million in 2021 value.

There are many indications of great wealth especially from inheritances with Jupiter and Mars in the 8th house of inheritances. Jupiter ruler of the 9th House of the father sits in the 8th House of inheritances with Mars ruler of the 8th house in the 8th house. This clearly indicates the inheritance that she received was from her father.

But another very interesting indicator of wealth is when Venus is in the 12th house. Venus is the only planet that will prosper and produce wealth instead of losses in the 12th house. This can be easily misunderstood since the 12th house is notoriously known for great loss.

12th h.	1st h.	2nd h.	3rd h.
♓ ♀ 16:08 UBh	♈ ASC 23:44 Bha	♉	♊ ☿℞ 17:39 Ard
11th h. ♒ ♅ 23:45 PBh ☋ 09:22 Sat ☉ 07:55 Sat	Gloria Vanderbilt Wed 02-20-1924 09:55:00 New York, NY,New York USA Timezone: 5 DST: 0 Latitude: 40N42'51 Longitude: 74W00'23 Ayanamsha : -22:47:44 Lahiri		♋ ♆℞ 25:53 Asl 4th h.
10th h. ♑ ☿ 16:03 Shr			♌ ☽ 07:17 Mag ☊ 09:22 Mag 5th h.
♐	♏ ♃ 24:03 Jye ♂ 27:34 Jye	♎ ♄℞ 09:27 Swa	♍
9th h.	8th h.	7th h.	6th h.

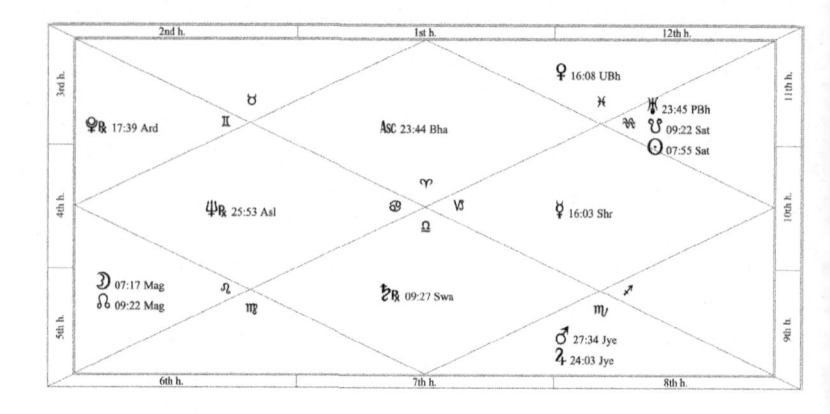

Private Client

Venus in 12th house
Great wealth, comes from the mother, Venus/Moon in Uttara Bhadrapada

This is a chart of a client who also inherited great family wealth, but a very interesting combination that denotes great wealth particularly coming from the mother can be seen by Venus in the 12th house exalted in Pisces conjunct the Moon indicator of the mother plus it rules the 4th house of mother and family. Furthermore, both Venus and the Moon sit in the nakshatra Uttara Bhadrapada which is one of the nakshatras that indicate inheritance.

On another note, it can be seen in the 8th House of inheritance as Mars ruler of the 8th house sits in the 8th house magnified by Rahu in Scorpio.

Also, Saturn rules the 11th house which is also the house of older siblings, and Saturn is conjunct Rahu and Mars, and she lost two of her older brothers to cancer. Furthermore, Mars is also the indicator for siblings, and this combination may be great for inheritances but it is extraordinarily difficult for siblings since Mars also rules the 8th house of death conjunct Saturn Rahu.

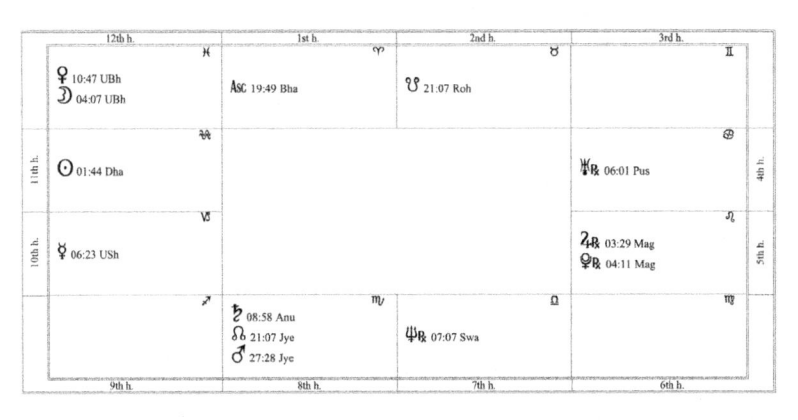

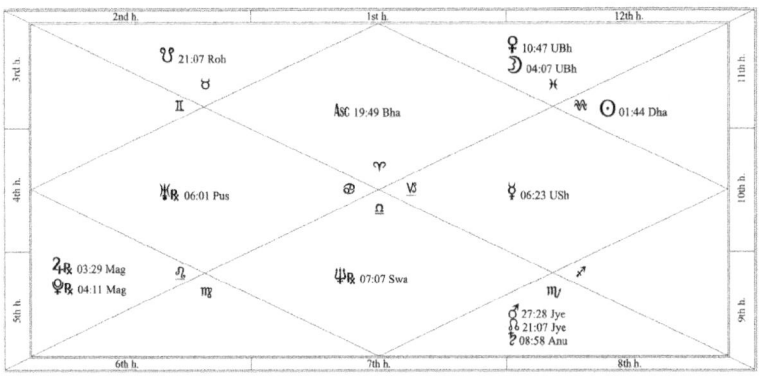

12th h.	1st h.	2nd h.	3rd h.
♓	♈ ASC 19:49 Bha	♉ ☋ 21:07 Roh	♊
♀ 10:47 UBh ☽ 04:07 UBh			

11th h.			4th h.
♒ ☉ 01:44 Dha			♋ ♅℞ 06:01 Pus

10th h.			5th h.
♑ ☿ 06:23 USh			♌ ♃℞ 03:29 Mag ♀℞ 04:11 Mag

9th h.	8th h.	7th h.	6th h.
♐ ♄ 08:58 Anu ☊ 21:07 Jye ♂ 27:28 Jye	♏ ♆℞ 07:07 Swa	♎	♍

Fixed Stars

Rigel: 23–24 degrees Taurus/Scorpio
Wealth and Money

There are fixed stars that are specific indicators for certain things in a chart. In this next group of charts are very wealthy individuals due to the fixed star Rigel.

The fixed star Rigel sits around 23–24 degrees of Taurus, planets within 23–24 degrees Taurus or the opposite sign of Scorpio is a strong indicator of wealth.

Below are eight individuals that have the degree marking of either 23–24 degrees of Taurus or Scorpio. Regardless of the house placements it is an indicator of wealth.

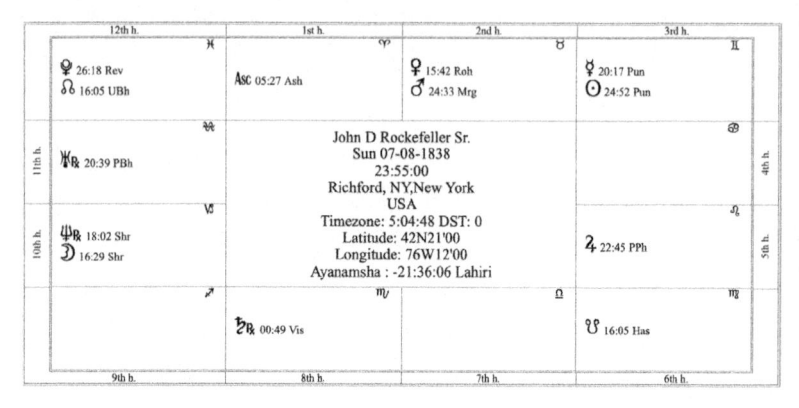

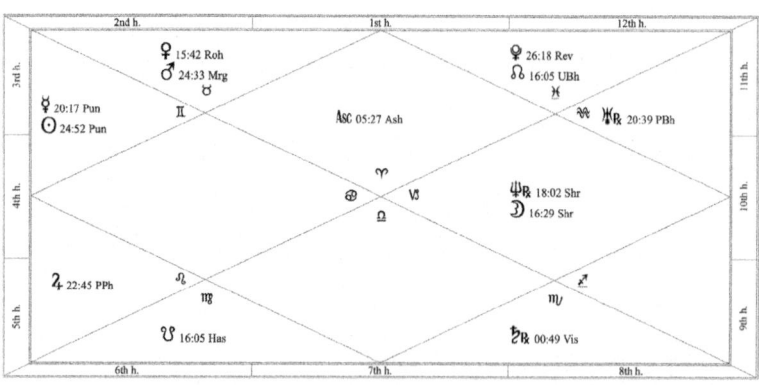

12th h.	1st h.	2nd h.	3rd h.
♀ 26:18 Rev ☊ 16:05 UBh	ASC 05:27 Ash	♀ 15:42 Roh ♂ 24:33 Mrg	☿ 20:17 Pun ☉ 24:52 Pun
♅R 20:39 PBh	John D Rockefeller Sr. Sun 07-08-1838 23:55:00 Richford, NY, New York USA		
♆R 18:02 Shr ☽ 16:29 Shr	Timezone: 5:04:48 DST: 0 Latitude: 42N21'00 Longitude: 76W12'00 Ayanamsha : -21:36:06 Lahiri	♃ 22:45 PPh	
	♄R 00:49 Vis		☋ 16:05 Has
9th h.	8th h.	7th h.	6th h.

John D. Rockefeller had an estimated net worth of $340 Billion at death. He was the head of the Standard Oil Company and one of the world's richest men of all time. His Mars is 24 degrees of Taurus in the 2nd house of money with Venus ruler of the 2nd house.

Planet's Houses and Rulers: 12th house

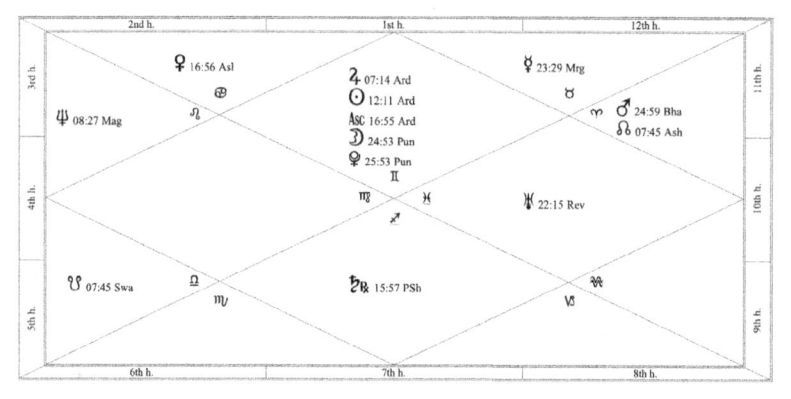

Chapter 13

Ross Perot was a businessman who had a net worth of $4 billion at the time of his death in 2019. Famous for his involvement in politics and his shrewd instinct for business, Perot was one of the richest people in the world for decades. He initially worked as a salesman for IBM before founding Electronic Data Systems in the early 1960s. After selling this company in the 1980s, Perot became a billionaire.

Amongst many other things in his chart that indicate his massive wealth he has Mercury at 23 degrees of Taurus.

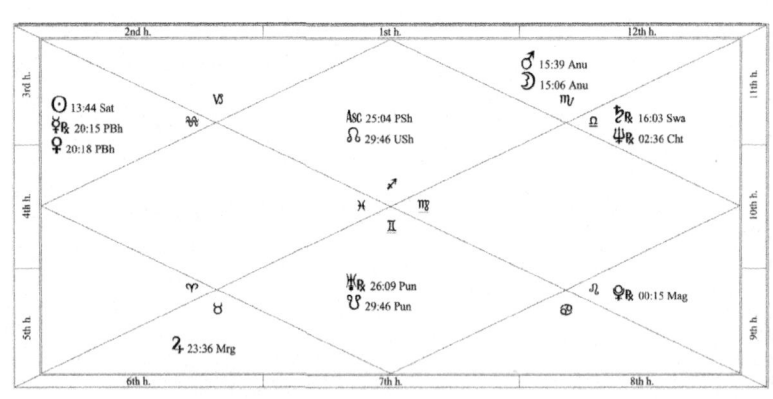

	4th h.	5th h.	6th h.	7th h.
	♓	♈	♉	♊
3rd h.	♀ 20:18 PBh ☿℞ 20:15 PBh ☉ 13:44 Sat ♒	Erdogan, Recep Tayyip Fri 02-26-1954 04:25:00 Istanbul, İstanbul Turkey Timezone: -2 DST: 0 Latitude: 41N01'00 Longitude: 28E57'00 Ayanamsha : -23:13:17 Lahiri	♃ 23:36 Mrg	♅℞ 26:09 Pun ☋ 29:46 Pun
2nd h.	♑			♋ 8th h.
	♐	♏	♎	♌ ♆℞ 00:15 Mag 9th h.
	☊ 29:46 USh Asc 25:04 PSh	☽ 15:06 Anu ♂ 15:39 Anu	♇ 02:36 Cht ♄℞ 16:03 Swa	♍
	1st h.	12th h.	11th h.	10th h.

Rigel: 23–24 degrees Taurus/Scorpio
Wealth and Money

Recep Tayyip Erdoğan is a Turkish politician, and the current ruler of Turkey has a net worth of $500 million. He has Jupiter 23 degrees of Taurus.

Planet's Houses and Rulers: 12th house

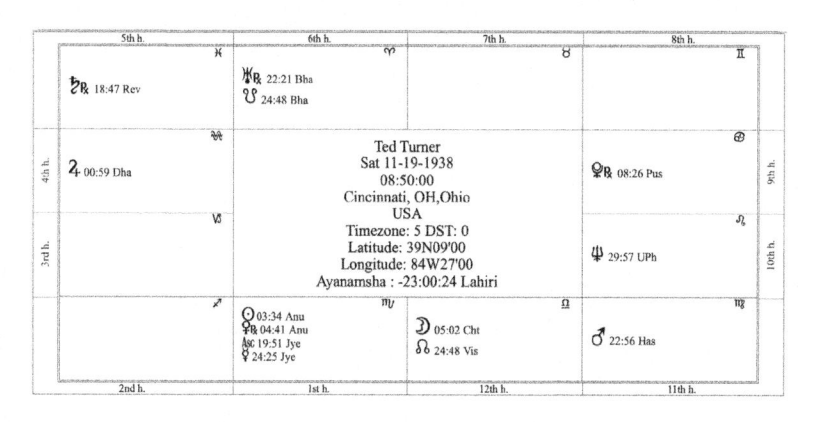

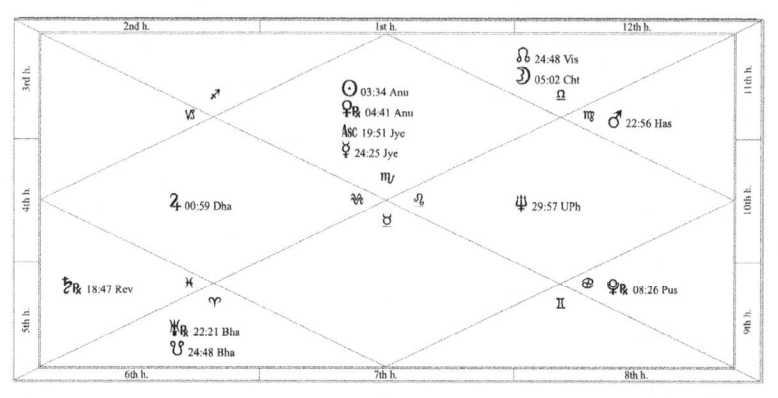

Chapter 13

5th h.	6th h.	7th h.	8th h.
♓	♈	♉	♊
♄℞ 18:47 Rev	♅℞ 22:21 Bha ☋ 24:48 Bha		

4th h. ♒			9th h. ⊕
♃ 00:59 Dha	Ted Turner Sat 11-19-1938 08:50:00 Cincinnati, OH, Ohio USA Timezone: 5 DST: 0 Latitude: 39N09'00 Longitude: 84W27'00 Ayanamsha: -23:00:24 Lahiri		♀℞ 08:26 Pus
3rd h. ♑			10th h. ♌
			♆ 29:57 UPh

♐	♍	♎	♏
☉ 03:34 Anu ♀℞ 04:41 Anu Asc 19:51 Jye ☿ 24:25 Jye	☽ 05:02 Cht ☊ 24:48 Vis		♂ 22:56 Has
2nd h.	1st h.	12th h.	11th h.

Ted Turner is a media giant and entrepreneur from Ohio who has a net worth of $2.2 billion dollars. Turner earned his fortune as the creator of CNN, TNT, TBS and as the former owner of the Atlanta Braves. Ted Turner has left his mark on the media landscape by creating CNN, WTBS, MGM, TNT, and Cartoon Network. He has Mercury, which is the planet of media and communications at 24 degrees of Scorpio.

133

My best Tools and Techniques

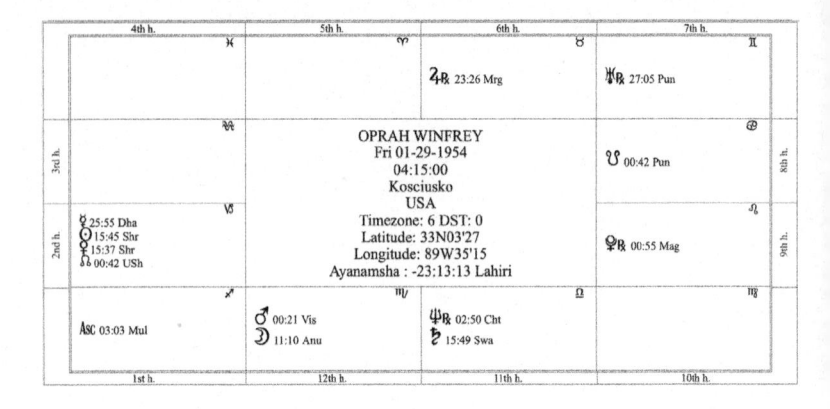

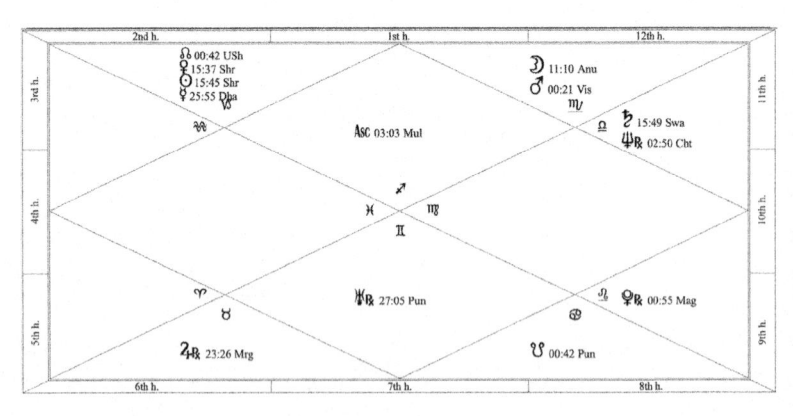

Astrologer's Secrets

	4th h.	5th h.	6th h.	7th h.
3rd h.	♓	♈ ♃℞ 23:26 Mrg	♉	♊ ♅℞ 27:05 Pun
	♒	OPRAH WINFREY Fri 01-29-1954 04:15:00 Kosciusko USA Timezone: 6 DST: 0 Latitude: 33N03'27 Longitude: 89W35'15 Ayanamsha: -23:13:13 Lahiri		♋ ☋ 00:42 Pun	8th h.
2nd h.	♑ ☊ 25:55 Dha ☉ 15:45 Shr ☿ 15:37 Shr ☋ 00:42 USh			♌ ♀℞ 00:55 Mag	9th h.
	♐ ASC 03:03 Mul	♏ ♂ 00:21 Vis ☽ 11:10 Anu	♎ ♆℞ 02:50 Cht ♄ 15:49 Swa	♍
	1st h.	12th h.	11th h.	10th h.

Oprah's net worth is $3.5 billion. Today she earns around $315 million per year thanks to her highly lucrative diversified media empire. Her Jupiter is 23 degrees Taurus.

134

Planet's Houses and Rulers: 12th house

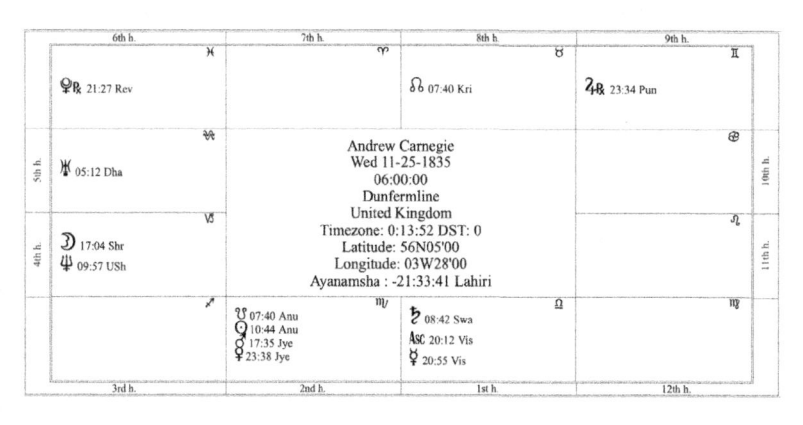

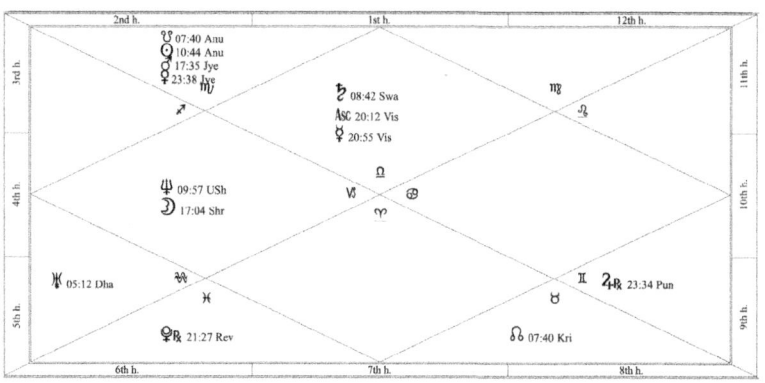

Chapter 13

6th h.	7th h.	8th h.	9th h.
♓ ♀℞ 21:27 Rev	♈	♉ ☊ 07:40 Kri	♊ ♃℞ 23:34 Pun
♒ ♅ 05:12 Dha (5th h.)	Andrew Carnegie Wed 11-25-1835 06:00:00 Dunfermline United Kingdom Timezone: 0:13:52 DST: 0 Latitude: 56N05'00 Longitude: 03W28'00 Ayanamsha : -21:33:41 Lahiri		⊕ (10th h.) ♌ (11th h.)
♑ ☽ 17:04 Shr ♆ 09:57 USh (4th h.)			
♐ ☋ 07:40 Anu ☉ 10:44 Anu ♂ 17:35 Jye ☿ 23:38 Jye	♏ ♄ 08:42 Swa Asc 20:12 Vis ☿ 20:55 Vis	♎	♍
3rd h.	2nd h.	1st h.	12th h.

2nd h.	1st h.	12th h.
☋ 07:40 Anu ☉ 10:44 Anu ♂ 17:35 Jye ♀ 23:38 Jye ♏ ♐ (3rd h.)	♄ 08:42 Swa Asc 20:12 Vis ☿ 20:55 Vis	♍ ♌ (11th h.)
♆ 09:57 USh ☽ 17:04 Shr (4th h.)	♎ ♑ ⊕ ♈	(10th h.)
♅ 05:12 Dha ♒ (5th h.) ♓		♊ ♃℞ 23:34 Pun ♉ (9th h.)
♀℞ 21:27 Rev (6th h.)	(7th h.)	☊ 07:40 Kri (8th h.)

During his lifetime, Andrew Carnegie had a peak, inflation-adjusted, net worth of $310 billion. That's enough to make him the 4th richest human being of all time. His Venus is 23 degrees Scorpio.

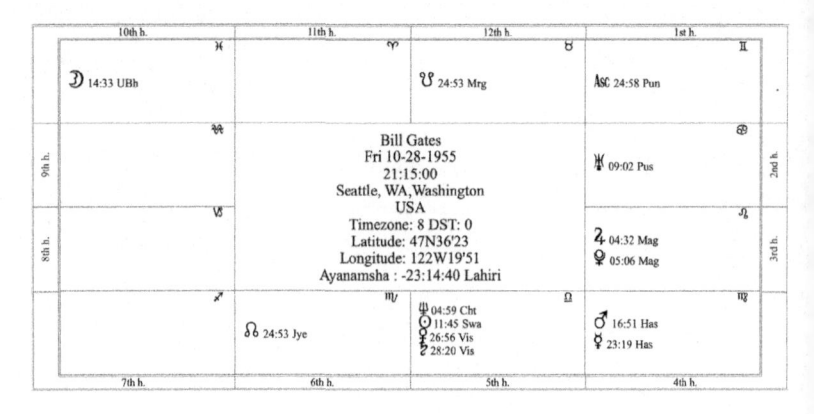

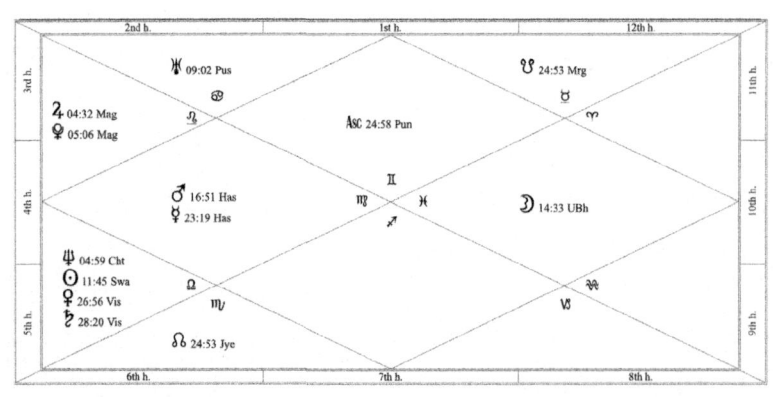

10th h.	11th h.	12th h.	1st h.
♓ ☽ 14:33 UBh	♈	♉ ☋ 24:53 Mrg	♊ ASC 24:58 Pun
♒	Bill Gates Fri 10-28-1955 21:15:00 Seattle, WA, Washington USA Timezone: 8 DST: 0 Latitude: 47N36'23 Longitude: 122W19'51 Ayanamsha : -23:14:40 Lahiri		♋ ♅ 09:02 Pus
♑			♌ ♃ 04:32 Mag ♀ 05:06 Mag
♐ ☊ 24:53 Jye	♏ ♆ 04:59 Cht ☉ 11:45 Swa ♀ 26:56 Vis ☿ 28:20 Vis	♎	♍ ♂ 16:51 Has ☿ 23:19 Has
7th h.	6th h.	5th h.	4th h.

Bill Gates is an American business magnate, founder and former chairman and CEO of Microsoft, philanthropist, and author. As of this writing, Bill Gates' net worth is $114 billion. Over much of the last 20 years, Bill Gates has been the richest person in the world. His Rahu is at 24 degrees Scorpio.

Planet's Houses and Rulers: 12th house

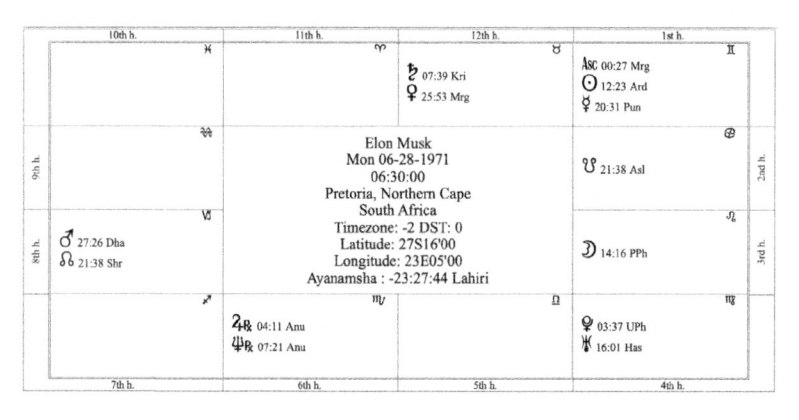

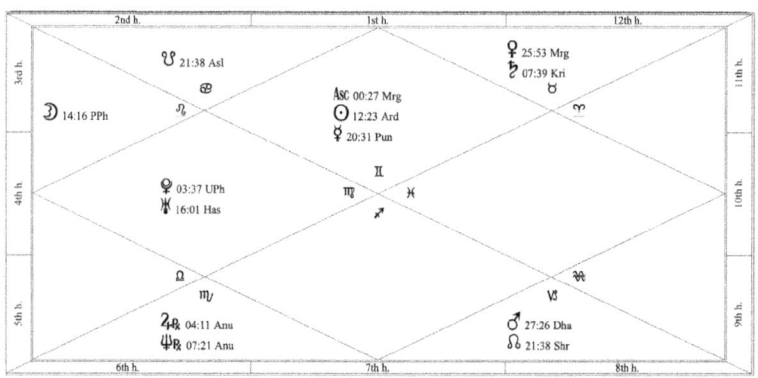

Chapter 13

10th h.	11th h.	12th h.	1st h.
♓	♈	♄ 07:39 Kri ♀ 25:53 Mrg	♉ Asc 00:27 Mrg ☉ 12:23 Ard ☿ 20:31 Pun ♊
♒ (9th h.)	Elon Musk Mon 06-28-1971 06:30:00 Pretoria, Northern Cape		� 21:38 Asl (2nd h.)
♑ ♂ 27:26 Dha (8th h.) ☋ 21:38 Shr	South Africa Timezone: -2 DST: 0 Latitude: 27S16'00 Longitude: 23E05'00 Ayanamsha: -23:27:44 Lahiri		♌ ☽ 14:16 PPh (3rd h.)
♐ 	♏ ♃℞ 04:11 Anu ♅℞ 07:21 Anu	♎	♍ ♀ 03:37 UPh ♆ 16:01 Has
7th h.	6th h.	5th h.	4th h.

Elon Musk's net worth is $168 billion. As of this writing, that makes him one of the richest people on the planet. Musk's fortune comes with his 20% stake in Tesla and his 48% stake in the privately held SpaceX. His Venus is 25 degrees Taurus. I give a degree and a half orb of influence with the 23–24 degrees of Taurus or Scorpio, on either side (22–25 egrees).

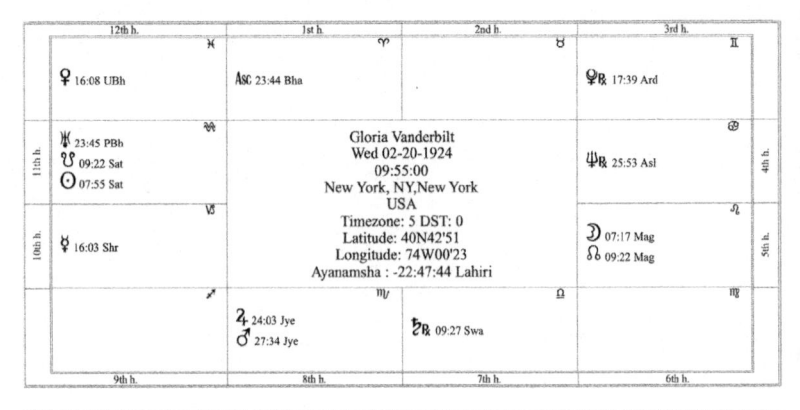

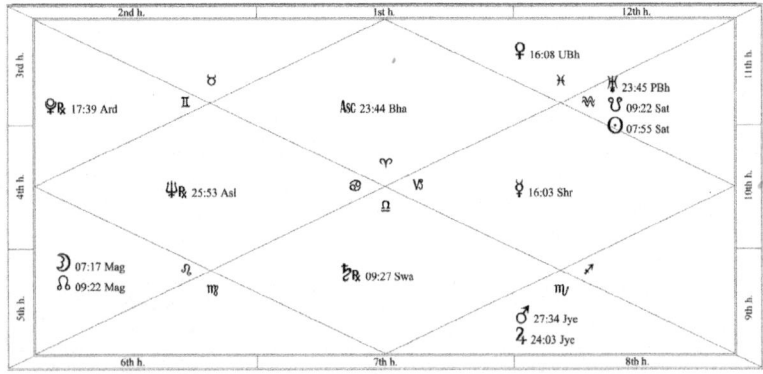

12th h.		1st h.		2nd h.		3rd h.
	♓	♈		♉		♊
♀ 16:08 UBh		Asc 23:44 Bha				♀℞ 17:39 Ard

	♒	Gloria Vanderbilt		⊕	
♅ 23:45 PBh ☊ 09:22 Sat ☉ 07:55 Sat		Wed 02-20-1924 09:55:00 New York, NY, New York USA		♆℞ 25:53 Asl	
	♑	Timezone: 5 DST: 0 Latitude: 40N42'51 Longitude: 74W00'23 Ayanamsha : -22:47:44 Lahiri			♌
☿ 16:03 Shr				☽ 07:17 Mag ☋ 09:22 Mag	

	♐	♏		♎		♍
		♃ 24:03 Jye ♂ 27:34 Jye		♄℞ 09:27 Swa		
9th h.		8th h.		7th h.		6th h.

Gloria Vanderbilt was said to have a net worth of $200 million, although the exact amount has never been revealed. Her Jupiter in the 8th house is 24 degrees Scorpio.

Regulus-leaders: 5–6 degrees of Leo

The fixed star Regulus which sits at 5–6 degrees of Leo is in the nakshatra Magha represents kings and leaders, as Magha's symbol is a king's throne. Oppositions as in 5–6 degrees Aquarius are significant too, but the nakshatra of a king's throne make the degree in Leo more powerful.

Donald Trump's ascendant sits at 6 degrees of Leo activating the leader qualities, which led him to lead his own companies and business as well as the Presidency of the United States.

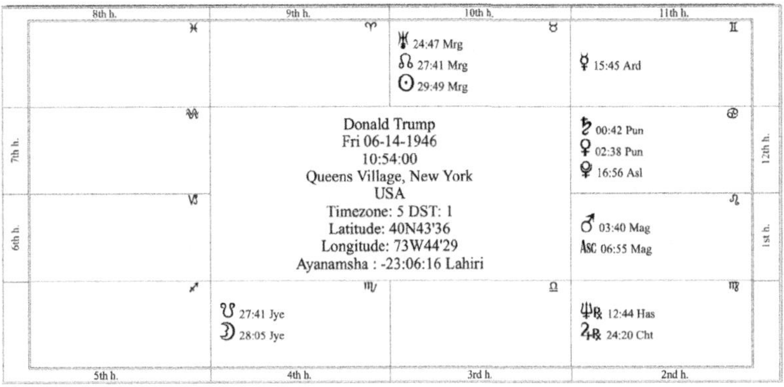
8th h.
9th h.
10th h.
11th h.
12th h.
1st h.
2nd h.
3rd h.
4th h.
5th h.
6th h.
7th h.
♅ 24:47 Mrg
☊ 27:41 Mrg
☉ 29:49 Mrg
☿ 15:45 Ard
♄ 00:42 Pun
♀ 02:38 Pun
♇ 16:56 Asl
♂ 03:40 Mag
Asc 06:55 Mag
♆℞ 12:44 Has
♃℞ 24:20 Cht
☋ 27:41 Jye
☽ 28:05 Jye
Donald Trump
Fri 06-14-1946
10:54:00
Queens Village, New York
USA
Timezone: 5 DST: 1
Latitude: 40N43'36
Longitude: 73W44'29
Ayanamsha : -23:06:16 Lahiri

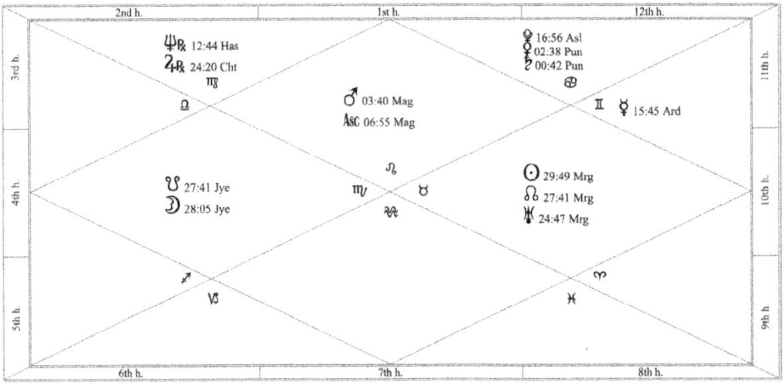
2nd h.
1st h.
12th h.
11th h.
10th h.
9th h.
8th h.
7th h.
6th h.
5th h.
4th h.
3rd h.
♆℞ 12:44 Has
♃℞ 24:20 Cht
♇ 16:56 Asl
♀ 02:38 Pun
♄ 00:42 Pun
♂ 03:40 Mag
Asc 06:55 Mag
☿ 15:45 Ard
☋ 27:41 Jye
☽ 28:05 Jye
☉ 29:49 Mrg
☊ 27:41 Mrg
♅ 24:47 Mrg

Spica-29 Virgo-0 degrees Libra: overnight sensation

Spica is thought to be the most auspicious star in the heavens and is said to represent great talent, with writing and the arts, but I have noticed many with this star prominent experience great stardom or success that comes overnight, as in suddenly and quickly.

North Indian Chart

5th h.	6th h.	7th h.	8th h.
♓	♈	♉	♊
	☋ 03:10 Kri		

4th h.
♀ 27:03 PBh
☉ 16:38 Sat
♄ 09:58 Sat
♂ 01:20 Dha
♒

Justin Bieber
Tue 03-01-1994
00:56:00
Stratford, Ontario
Canada
Timezone: 5 DST: 0
Latitude: 43N22'00
Longitude: 80W59'00
Ayanamsha : -23:46:47 Lahiri

9th h. ♋

3rd h.
☿℞ 29:44 Dha
⛢ 01:05 USh
♑

10th h. ♌

♆ 28:45 USh
♐

☊ 03:10 Vis
♀ 04:17 Anu
Asc 05:14 Anu
♏

☽ 00:50 Cht
♃℞ 20:52 Vis
♎

♍

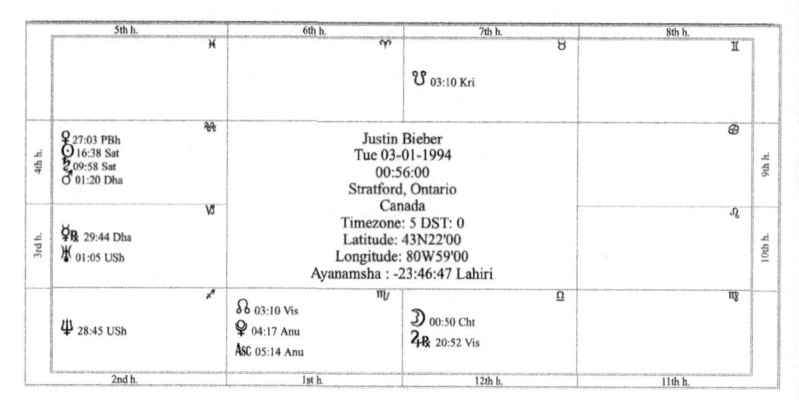

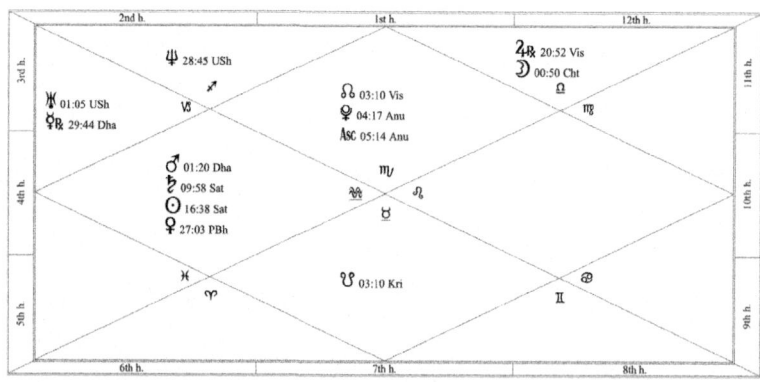

| 2nd h. | 1st h. | 12th h. | 11th h. |

South Indian Chart

2nd h.	1st h.	12th h.	
♆ 28:45 USh ♐		♃℞ 20:52 Vis ☽ 00:50 Cht ♎	11th h.
⛢ 01:05 USh ☿℞ 29:44 Dha ♑	☊ 03:10 Vis ♀ 04:17 Anu Asc 05:14 Anu	♍	
♂ 01:20 Dha ♄ 09:58 Sat ☉ 16:38 Sat ♀ 27:03 PBh	♏ ♒ ♌ ☉		10th h.
♓ ♈	☋ 03:10 Kri	♋ ♊	9th h.
6th h.	7th h.	8th h.	

Justin Bieber is a singer, played an influential role in modern-day popular music. He signed with RBMG Records in 2008, gaining recognition with the release of his debut seven-track EP *My World* (2009) and soon establishing himself as a teen idol. His overnight sensation occurred from a YouTube video! Bieber has his Moon at 0 degrees Libra.

Planet's Houses and Rulers: 12th house

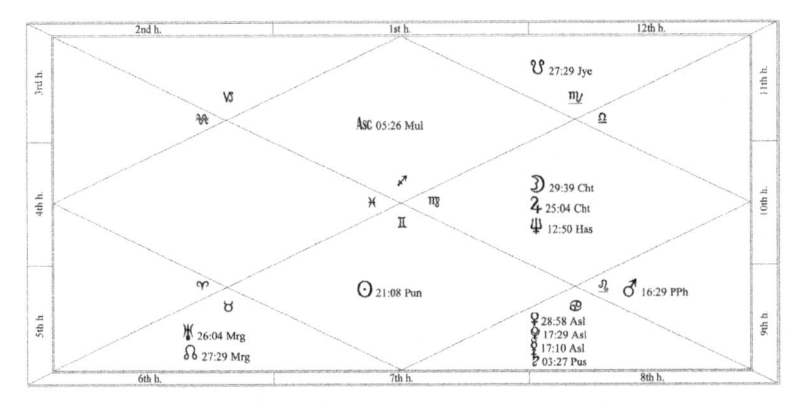

Chapter 13

```
4th h.        | 5th h.              | 6th h.           | 7th h.
    ♓         |       ♈             |      ♉           |          ♊
              | ♅ 26:04 Mrg         | ☉ 21:08 Pun
              | ☊ 27:29 Mrg         |
    ♒         |                     |                  | ☿ 03:27 Pus
              | Sylvester Stallone  |                  | ♀ 17:10 Asl
              | Sat 07-06-1946      |                  | ♀ 17:29 Asl
              | 19:20:00            |                  | ⊕ 28:58 Asl
              | New York, NY, New York |
              | USA                 |
    ♑         | Timezone: 5 DST: 1  |                  |    ♌
              | Latitude: 40N42'51  |                  | ♂ 16:29 PPh
              | Longitude: 74W00'23 |
              | Ayanamsha: -23:06:20 Lahiri |
    ♐         |        ♏            |       ♎          |     ♍
ASC 05:26 Mul | ☋ 27:29 Jye         |                  | ♆ 12:50 Has
              |                     |                  | ♃ 25:04 Cht
              |                     |                  | ☽ 29:39 Cht
1st h.        | 12th h.             | 11th h.          | 10th h.
```

Sylvester Stallone is actor and filmmaker. After his beginnings as a struggling actor for a number of years he achieved his greatest critical and commercial success as an actor and screenwriter, starting in 1976 with his role as boxer Rocky Balboa, Rocky is portrayed as an underdog boxer who fights numerous brutal opponents, and wins the world heavyweight championship twice. After years of struggles he made it overnight with the movie Rocky. Stallone has his Moon at 29 degrees Virgo.

Algol 2–3 degrees Taurus

Algol historically, the star has received a strong association with bloody violence across a wide variety of cultures. In the

Tetrabiblos, the 2nd-century astrological text of the Alexandrian astronomer Ptolemy, Algol is referred to as "the Gorgon of Perseus" and associated with death by decapitation: a theme which mirrors the myth of the hero Perseus's victory over the snake-haired Gorgon Medusa. In the astrology of fixed stars, Algol is considered one of the unluckiest stars in the sky.

This can indicate people who lose their head and suffer extreme problems, sometimes even with addictions. Those who are born May 16–18 will have their Sun conjunct this star and have major issues with addictions or have a family member with addictions or severe problems.

This is the chart of an individual who suffered severe trauma or difficulties, and was attacked savagely, arms cut off and raped 09/29 1978.

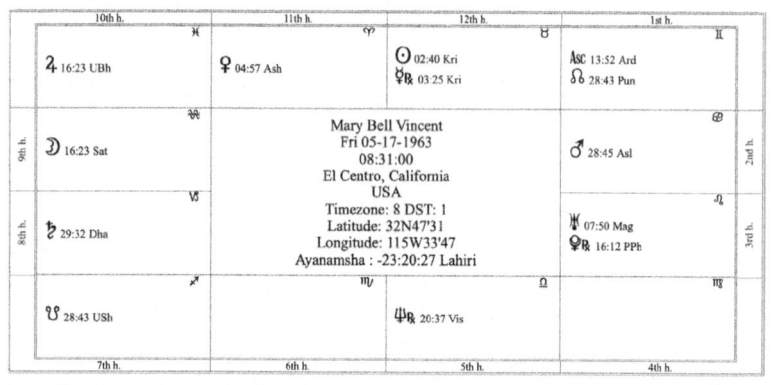

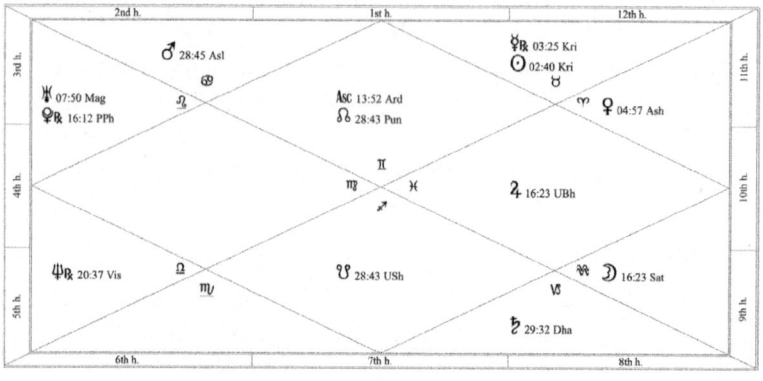

10th h.	11th h.	12th h.	1st h.
♃ 16:23 UBh	♀ 04:57 Ash	☉ 02:40 Kri ☿℞ 03:25 Kri	ASC 13:52 Ard ☊ 28:43 Pun
☽ 16:23 Sat	Mary Bell Vincent Fri 05-17-1963 08:31:00 El Centro, California USA Timezone: 8 DST: 1 Latitude: 32N47'31 Longitude: 115W33'47 Ayanamsha : -23:20:27 Lahiri		♂ 28:45 Asl
♄ 29:32 Dha			♅ 07:50 Mag ♀℞ 16:12 PPh
☋ 28:43 USh		♆℞ 20:37 Vis	
7th h.	6th h.	5th h.	4th h.

142

Chapter 14

Planet's Important combinations and Aspects

Saturn conjunct Mars. Diligence and power to achieve, overcome obstacles

Dolly Parton is singer-songwriter, actor, philanthropist, and businesswoman, known primarily for her work in country music. She was born in a one-room cabin in Tennessee. She is the fourth of twelve children. She describes her childhood as being "Dirt Poor".

She has acquired enormous success and wealth and I believe this can be attributed to the powerful strong ability to overcome great obstacles with her exact Mars and Saturn conjunction. Furthermore, this conjunction is accentuated with Rahu, which magnifies the planets that it is conjunct. The 11th house is an Upachaya house (3, 6, 10 and 11) indicating growth and improvement over time. When natural malefic planets are in Upachaya houses they give the drive and ambition to overcome obstacles and create success.

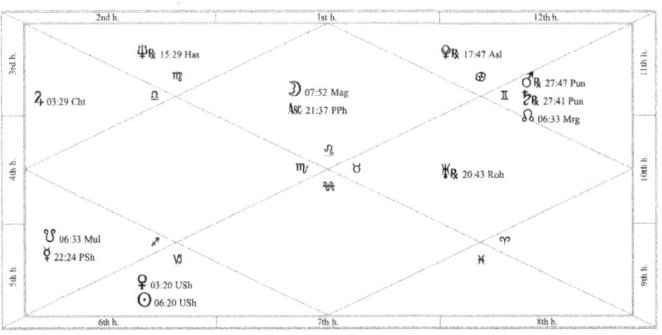

143

Venus conjunct Rahu: Marriage to a Foreigner

Venus is the planet of relationships and Rahu is the indicator of foreigners, so when they are conjunct there is an attraction to foreigners, and many times can indicate marriage to a foreigner. Maria Shriver is a Kennedy, the daughter of Eunice Kennedy, the sister to late U.S. president John F. Kennedy. She married actor, and former governor of California who was born and raised in Austria, Arnold Schwarzenegger. Not only is Venus conjunct Rahu but both are in the 7th house of marriage.

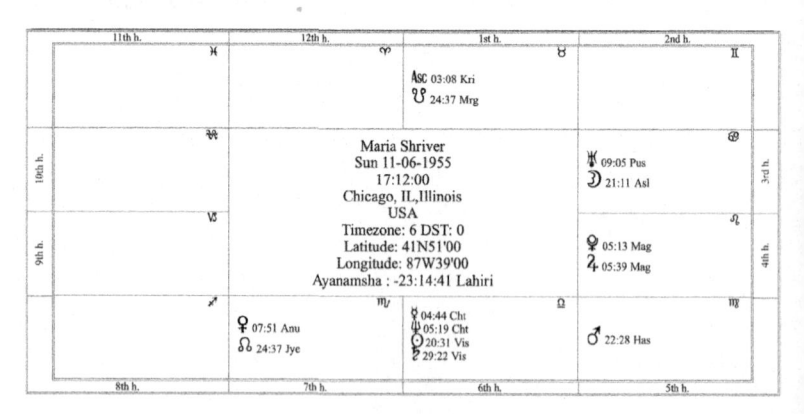

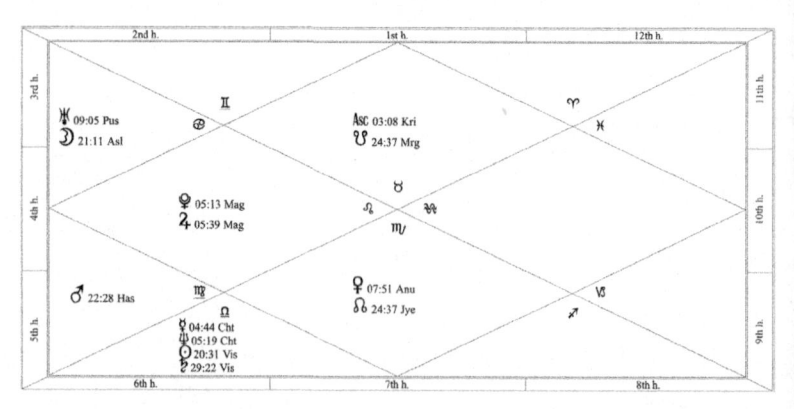

11th h.	12th h.	1st h.	2nd h.
♓	♈	♉ ASC 03:08 Kri / ☋ 24:37 Mrg	♊
♒	Maria Shriver Sun 11-06-1955 17:12:00 Chicago, IL, Illinois USA Timezone: 6 DST: 0 Latitude: 41N51'00 Longitude: 87W39'00 Ayanamsha: -23:14:41 Lahiri		♋ ♅ 09:05 Pus / ☽ 21:11 Asl
♑			♌ ♀ 05:13 Mag / ♃ 05:39 Mag
♐ ♀ 07:51 Anu / ☊ 24:37 Jye	♏	♎ ☿ 04:44 Cht / ♆ 05:19 Cht / ☉ 20:31 Vis / ♄ 29:22 Vis	♍ ♂ 22:28 Has
8th h.	7th h.	6th h.	5th h.

144

Mars conjunct Ketu can be an injury

Mars with Ketu is a very difficult conjunction, and many times represents injury or even attacks as they were tightly conjunct on September 11th, 2001, in Sagittarius. They are both very fiery and cause great destruction together. In Vedic astrology they are likened to each other, they are both said to burn.

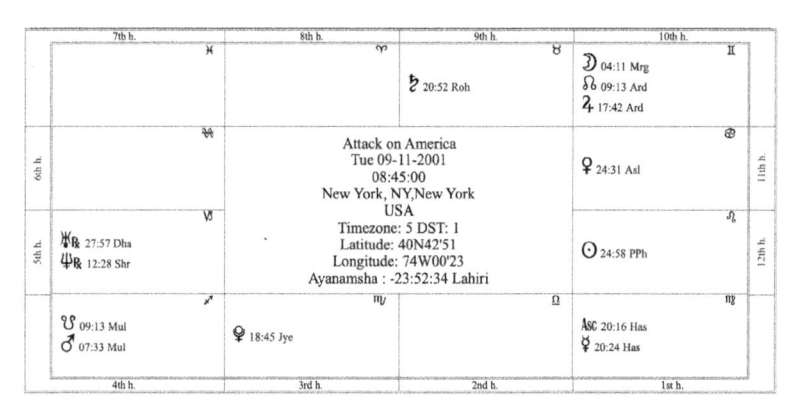

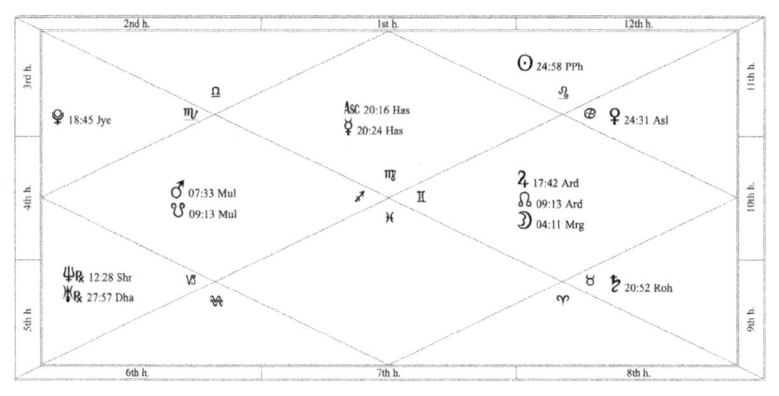

7th h.	8th h.	9th h.	10th h.
♓	♈ ♄ 20:52 Roh	♉	☽ 04:11 Mrg ☊ 09:13 Ard ♃ 17:42 Ard ♊
♒	Attack on America Tue 09-11-2001 08:45:00 New York, NY, New York USA Timezone: 5 DST: 1 Latitude: 40N42'51 Longitude: 74W00'23 Ayanamsha: -23:52:34 Lahiri		⊕ ♀ 24:31 Asl
♅ ℞ 27:57 Dha ♆ ℞ 12:28 Shr ♑			☉ 24:58 PPh ♌
♐ ☋ 09:13 Mul ♂ 07:33 Mul	♀ 18:45 Jye ♍	♎	Asc 20:16 Has ☿ 20:24 Has ♍
4th h.	3rd h.	2nd h.	1st h.

Mars/Ketu: Injury

Chalino was a singer, recorded 9 albums and died in a car crash 03/27/2004 at a very young age. His Mars and Ketu are very strong in Scorpio but are additionally in the 6th house of accidents with Uranus. Uranus is also an indicator of accidents, all three together can cause accidents.

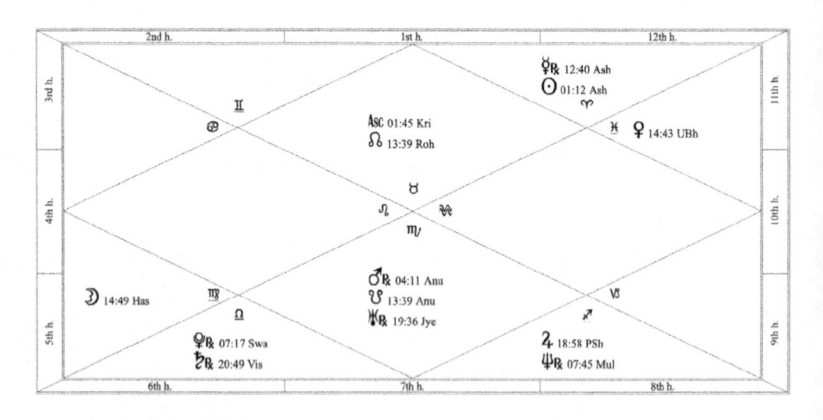

11th h.	12th h.	1st h.	2nd h.
♓ ♀ 14:43 UBh	☉ 01:12 Ash ☿℞ 12:40 Ash ♈	ASC 01:45 Kri ☊ 13:39 Roh ♉	♊
♒ 10th h.	Aden Sanchez Chalino Sat 04-14-1984 07:00:00 Torrance, California USA Timezone: 8 DST: 0 Latitude: 33N50'09 Longitude: 118W20'26 Ayanamsha : -23:37:58 Lahiri		♋ 3rd h.
♑ 9th h.			♌ 4th h.
8th h. ♐ ♃ 18:58 PSh ♅℞ 07:45 Mul	7th h. ♂℞ 04:11 Anu ☋ 13:39 Anu ♆℞ 19:36 Jye ♍	6th h. ♀℞ 07:17 Swa ♄℞ 20:49 Vis ♎	5th h. ☽ 14:49 Has ♍

Mars/Ketu: Accident

Brian Epstein was The Beatles manager who died of an accidental drug overdose. This can be seen by the Mars Ketu, plus Pluto in the 11th house. Mars is the ruler of the 8th house, debilitated with Ketu, making Mars a first rate damaging malefic especially with Ketu.

Beatles Manager, died of drug overdose: 08/27/1967

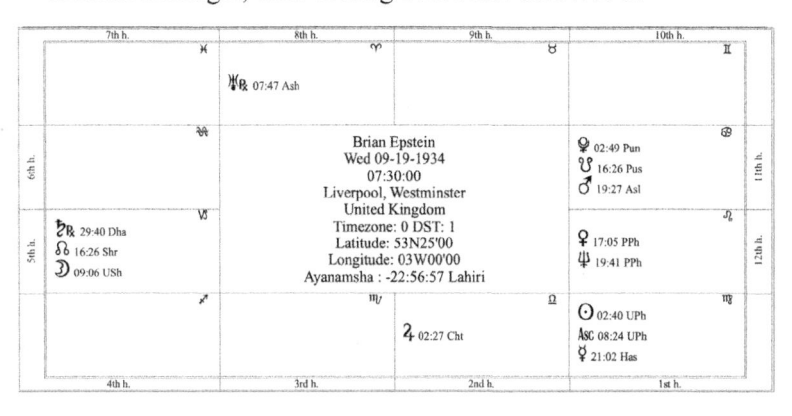

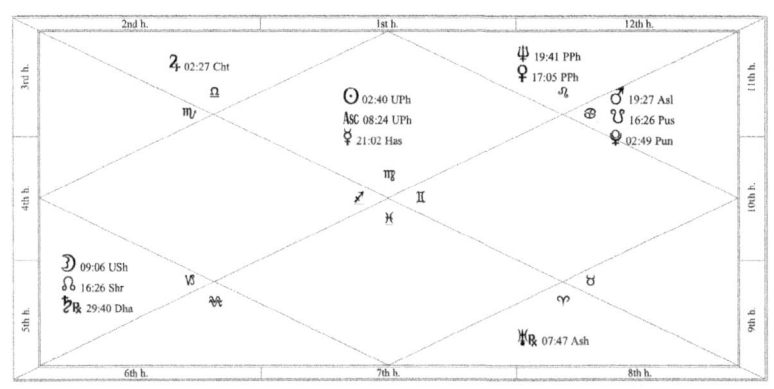

	7th h.	8th h.	9th h.	10th h.
6th h.	♓ ♅℞ 07:47 Ash	♈	♉	♊
	♒	Brian Epstein Wed 09-19-1934 07:30:00 Liverpool, Westminster United Kingdom Timezone: 0 DST: 1 Latitude: 53N25'00 Longitude: 03W00'00 Ayanamsha: -22:56:57 Lahiri	♀ 02:49 Pun ☋ 16:26 Pus ♂ 19:27 Asl	11th h.
5th h.	♑ ♄℞ 29:40 Dha ☊ 16:26 Shr ☽ 09:06 USh		♀ 17:05 PPh ♆ 19:41 PPh	12th h.
4th h.	♐	♏ ♃ 02:27 Cht	♎ ☉ 02:40 UPh ASC 08:24 UPh ☿ 21:02 Has	1st h.
		3rd h.	2nd h.	

Jupiter aspecting Rahu

Jupiter is the karaka for children, and when in aspect to Rahu can cause problems with children. In the next set of charts we will look at Jupiter's aspect to Rahu in terms of it creating problems for children. The aspects for Jupiter in connection to Rahu are a conjunction opposition and the trine aspect which sits five and nine placements from each other. These effects come into play regardless of what houses Jupiter or Rahu sit in. In these examples below Jupiter sits 5 placements from Rahu, remember the 5th house represents children and so does Jupiter.

147

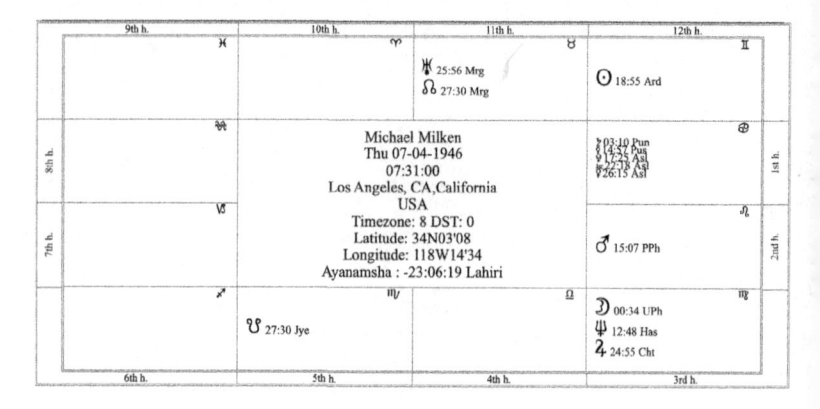

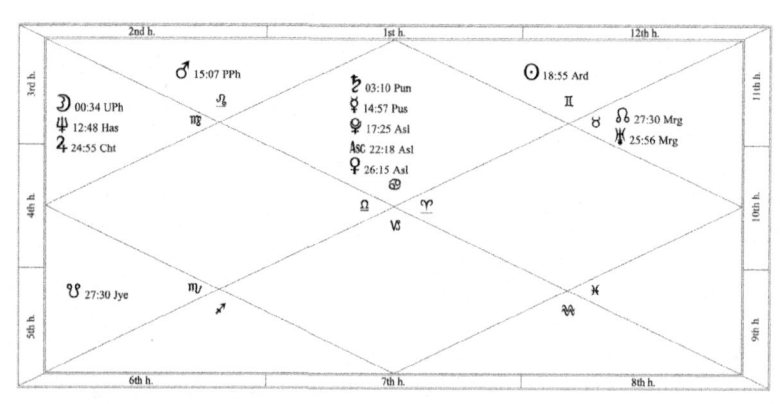

9th h.	10th h. ♈	11th h. ♉ ☒ 25:56 Mrg ☊ 27:30 Mrg	12th h. ♊ ☉ 18:55 Ard
8th h. ♒	Michael Milken Thu 07-04-1946 07:31:00 Los Angeles, CA,California USA Timezone: 8 DST: 0 Latitude: 34N03'08 Longitude: 118W14'34 Ayanamsha: -23:06:19 Lahiri		1st h. ♋ ♄ 03:10 Pun ☿ 14:57 Pun ♀ 17:25 Asl Asc 22:18 Asl ♀ 26:15 Asl
7th h. ♑			2nd h. ♌ ♂ 15:07 PPh
6th h. ♐ ☋ 27:30 Jye	5th h. ♍	4th h. ♎	3rd h. ♍ ☽ 00:34 UPh ♆ 12:48 Has ♃ 24:55 Cht

2nd h.	1st h.	12th h.
3rd h. ♂ 15:07 PPh ☽ 00:34 UPh ♆ 12:48 Has ♃ 24:55 Cht	♄ 03:10 Pun ☿ 14:57 Pus ♀ 17:25 Asl Asc 22:18 Asl ♀ 26:15 Asl	☉ 18:55 Ard ☊ 27:30 Mrg ☒ 25:56 Mrg 11th h.
4th h.		10th h.
5th h. ☋ 27:30 Jye		9th h.
6th h.	7th h.	8th h.

Michael Milken is a financier. He is known for his role in the development of the market for high-yield bonds ("junk bonds"), and his conviction and sentence following a guilty plea on felony charges for violating U.S. securities laws. He has a net worth of $6 billion as of 2022.

Aside from his notoriety and wealth Milken has two children with epilepsy. In his chart Jupiter is aspected by Rahu. Jupiter is 5 signs/houses away (trine) from Rahu.

Planet's Important combinations and Aspects

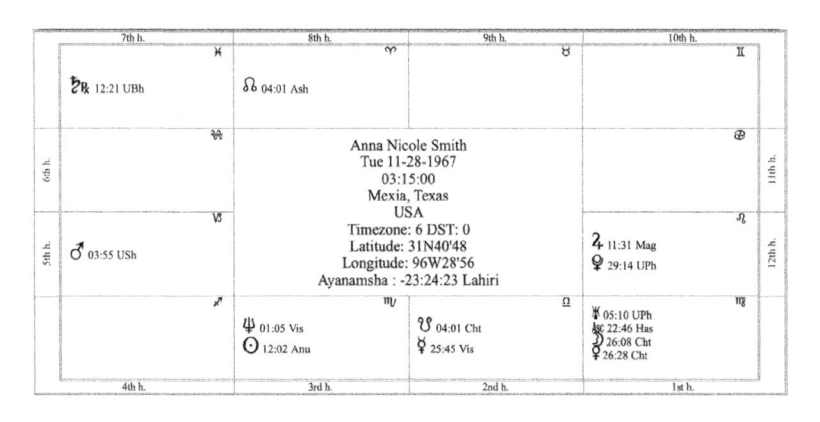

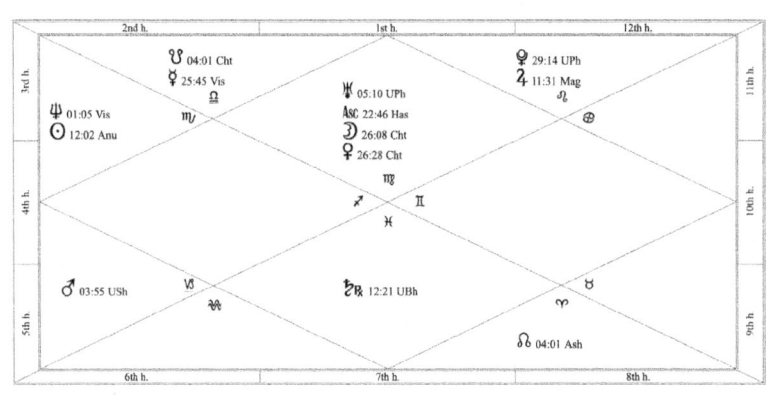

Chapter 14

7th h.	8th h.	9th h.	10th h.
♓ ♄℞ 12:21 UBh	♈ ☊ 04:01 Ash	♉	♊
♒	Anna Nicole Smith Tue 11-28-1967 03:15:00 Mexia, Texas USA Timezone: 6 DST: 0 Latitude: 31N40'48 Longitude: 96W28'56 Ayanamsha : -23:24:23 Lahiri		⊕
♑ ♂ 03:55 USh			♌ ♃ 11:31 Mag ♀ 29:14 UPh
♐	♏ ♆ 01:05 Vis ☉ 12:02 Anu	♎ ☋ 04:01 Cht ☿ 25:45 Vis	♍ ♅ 05:10 UPh Asc 22:46 Has ☽ 26:08 Cht ♀ 26:28 Cht
4th h.	3rd h.	2nd h.	1st h.

Anna Nicole Smith was a model, actor, and TV personality. She was known for her outrageous behavior and addiction to drugs. After giving birth to her daughter her son Daniel was visiting her in her hospital room when he died of a drug overdose.

In Smith's chart Jupiter sits five placements in a trine from Rahu. Furthermore, Rahu sits in the 8th House of death while Jupiter is in the 12th House of hospitals and losses.

149

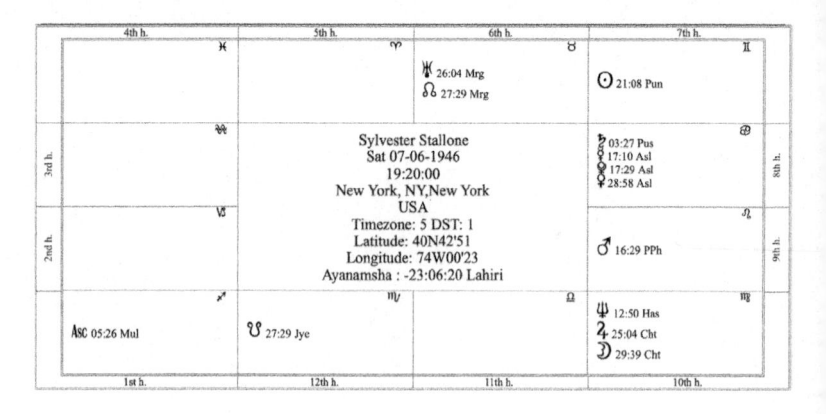

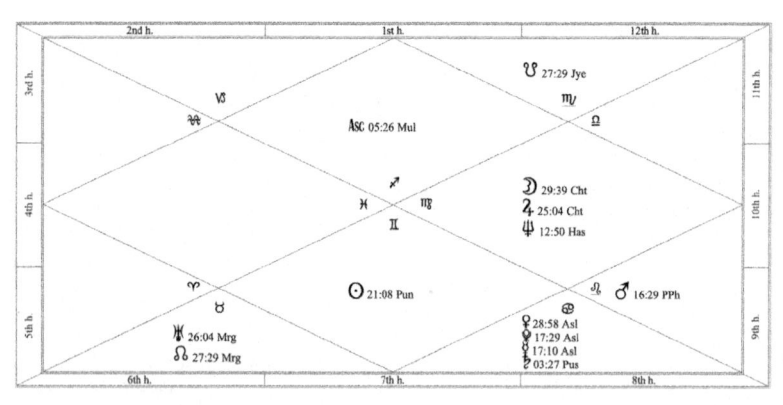

Rahu trine Jupiter: Loss of a Son

Sylvester Stallone lost his son Sage to heart disease in 2012 he was 36 years old. Stallone has Jupiter trine Rahu, Jupiter is five signs away from Rahu.

Planet's Important combinations and Aspects

Chapter 14

9th h.	10th h.	11th h.	12th h.
♓	♈	♉	♊
		♃ 23:18 Roh	♅ ℞ 26:21 Pun

8th h.
♒
☿ 22:43 PBh
♀ 11:12 Sat
☉ 06:24 Dha

John Travolta
Thu 02-18-1954
14:53:00
Englewood, New Jersey
USA
Timezone: 5 DST: 0
Latitude: 40N54'00
Longitude: 73W59'00
Ayanamsha : -23:13:16 Lahiri

☊ 00:22 Pun
Asc 05:52 Pus

1st h.
♋

7th h.
♑
☋ 00:22 USh

♀℞ 00:26 Mag
☽ 17:57 PPh

2nd h.
♌

6th h. ♐
♂ 11:44 Anu

5th h. ♏
♆℞ 02:42 Cht
♄℞ 16:07 Swa

4th h. ♎

3rd h. ♍

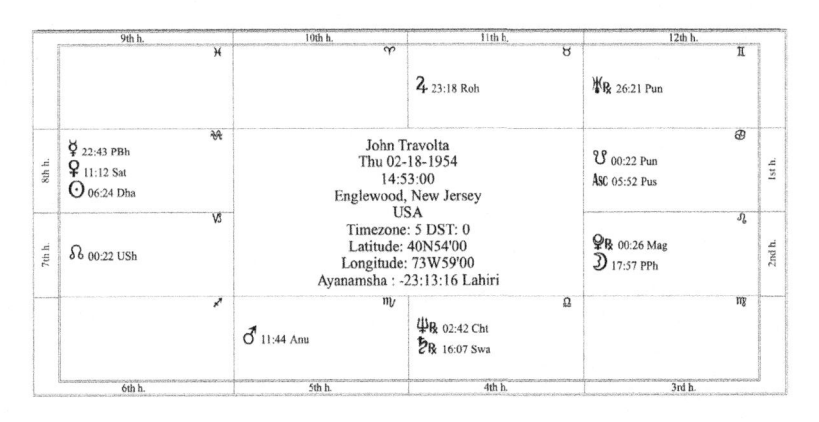

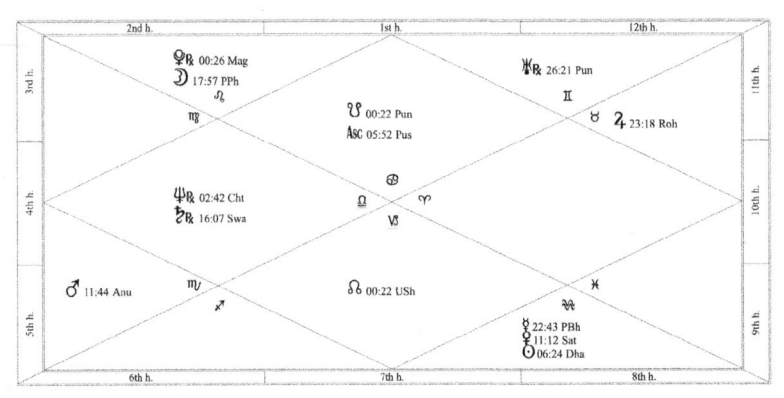

John Travolta is an actor well known for starring in the movies, Saturday Night Fever and Grease. Travolta's son, Jett was the eldest son of John Travolta and Kelly Preston, who died at the age of 16 in 2009. He had a history of seizures from the age of two. In John's chart he has Jupiter five placements from Rahu by sign forming a trine aspect.

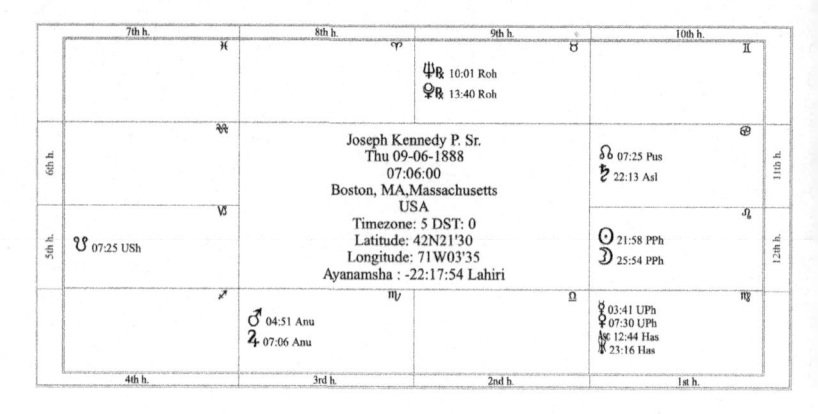

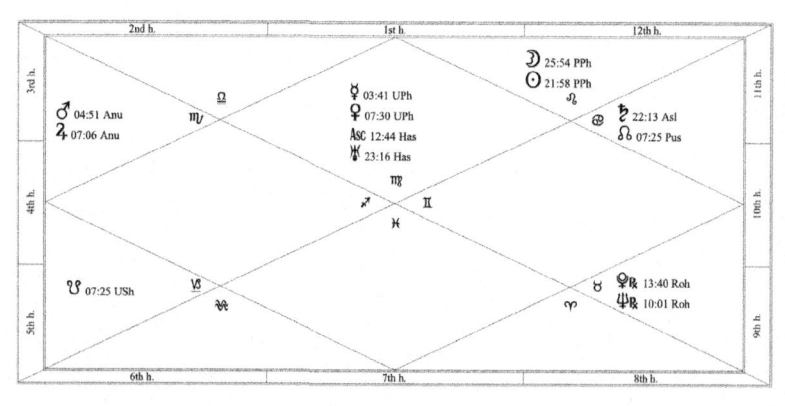

```
   7th h.        |     8th h.      |      9th h.           |    10th h.
                 |   ♓             |  ♈                    |           ♊
                 |                 | ♆℞ 10:01 Roh          |
                 |                 | ♀℞ 13:40 Roh          |
─────────────────┼─────────────────┴───────────────────────┼─────────────────
            ♒    | Joseph Kennedy P. Sr.                   |            ⊕
                 | Thu 09-06-1888                          | ☊ 07:25 Pus
                 | 07:06:00                                | ♄ 22:13 Asl
6th h.      ♑    | Boston, MA,Massachusetts                |            ♌   11th h.
                 | USA                                     |
                 | Timezone: 5 DST: 0                      |
5th h.  ☋ 07:25 USh | Latitude: 42N21'30                   | ☉ 21:58 PPh    12th h.
                 | Longitude: 71W03'35                     | ☽ 25:54 PPh
                 | Ayanamsha : -22:17:54 Lahiri            |
─────────────────┼─────────────────┬───────────────────────┼─────────────────
            ♐    |     ♍           |    ♎                  |           ♍
  ♂ 04:51 Anu    |                 |                       | ☿ 03:41 UPh
  ♃ 07:06 Anu    |                 |                       | ♀ 07:30 UPh
                 |                 |                       | Asc 12:44 Has
                 |                 |                       | ♅ 23:16 Has
   4th h.        |    3rd h.       |    2nd h.             |    1st h.
```

Jupiter trine Rahu: Joseph Kennedy Sr.

As we know Joseph Kennedy senior lost four of his children violently, and he has Jupiter five placements away from Rahu. When someone experiences such an extreme loss with children there will be many variables that indicate this.

Rahu conjunct Saturn
Karmic indicator

Rahu conjunct Saturn will always be a huge indicator of powerful karma. Saturn is perceived as a very difficult limiting malefic planet but when it is in combination with Rahu it brings a huge karmic destiny of extremes and greatness.

4th h. ♓	5th h. ♈	6th h. ♉	7th h. ♊
♀ 29:42 Rev ♂ 23:53 Rev	☿ 18:41 Bha	☉ 10:26 Roh ⛢ 19:32 Roh	♄ 15:57 Ard ☋ 16:32 Ard
3rd h. ♒	Priscilla Presley Thu 05-24-1945 22:40:00 Brooklyn Naval Station 7 USA Timezone: 5 DST: 1 Latitude: 40N42'00 Longitude: 73W58'00 Ayanamsha : -23:05:22 Lahiri		♀ 15:04 Pus — 8th h.
2nd h. ♑			♃ 24:35 PPh — 9th h. ♌
1st h. ♐ ☊ 16:32 PSh ASC 12:58 Mul	12th h. ♏ ☽ 18:31 Swa	11th h. ♎	10th h. ♍ ♆℞ 10:40 Has

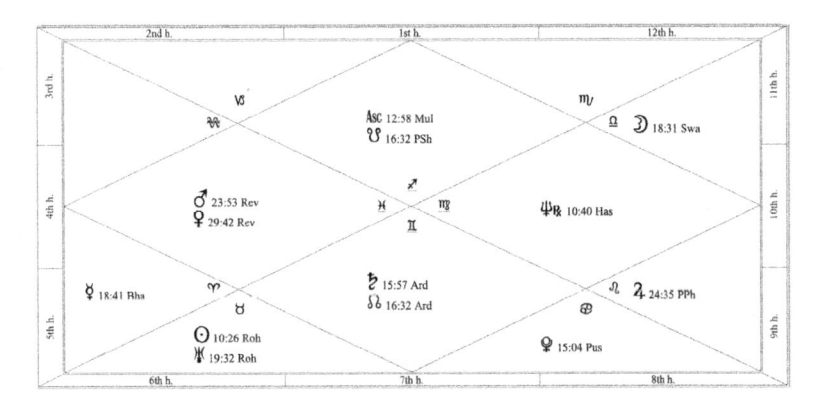

2nd h.	1st h.	12th h.
3rd h. ♒ ♑	ASC 12:58 Mul ☊ 16:32 PSh	♏ ☽ 18:31 Swa — 11th h.
4th h. ♂ 23:53 Rev ♀ 29:42 Rev	♐ ♓ ♍ ♊	♆℞ 10:40 Has — 10th h.
5th h. ☿ 18:41 Bha ♈ ♉ ☉ 10:26 Roh ⛢ 19:32 Roh	6th h. ♄ 15:57 Ard ☋ 16:32 Ard	♌ ♃ 24:35 PPh ♀ 15:04 Pus — 9th h. / 8th h.

Saturn/Rahu: Greatness and Extremes in house they occupy

7th house marriage partner

In the chart for Priscilla Presley, ex-wife of Elvis Presley she has Saturn conjunct Rahu indicating an extremely powerful and famous husband. Many speak about the power and greatness of Saturn, but when it is conjunct Rahu it is magnified even more.

North Indian Chart (top)

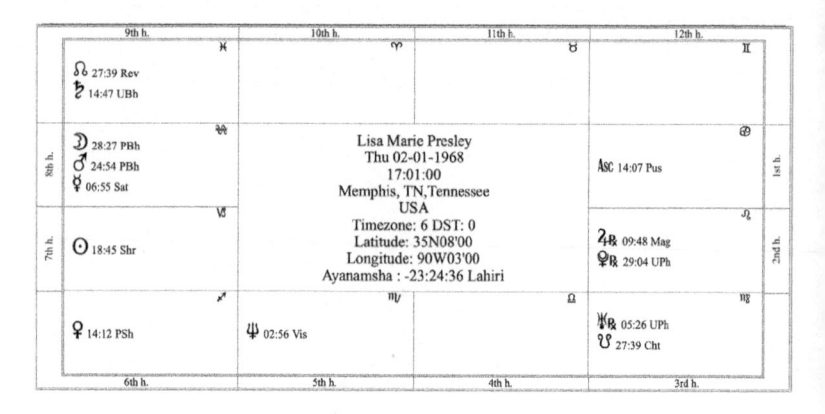

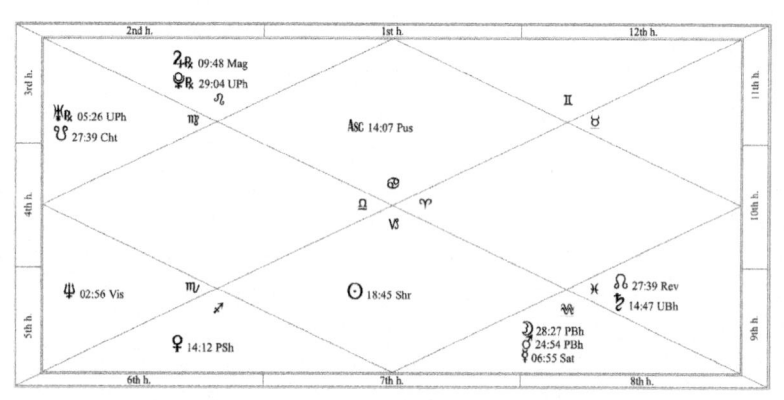

9th h.	10th h.	11th h.	12th h.
♓	♈	♉	♊
☊ 27:39 Rev ♄ 14:47 UBh			Asc 14:07 Pus
♒			♋
☽ 28:27 PBh ♂ 24:54 PBh ☿ 06:55 Sat	Lisa Marie Presley Thu 02-01-1968 17:01:00 Memphis, TN, Tennessee USA		
♑	Timezone: 6 DST: 0 Latitude: 35N08'00 Longitude: 90W03'00 Ayanamsha: -23:24:36 Lahiri		♌
☉ 18:45 Shr			♃R 09:48 Mag ♀R 29:04 UPh
♐	♏	♎	♍
♀ 14:12 PSh	♆ 02:56 Vis		♅R 05:26 UPh ☋ 27:39 Cht
6th h.	5th h.	4th h.	3rd h.

Saturn conjunct Rahu
9th house of Father

In the case of Lisa Marie Presley, daughter of Elvis Presley, she has Saturn conjunct Rahu in the 9th House of the father. This is also a representation of the power, success, and fame her father had in his lifetime with Saturn conjunct Rahu in the 9th house of the father.

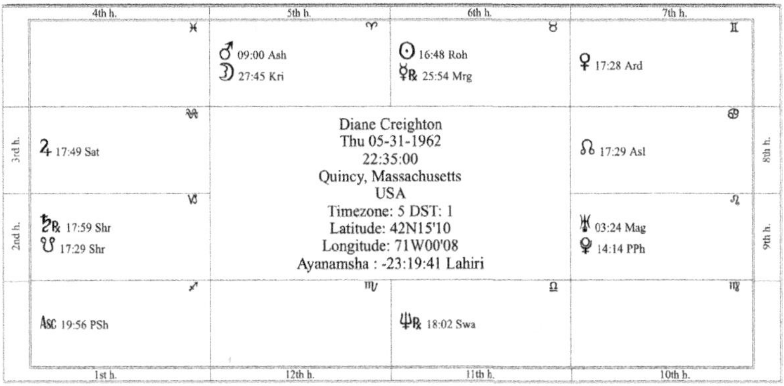

Planet's Important combinations and Aspects

Chapter 14

	4th h.	5th h.	6th h.	7th h.
	♓	♈	♉	♊
3rd h.	♒	♂ 09:00 Ash ☽ 27:45 Kri	☉ 16:48 Roh ☿ ℞ 25:54 Mrg	♀ 17:28 Ard
	♃ 17:49 Sat	Diane Creighton Thu 05-31-1962 22:35:00 Quincy, Massachusetts USA Timezone: 5 DST: 1 Latitude: 42N15'10 Longitude: 71W00'08 Ayanamsha : -23:19:41 Lahiri		☊ 17:29 Asl	8th h.
2nd h.	♑ ♄℞ 17:59 Shr ☋ 17:29 Shr			♅ 03:24 Mag ♀ 14:14 PPh	9th h.
	♐	♏	♎	♍
	Asc 19:56 PSh		♆℞ 18:02 Swa	
	1st h.	12th h.	11th h.	10th h.

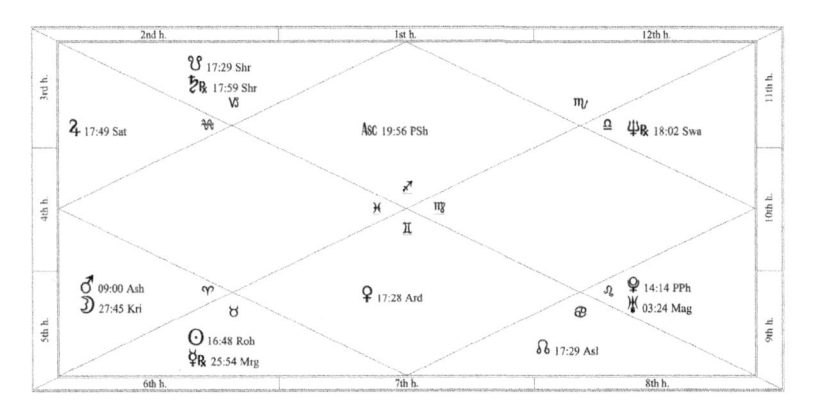

Saturn and Ketu

Saturn conjunct Ketu represents deep loss and represents a certain karma in life. The house that they sit in indicates where the extreme loss and profound karmic lesson occurs in life.

Diane Creighton was a model who died from Anorexia. The 2nd house rules the mouth in terms of drink, food intake and the voice. Difficult planets in the 2nd house may indicate losses in terms of the voice but also affect how someone eats, as it did for Karen Carpenter. In Creighton's chart both Saturn and Ketu represent a loss or denial affecting the 2nd

155

house of the food she eats. Both planets represent a problem with eating. She denied herself the food her body needed that caused her death. There is a karmic issue apparently from past lives or childhood that caused her to starve herself to death. Ketu can also indicate the past, or past lives.

Additionally, since the 2nd house does deal with self-esteem, or self-value, Saturn and Ketu would lead one to believe they are never good enough. In this case her body image was the factor.

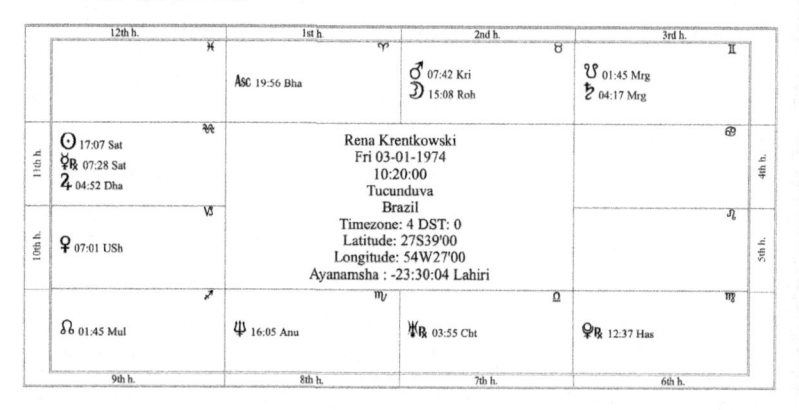

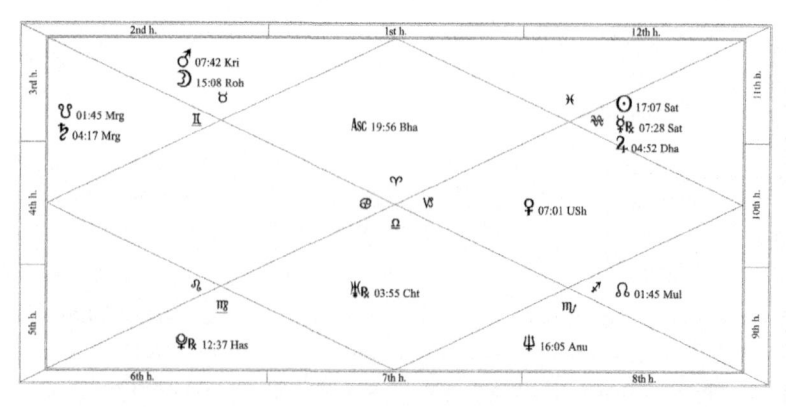

12th h.	1st h.	2nd h.	3rd h.
	ASC 19:56 Bha	♂ 07:42 Kri ☽ 15:08 Roh	☊ 01:45 Mrg ♄ 04:17 Mrg
☉ 17:07 Sat ☿R 07:28 Sat ♃ 04:52 Dha	Rena Krentkowski Fri 03-01-1974 10:20:00 Tucunduva Brazil Timezone: 4 DST: 0 Latitude: 27S39'00 Longitude: 54W27'00 Ayanamsha : -23:30:04 Lahiri		
♀ 07:01 USh			
☋ 01:45 Mul	♆ 16:05 Anu	♅R 03:55 Cht	♀R 12:37 Has
9th h.	8th h.	7th h.	6th h.

Rena Krentkowski was a triplet. In her third House of siblings sits Saturn with Ketu indicating an extreme associated

Planet's Important combinations and Aspects

with siblings. In the case of triplets because you are one of three you will not get the attention deserved or needed from the mother. There is a unique karma associated with siblings with this placement in the 3rd house.

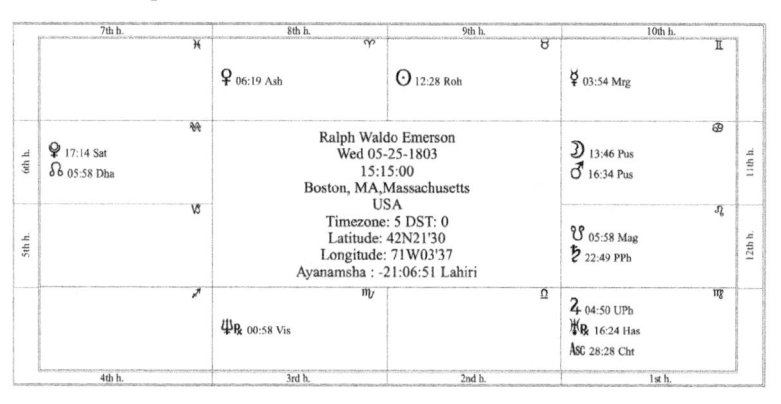

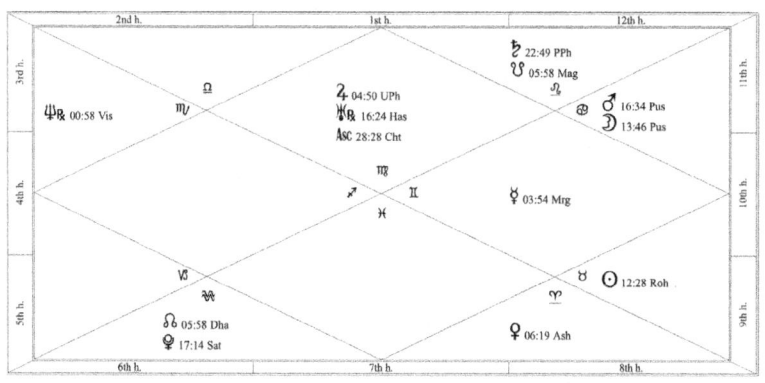

7th h.	8th h.	9th h.	10th h.
♓	♈	♉	♊
♀ 06:19 Ash	☉ 12:28 Roh	☿ 03:54 Mrg
♒ (6th h.) ♀ 17:14 Sat ☋ 05:58 Dha	Ralph Waldo Emerson Wed 05-25-1803 15:15:00 Boston, MA, Massachusetts USA Timezone: 5 DST: 0 Latitude: 42N21'30 Longitude: 71W03'37 Ayanamsha: -21:06:51 Lahiri	☽ 13:46 Pus ♂ 16:34 Pus (11th h.)
♑ (5th h.)		☊ 05:58 Mag ♄ 22:49 PPh (12th h.)
♐ (4th h.) ♆℞ 00:58 Vis	♏ (3rd h.)	♎ (2nd h.) ♃ 04:50 UPh ♅℞ 16:24 Has Asc 28:28 Cht (1st h.) ♍

2nd h.	1st h.	12th h.
	♄ 22:49 PPh ☊ 05:58 Mag	
♎ ♆℞ 00:58 Vis ♏	♃ 04:50 UPh ♅℞ 16:24 Has Asc 28:28 Cht ♌	♂ 16:34 Pus ☽ 13:46 Pus (11th h.)
(4th h.)	♍ ♐ ♊ ♓	☿ 03:54 Mrg (10th h.)
(5th h.) ♑ ♒ ☋ 05:58 Dha ♀ 17:14 Sat		♉ ☉ 12:28 Roh ♈ ♀ 06:19 Ash (9th h.) (8th h.)
6th h.	7th h.	

Saturn and Ketu: Unique talent or loss, Gift, Curse or Spirituality

Ralph Waldo Emerson was a philosopher and poet who led the transcendentalist movement of the mid-19th century. Emerson gradually moved away from the religious and social beliefs of his contemporaries, formulating and expressing the philosophy of transcendentalism. Emerson philosophically considered, the universe is composed of Nature and the Soul, rejecting views of God as separate from the world.

In my opinion Emerson was way ahead of his time. With Saturn and Ketu in the 12th house he had a vision of the karmas of the soul beyond this world. His Saturn and Ketu in Leo ruled by the Sun sits in the 9th House of spirituality and truth. A connection between the 9th house and the 12th house may be one of the most spiritual combinations in a chart. As both houses are connected to planet Jupiter which rules both Sagittarius and Pisces, Jupiter is the planet of spirituality.

The 12th house pertains to isolation, separation but deep spiritual surrender as it represents the end of life. Planets here can represent profound spirituality as in the case of both Saturn and Ketu as indicators of moksha which is spiritual liberation from this world. Emerson was profoundly spiritually aware with this placement as all three are indicators of karma, moksha and spiritual realization.

Chapter 15

Rahu and Ketu Fated Destiny

Both Rahu and Ketu are considered harbingers of our destiny, either future or past. They both relate to our karma. Either Rahu or Ketu closely conjunct the ascendant indicates a life with a certain fated destiny.

When Rahu is conjunct the ascendant there is a fated destiny of extremes that appears like life's events are out of your control. When Ketu is on the ascendant, the individual never feels connected or a part of this world; there is a sense of alienation and disconnection. Both can represent incredible extremes fraught with problems and possible losses.

The next set of charts will represent the karma and the destiny of extremes either Rahu or Ketu represent when they're conjunct the ascendant.

Ketu on Ascendant

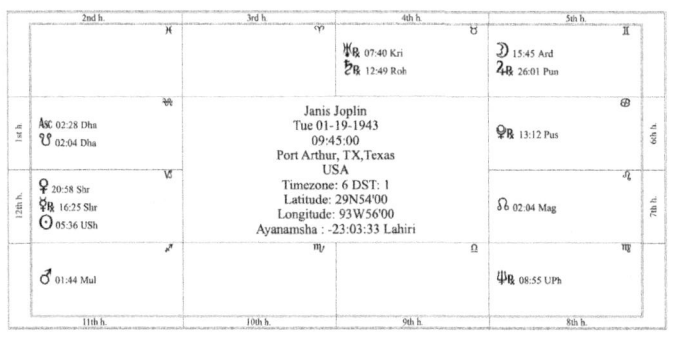

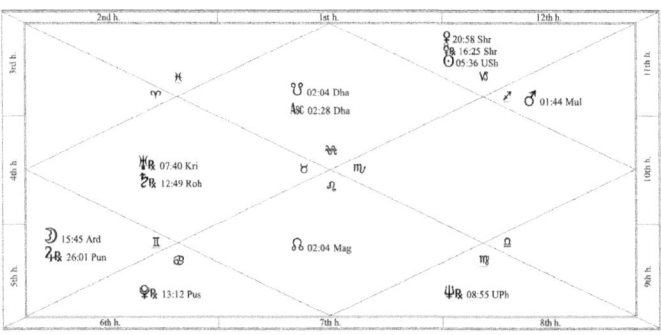

Janis Joplin, a rock and roll legend, always felt like an outcast from an early age growing up in conservative Texas. She found herself through singing but could never overcome her insecurities from not fitting in with her home and family and her personal appearance. To help cope with her insecurities and self-doubt she became addicted to drugs and alcohol which ultimately took her life by age 27. Her destiny brought her into massive fame and recognition through her talent. Many talented people never become famous, but it was Joplin's destiny. She had Ketu exactly on the Ascendant indicating she felt like an outcast and never truly fit in.

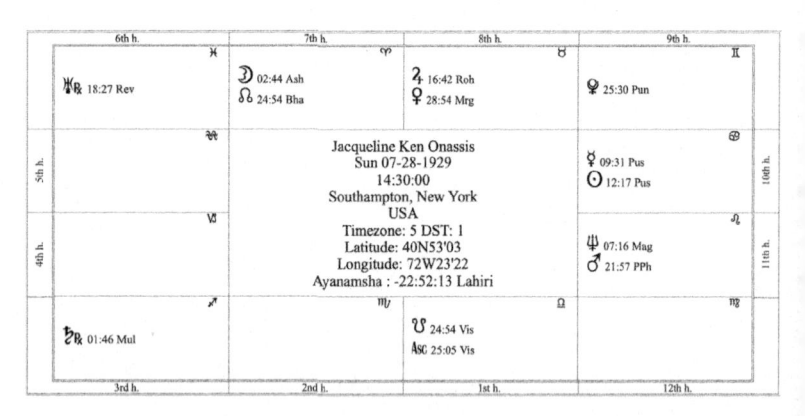

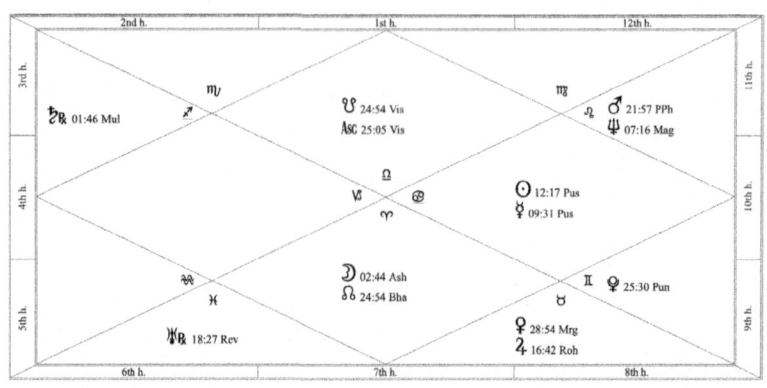

6th h.	7th h.	8th h.	9th h.
♅ 18:27 Rev	☽ 02:44 Ash ☋ 24:54 Bha	♃ 16:42 Roh ♀ 28:54 Mrg	♀ 25:30 Pun
5th h.	Jacqueline Ken Onassis Sun 07-28-1929 14:30:00 Southampton, New York USA Timezone: 5 DST: 1 Latitude: 40N53'03 Longitude: 72W23'22 Ayanamsha : -22:52:13 Lahiri	☿ 09:31 Pus ☉ 12:17 Pus	10th h.
4th h.		♆ 07:16 Mag ♂ 21:57 PPh	11th h.
3rd h.	2nd h.	1st h.	12th h.
♄ 01:46 Mul		☊ 24:54 Vis Asc 25:05 Vis	

Ketu on Ascendant – Great Losses

Jacqueline Kennedy Onassis was one of the most photographed women in the world in her day, but all she wanted to do was escape the world and the paparazzi. Her life was one of extreme karmic destiny, especially since Rahu is in the 7th house with the Moon indicating a famous and influential marriage partner. Both of her husbands were extremely famous and wealthy, President John F Kennedy, and the extremely wealthy Greek shipping magnate, Aristotle Onassis.

It is believed that Jackie married Onassis in order to escape the threats on her life after her husband's assassination. He brought her to live on one of his private Greek islands, Skorpios. Here again is an example of Ketu on the ascendant indicating a need to escape from the world.

As Ketu sits exactly on her ascendant, her life involved many profound losses, just as Janis Joplin's life was one of extremes with heavy losses as was Jacqueline Kennedy Onassis' life.

Rahu on Ascendant – A Fated Life or Destiny

When Rahu is on the ascendant this sets someone up for an extreme destiny where one feels like they are not in control of their fate and their future. There are certain events that are destined to occur in a life that has Rahu on the ascendant, their life is very fated.

North Indian Chart

8th h.	9th h.	10th h.	11th h.
♓	♈	♉	♊ ♂ ℞ 25:12 Pun

Left side (7th h., 6th h.):
♒
☊ 18:27 Sat
☽ 04:06 Dha

♑

Center:
KENNEDY JOHN JR
Fri 11-25-1960
00:22:00
WASHINGTON, DC, District of Columbia
USA
Timezone: 5 DST: 0
Latitude: 38N53'42
Longitude: 77W02'12
Ayanamsha : -23:18:33 Lahiri

Right side (12th h., 1st h.):
♋
♌
♅ 02:28 Mag
♀ 14:45 PPh
☋ 18:27 PPh
Asc 18:39 PPh

5th h.	4th h.	3rd h.	2nd h.
♐ ♄ 22:14 PSh, ♀ 18:35 PSh, ♃ 12:30 Mul	♏ ☉ 09:38 Anu	♎ ♆ 16:26 Swa, ☿ 19:55 Swa	♍

South Indian Chart

2nd h.	1st h.	12th h.	11th h.
♆ 16:26 Swa, ☿ 19:55 Swa ♎	♅ 02:28 Mag, ♀ 14:45 PPh, ☋ 18:27 PPh, Asc 18:39 PPh	♋	♊ ♂ ℞ 25:12 Pun

(4th h.) ☉ 09:38 Anu — ♏ ♌ ♉ (10th h.)

(5th h.) ♃ 12:30 Mul, ♀ 18:35 PPh, ♄ 22:14 PSh — ♐ — ☽ 04:06 Dha, ☊ 18:27 Sat — ♑ — ♓ — ♈ (9th h.)

| 6th h. | 7th h. | 8th h. |

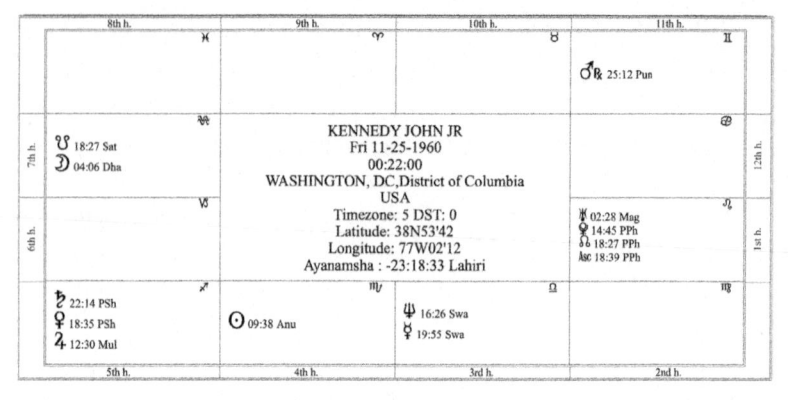

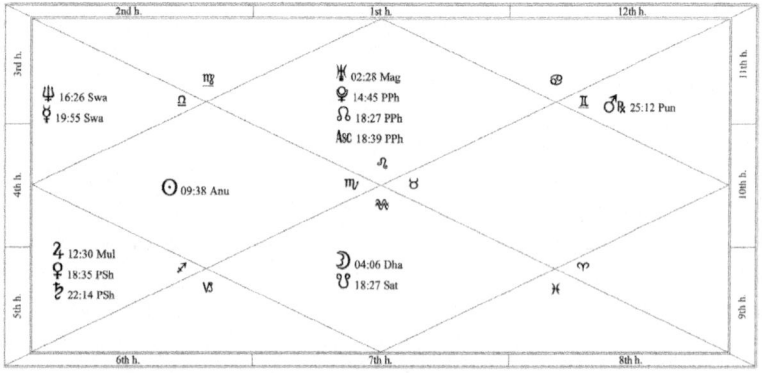

John Kennedy junior, the son of President Kennedy appeared to have a fated destiny. At age three his father was assassinated, and his mother Jacqueline Kennedy Onassis escaped the United States to a Greek island Skorpios provided by her new husband Aristotle.

Everyone wanted John Kennedy Jr to go into law and politics. He finally passed the New York bar exam on his third try. He did not want to be the things others were pushing him into. When he followed his heart and began writing and publishing his magazine- George, he became alive with excitement for the future. It wasn't soon after this that he was involved in a fatal and fated plane crash that he was piloting with his wife Carolyn and her sister Lauren. He was only 38 years old.

Chapter 15

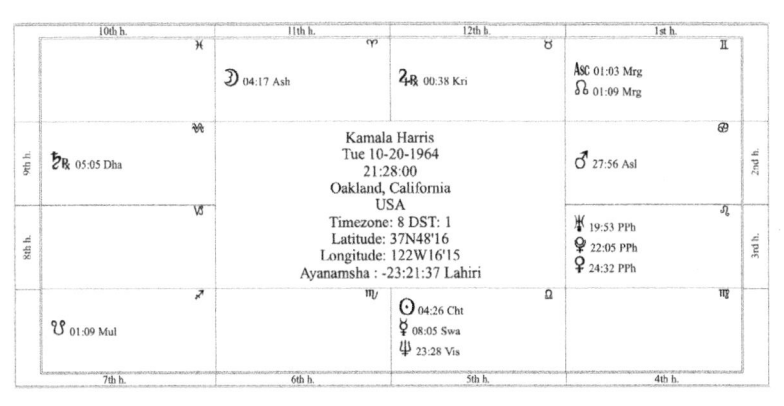

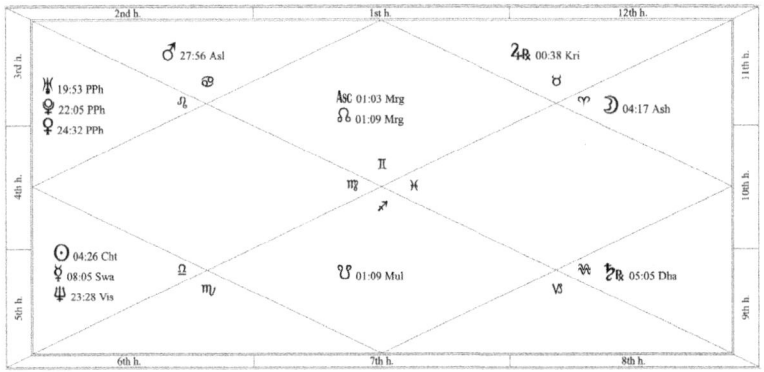

10th h.	11th h.	12th h.	1st h.
♓	♈	♉	♊
☽ 04:17 Ash	♃R 00:38 Kri	Asc 01:03 Mrg ☊ 01:09 Mrg	

9th h.			2nd h.
♒	Kamala Harris Tue 10-20-1964 21:28:00 Oakland, California USA Timezone: 8 DST: 1 Latitude: 37N48'16 Longitude: 122W16'15 Ayanamsha: -23:21:37 Lahiri		♋
♄R 05:05 Dha			♂ 27:56 Asl

8th h.			3rd h.
♑			♌
			♅ 19:53 PPh ♀ 22:05 PPh ☿ 24:32 PPh

7th h.	6th h.	5th h.	4th h.
♐	♏	☉ 04:26 Cht ☿ 08:05 Swa ♆ 23:28 Vis	♎ ♍
☋ 01:09 Mul			

Kamala Harris the vice president of the United States in 2021 has a certain fated destiny as Rahu exactly conjuncts her ascendant. It is her destiny to be chosen as the first female vice president of the United States. As she is in office during very turbulent times, I believe many fated events are still due to come in her life.

Benefic planets, Jupiter or Venus in their own sign or exalted with Ketu manifests greatness for that house

When a benefic planet is conjunct Ketu and it is in its sign of rulership or exalted, this will bring great benefits and effects to the house, and what the house represents that they are in.

You would think since Ketu represents losses that this would represent an extreme loss but essentially it has a powerful reverse in effects and brings enormous gains relative to the house that they are in.

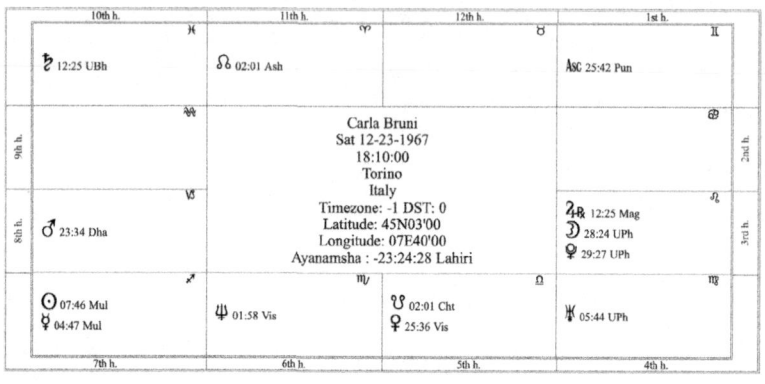

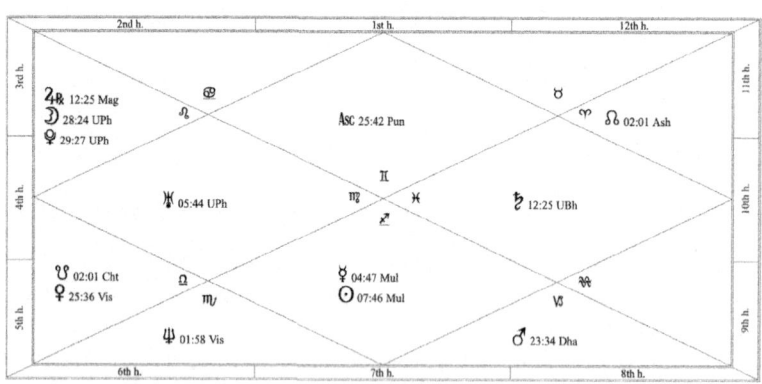

Carla Bruni was a supermodel, turn singer and married former French President Nicolas Sarkozy. Her Venus is conjunct Ketu in Libra in the 5th house of creativity and talent. She was beautiful, enormously talented, known all over the world and lived the life of luxury as the president's wife in France.

Planets Combust or Cazimi – Stationary Planets

Planets too close to the Sun are combust, meaning they are burnt, weakened or destroyed by the Sun. But if a planet sits less than a degree from the Sun it is Cazimi, meaning the planet unites and becomes one with the Sun, and the Sun will emit the power and energy of that planet that it is combined with. Cazimi planets are very rare. Combust planets are weaker when they are closest to the Sun, in orb of 8 degrees is strong but an orb of 1 to 3 degrees is catastrophic. The areas ruled by the planet seemed to be destroyed.

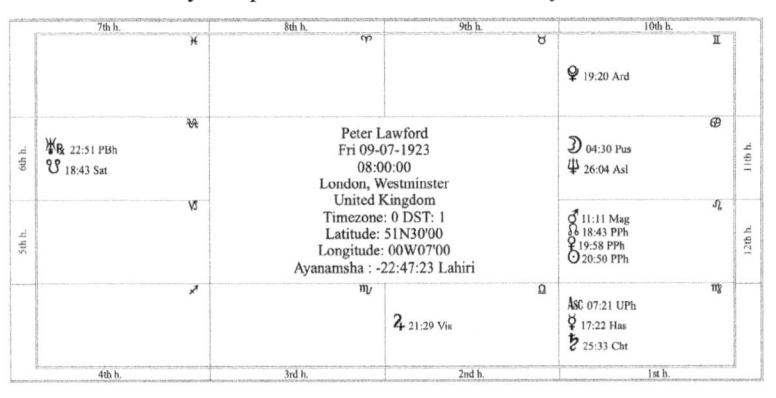

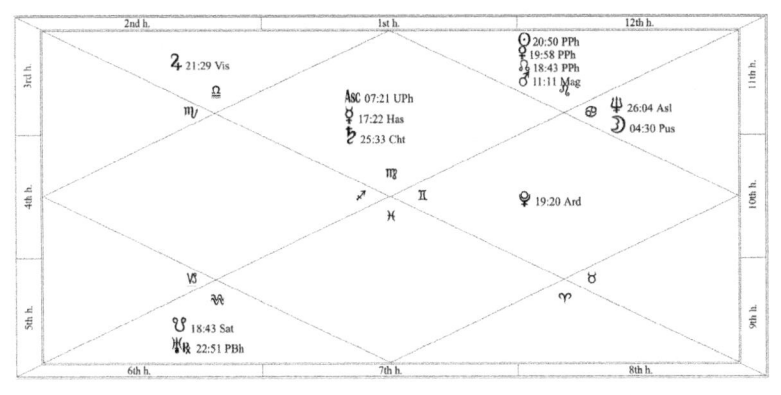

Peter Lawford, a famous actor, was married four times and one of his wives was Patricia Kennedy, sister to John F

Kennedy. He had great difficulty with relationships. He was believed to have ties with the mafia.

His Venus and Sun are one degree apart making this the deepest darkest combustion possible. In order to be Cazimi planets must be almost the same degree as the Sun.

Furthermore, Venus sits with malefic Rahu and Mars all at the same time. So, Venus is conjunct three powerful natural malefics in the 12th House of loss, representing his extreme problems and difficulties in marriage. Venus particularly in a man's chart represents the wife and relationships.

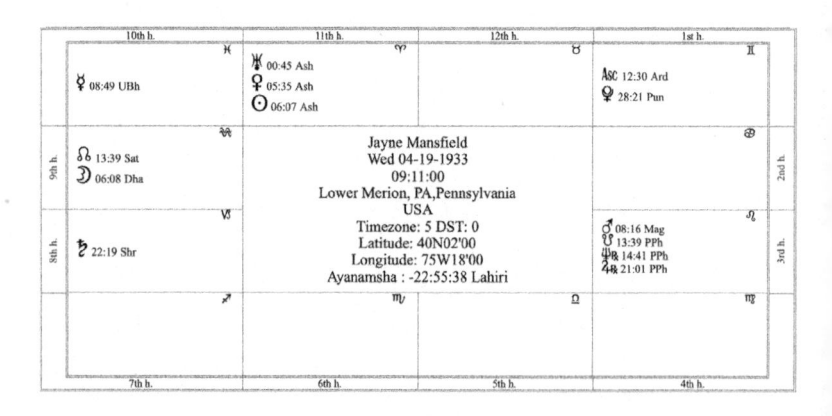

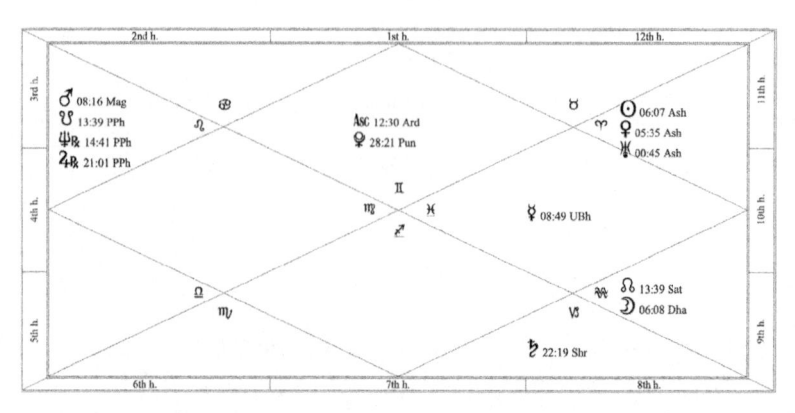

	10th h.	11th h.	12th h.	1st h.
	☿ 08:49 UBh	♅ 00:45 Ash ♀ 05:35 Ash ☉ 06:07 Ash		ASC 12:30 Ard ♀ 28:21 Pun
9th h.	☊ 13:39 Sat ☽ 06:08 Dha	Jayne Mansfield Wed 04-19-1933 09:11:00 Lower Merion, PA, Pennsylvania USA Timezone: 5 DST: 0 Latitude: 40N02'00 Longitude: 75W18'00 Ayanamsha : -22:55:38 Lahiri		2nd h.
8th h.	♄ 22:19 Shr			♂ 08:16 Mag ☋ 13:39 PPh ♆℞ 14:41 PPh ♃℞ 21:01 PPh	3rd h.
	7th h.	6th h.	5th h.	4th h.

Jayne Mansfield was an actress, singer, nightclub entertainer, and *Playboy* Playmate. A sex symbol of the 1950s and early 1960s while under contract at 20th Century Fox, Mansfield was known for her well-publicized personal life and publicity stunts. Her film career was short-lived, but she had several box-office successes.

She was married 4 times before her tragic death in a car crash at age 34. Venus is severely combust the Sun, causing major marital problems. Mars as the ruling planet of the Sun and Venus conjunction in Aries is conjunct Ketu and Neptune in the 3rd house. This is significant because Mars conjunct Ketu represents, as noted before, accidents and injury. Her car crash is noted to be due to a fog that was the mist being sprayed in the streets to control mosquitoes close to New Orleans. Mars and Ketu represent accidents and injury plus Neptune rules over fog that caused the crash.

When Venus is combust the Sun, it is said that there is an early relationship that does not work out, and that relationship subconsciously taints the way one feels about future relationships, essentially causing problems in relationships.

4th h.	5th h.	6th h.	7th h.
♓	♈ ♃℞ 23:26 Mrg	♉ ♅℞ 27:05 Pun	♊
3rd h. ♒	OPRAH WINFREY Fri 01-29-1954 04:15:00 Kosciusko USA		☊ 00:42 Pun 8th h. ♋
2nd h. ☿ 25:55 Dha ☉ 15:45 Shr ♀ 15:37 Shr ☋ 00:42 USh ♑	Timezone: 6 DST: 0 Latitude: 33N03'27 Longitude: 89W35'15 Ayanamsha : -23:13:13 Lahiri		♀℞ 00:55 Mag 9th h. ♌
Asc 03:03 Mul ♐	♂ 00:21 Vis ☽ 11:10 Anu ♍	♆℞ 02:50 Cht ♄ 15:49 Swa ♎	♍
1st h.	12th h.	11th h.	10th h.

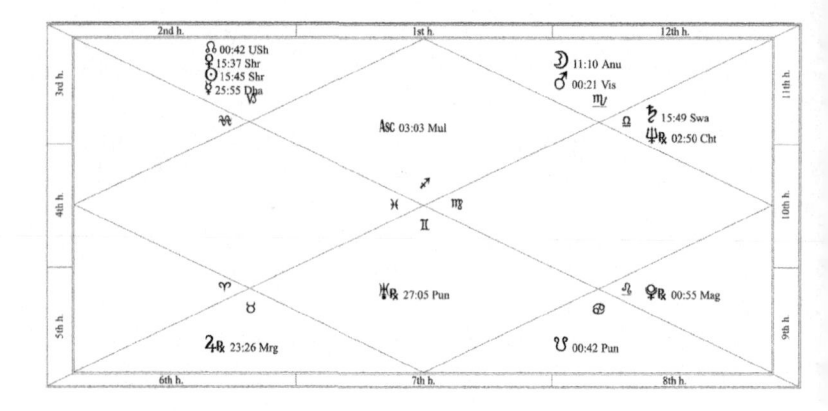

```
┌─────────────────┬─────────────────┬─────────────────┐
│    2nd h.       │    1st h.       │    12th h.      │
│  ☊ 00:42 USh    │                 │  ☽ 11:10 Anu    │
│  ☉ 15:37 Shr    │                 │  ♂ 00:21 Vis    │
│  ☿ 15:45 Shr    │                 │     ♍           │
│  ♀ 25:55 Dha    │  ASC 03:03 Mul  │                 │
│       ♒         │                 │  ♎ ♄ 15:49 Swa  │
│                 │        ♐        │     Ψ℞ 02:50 Cht│
│                 │     ♓    ♍      │                 │
│                 │        ♊        │                 │
│       ♈         │                 │     ♌  ♀℞ 00:55 │
│       ♉         │  ♅℞ 27:05 Pun   │     ⊕      Mag  │
│                 │                 │                 │
│  ♃℞ 23:26 Mrg   │  ☋ 00:42 Pun    │                 │
│    6th h.       │    7th h.       │    8th h.       │
└─────────────────┴─────────────────┴─────────────────┘
```

Cazimi planet: Venus

Oprah Winfrey has Venus so close to the Sun that it is Cazimi, meaning the Sun unites as one with Venus. The Sun emits the essence of Venus, this becomes a powerful influence for Venus energies, but I have noticed when Venus is Cazimi it gives good wealth and money, but it hurts the effects of relationships and marriage. Oprah has had difficult relationships probably because she works all the time, married to her career. So, the effects of Cazimi with Venus destroy relationships as Winfrey has never been married.

Stationary Planets

A stationary planet is when a planet slows down and changes direction either before it goes retrograde or before it goes direct. When this happens, the planet appears to be stationary, enhancing and empowering the planet's energy. A stationary planet is said to be the most powerful planet in a chart.

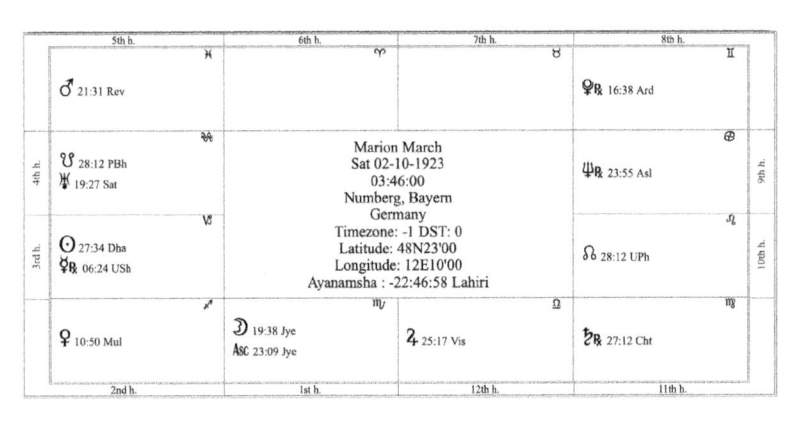

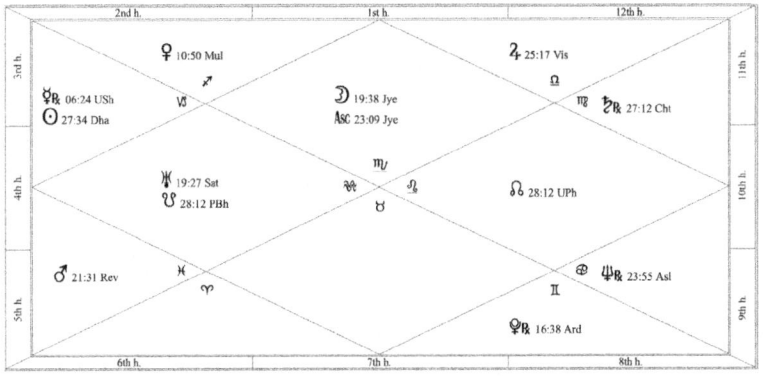

5th h.	6th h.	7th h.	8th h.
♓ ♂ 21:31 Rev	♈	♉ ♀℞ 16:38 Ard	♊
♒ ☊ 28:12 PBh ♅ 19:27 Sat	Marion March Sat 02-10-1923 03:46:00 Numberg, Bayern Germany	♆℞ 23:55 Asl	⊕
♑ ☉ 27:34 Dha ☿℞ 06:24 USh	Timezone: -1 DST: 0 Latitude: 48N23'00 Longitude: 12E10'00 Ayanamsha : -22:46:58 Lahiri	☊ 28:12 UPh	♌
♐ ♀ 10:50 Mul	♏ ☽ 19:38 Jye Asc 23:09 Jye	♎ ♃ 25:17 Vis	♍ ♄℞ 27:12 Cht
2nd h.	1st h.	12th h.	11th h.

Mercury Stationed: Brilliant Mind

Marian March was a top professional, co-authoring with Joan McEvers a best-selling six volume series entitled, "The Only Way to Learn Astrology". Aside from her books, Marion co-founded Aquarius Workshops and edited the "Aspects" journal. She lived in Switzerland and spoke many languages before immigrating to the United States.

Her Mercury was stationed in the 3rd house of communications and writing. It is conjunct the Sun ruler of the 10th house of career. Mercury rules the 8th house of metaphysics, psychology, and astrology.

Chapter 16

Eclipses

An eclipse is when there is a new Moon or a full Moon that is conjunct either Rahu or Ketu. There is a new Moon and a full moon every month but the only time they come together with the nodes of the Moon, Rahu or Ketu is twice a year. When the new Moon is conjunct Rahu and six months later when the new Moon is conjunct Ketu. The new Moon conjunct, either Rahu or Ketu is a solar eclipse and happens twice a year.

The lunar eclipse happens either two weeks before or after a solar eclipse. It is when the Sun and Moon are in opposition, which is a full Moon conjunct either Rahu or Ketu. There is a lunar eclipse usually twice a year when the Sun will be conjunct Rahu and the Moon will be conjunct Ketu. Then occur six months apart the Sun will conjunct Ketu and the Moon conjunct Rahu.

Eclipses are when either the Sun or the Moon are eclipsed by a shadow. It is a time of inner reflection because within the darkness of these shadows something hidden will reveal secrets to uncover the truth of our lives. When the unknown becomes known we will experience an awakening or an epiphany.

The nodes of the Moon, Rahu which is the north node and Ketu which is the South node, takes 18 1/2 years to transit through all 12 signs of the zodiac. Therefore, to better understand what the eclipse will reveal out of the darkness can be detected by looking back at what occurred 18 1/2 years prior when the nodes of the Moon were in the same sign as before.

Eclipses are powerful tools to better understand our lives as well as make future predictions. The true essence of the eclipse can be detected by the sign and the house that they are in a birth chart.

Eclipses of 1998 and 2016 – Scandal for Clintons 18 ½ years later

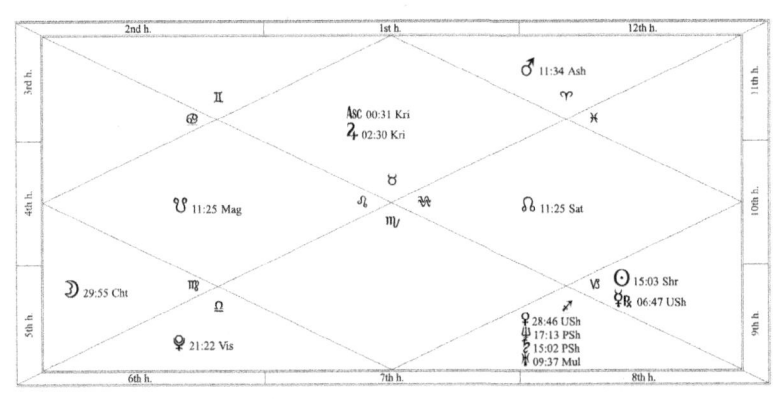

	11th h.	12th h.	1st h.	2nd h.
	♓	♈ ♂ 11:34 Ash	Asc 00:31 Kri ♃ 02:30 Kri ♉	♊
10th h.	♒ ☊ 11:25 Sat	Monica Lewinsky Scandal Sat 01-28-1989 12:00:00 Washington, District of Columbia USA Timezone: 5 DST: 0 Latitude: 38N53'42 Longitude: 77W02'11 Ayanamsha: -23:42:24 Lahiri		⊕ 3rd h.
9th h.	♑ ☉ 15:03 Shr ☿ ℞ 06:47 USh		♌ ☋ 11:25 Mag	♌ 4th h.
	♀ 28:46 USh ♆ 17:13 PSh ♄ 15:02 PSh ♇ 09:37 Mul ♐	♏	♎ ☽ 21:22 Vis	♍ ☽ 29:55 Cht
	8th h.	7th h.	6th h.	5th h.

The eclipses have an 18 ½ year cycle and can expose events from the previous 18 ½ years. 1998 was the time of the Monika Lewinsky scandal, but it was during the 2016 presidential election when Rahu and Ketu returned to the same placements, (Ketu in Aquarius and Rahu in Leo) as the Monica Lewinsky scandal.

In 2016 Hillary Clinton was running for president, without the birth time for Hillary Clinton I analyzed the chart of her daughter Chelsea Clinton to see the results of the elections according to the eclipses. In Chelsea's chart Ketu was transiting over her natal Sun, and her Sun happens to be in the 8th house from her natal Moon representing her mother.

18 1/2 years ago during the Monica Lewinsky trial in 1998 Ketu was in the same position representing losses. At this time it was on Chelsea's Sun which is the indicator for the father in a chart, but also indicates a feeling of loss in 2016, indicating her mother's loss of the presidency.

Tim Kaine was Hillary Clinton's vice president running mate. He was born two days before Chelsea putting his Sun close to where Ketu was transiting indicating again a possible loss.

Even though we do not have Hillary Clinton's birth time, we do know that her natal Moon is in Aquarius where transcending Ketu was during the 2016 elections as well as in 1998 when she suffered great loss, disgrace and scandal concerning her husband Bill Clinton.

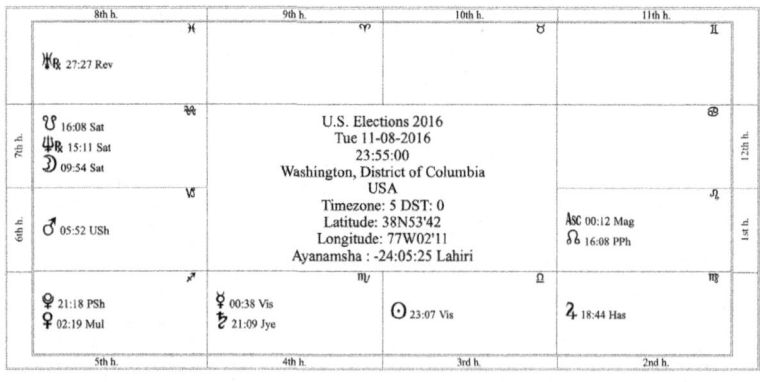

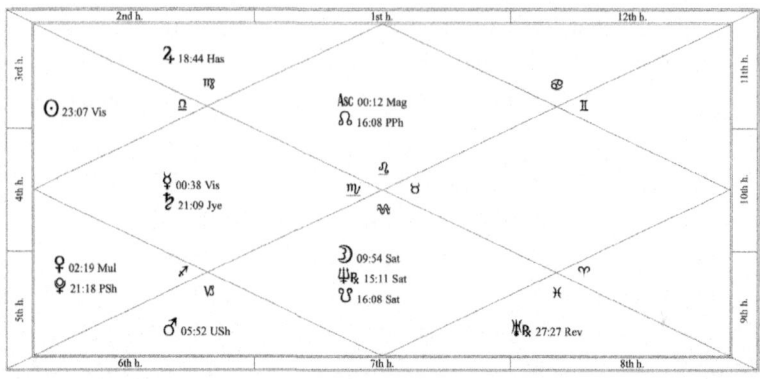

	8th h.	9th h.	10th h.	11th h.
	♆℞ 27:27 Rev			
7th h.	☋ 16:08 Sat ♅℞ 15:11 Sat ☽ 09:54 Sat	U.S. Elections 2016 Tue 11-08-2016 23:55:00 Washington, District of Columbia USA Timezone: 5 DST: 0 Latitude: 38N53'42 Longitude: 77W02'11 Ayanamsha : -24:05:25 Lahiri		12th h.
6th h.	♂ 05:52 USh		ASC 00:12 Mag ☊ 16:08 PPh	1st h.
	♀ 21:18 PSh ♀ 02:19 Mul	☿ 00:38 Vis ♄ 21:09 Jye	☉ 23:07 Vis	♃ 18:44 Has
	5th h.	4th h.	3rd h.	2nd h.

172

Eclipses

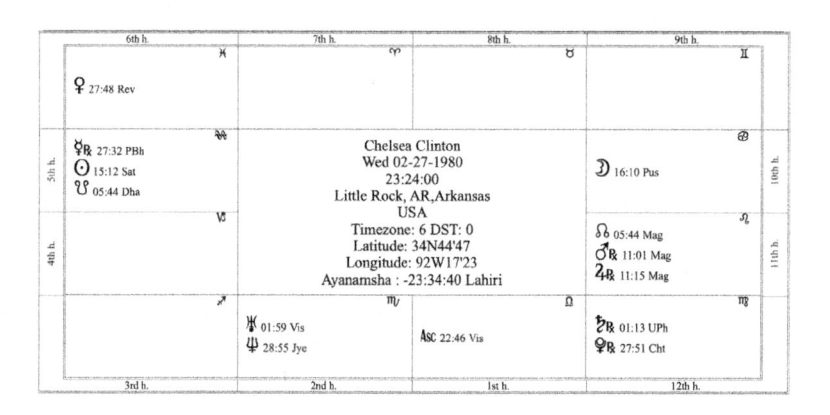

Chapter 16

6th h.	7th h.	8th h.	9th h.
♓ ♀ 27:48 Rev	♈	♉	♊
♒ ☿℞ 27:32 PBh ☉ 15:12 Sat ☊ 05:44 Dha	Chelsea Clinton Wed 02-27-1980 23:24:00 Little Rock, AR,Arkansas USA Timezone: 6 DST: 0 Latitude: 34N44'47 Longitude: 92W17'23 Ayanamsha : -23:34:40 Lahiri		☽ 16:10 Pus
♑			♌ ☋ 05:44 Mag ♂ 11:01 Mag ♃℞ 11:15 Mag
♐	♏ ⛢ 01:59 Vis ♆ 28:55 Jye	♎ Asc 22:46 Vis	♍ ♄℞ 01:13 UPh ☿℞ 27:51 Cht
3rd h.	2nd h.	1st h.	12th h.

Eclipse on Chelsea's Sun: 8th from her Moon

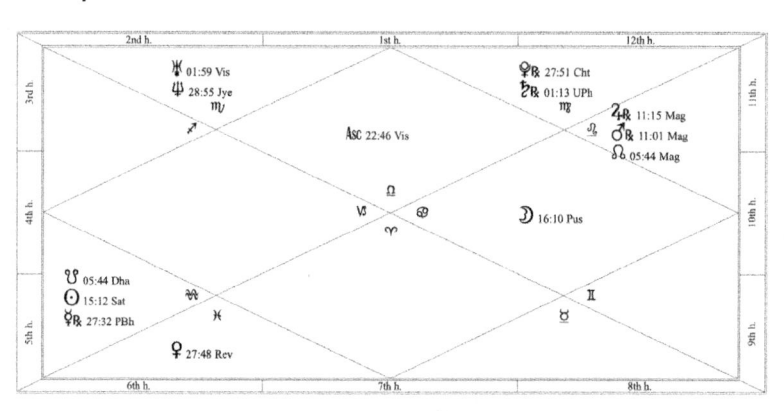

Diamond chart:
- 2nd h.: ⛢ 01:59 Vis, ♆ 28:55 Jye (♏)
- 1st h.: Asc 22:46 Vis
- 12th h.: ☿℞ 27:51 Cht, ♄℞ 01:13 UPh (♍), ♃℞ 11:15 Mag, ♂ 11:01 Mag, ☋ 05:44 Mag
- 11th h.
- 3rd h.
- 4th h.
- 10th h.: ☽ 16:10 Pus
- 5th h.: ☊ 05:44 Dha, ☉ 15:12 Sat, ☿℞ 27:32 PBh (♒), ♀ 27:48 Rev (♓)
- 6th h., 7th h., 8th h., 9th h.

1st h.	2nd h.	3rd h.	4th h.
♓ Asc 11:39 UBh	♈ ☊ 09:33 Ash	♉ ☽ 10:54 Roh	♊
♒ ☉ 14:11 Sat ☿ 09:44 Sat	Tim Kaine Wed 02-26-1958 07:59:00 Saint Paul, MN,Minnesota USA Timezone: 6 DST: 0 Latitude: 44N56'40 Longitude: 93W05'36 Ayanamsha : -23:16:32 Lahiri		⛢℞ 15:12 Pus
♑ ♀ 08:43 USh			♌ ☿℞ 07:38 Mag
♐ ♂ 23:06 PSh ♄ 01:18 Mul	♏ ♃℞ 08:11 Swa ☋ 09:33 Swa ♆℞ 11:22 Swa	♎	♍
10th h.	9th h.	8th h.	7th h.

173

Astrologer's Secrets — My best Tools and Techniques

Hilary's Vice President: Tim Kane Eclipse on his Sun

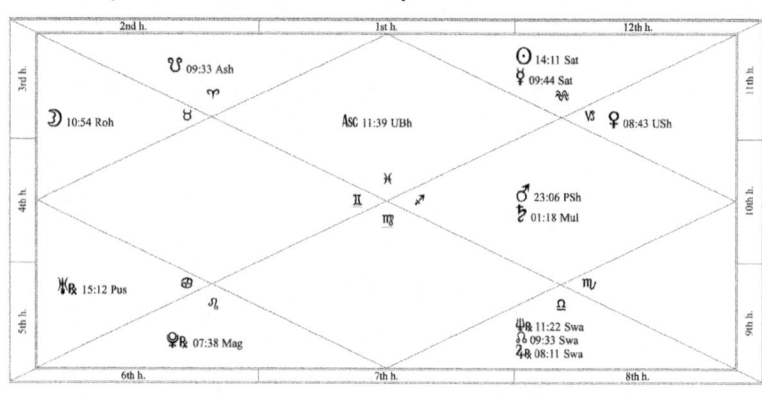

Chart 1 (North Indian style):

- 2nd h.: ☋ 09:33 Ash (Ari)
- 1st h.: ASC 11:39 UBh
- 12th h.: ☉ 14:11 Sat; ☿ 09:44 Sat
- 3rd h.: ☽ 10:54 Roh (Tau)
- 11th h.: ♄ 08:43 USh; ♀ 08:43 USh (Cap)
- 4th h.: (Gem / Vir / Sag / Pis)
- 10th h.: ♂ 23:06 PSh; ♃ 01:18 Mul
- 5th h.: ♅ ℞ 15:12 Pus (Can)
- 9th h.: ♆ ℞ 11:22 Swa; ☊ 09:33 Swa; ♃ 08:11 Swa
- 6th h.: ♀ ℞ 07:38 Mag (Leo)
- 7th h.
- 8th h.

Chart 2 (South Indian style):

Hillary Rodham Clinton
Sun 10-26-1947
02:18:00
Chicago, IL, Illinois
USA
Timezone: 6 DST: 0
Latitude: 41N51'00
Longitude: 87W39'00
Ayanamsha : -23:07:26 Lahiri

- 8th h. (Pis)
- 9th h. (Ari): ☊ 00:27 Kri
- 10th h. (Tau): ♅ ℞ 02:48 Mrg
- 11th h. (Gem)
- 7th h. (Aqu): ☽ 26:43 PBh
- 12th h. (Can): ♂ 20:45 Asl; ♀ 21:43 Asl; ♄ 28:10 Asl
- 6th h. (Cap)
- 1st h. (Leo): ASC 21:45 PPh
- 5th h. (Sag): ☋ 00:27 Vis; ♃ 07:20 Anu
- 4th h. (Sco)
- 3rd h. (Lib): ☉ 08:56 Swa; ♀ 22:48 Vis; ☿ ℞ 28:17 Vis
- 2nd h. (Vir): ♆ 18:13 Has

Eclipses over Hilary's Moon at time of elections

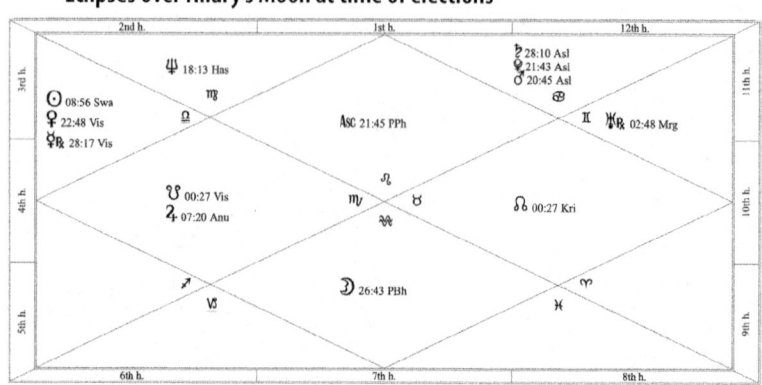

Chart 3 (North Indian style):

- 2nd h.: ♆ 18:13 Has (Vir)
- 1st h.: ASC 21:45 PPh
- 12th h.: ♄ 28:10 Asl; ♀ 21:43 Asl; ♂ 20:45 Asl (Can)
- 3rd h.: ☉ 08:56 Swa; ♀ 22:48 Vis; ☿ ℞ 28:17 Vis (Lib)
- 11th h.: ♅ ℞ 02:48 Mrg (Gem)
- 4th h.: ☋ 00:27 Vis; ♃ 07:20 Anu (Sco)
- 10th h.: ☊ 00:27 Kri (Ari)
- 5th h. (Sag)
- 9th h. (Pis)
- 6th h.
- 7th h.: ☽ 26:43 PBh
- 8th h.

174

Chapter 17

Vedic Astrology Concepts that work!

Lakshmi Yoga, Pancha Maha Purusha Yoga, Sade Sati, Gandanta Planets, Saturn Return

Lakshmi Yoga

Lakshmi yoga represents great wealth as Lakshmi is the goddess of wealth and prosperity. In order to have a Lakshmi yoga, the first requirement is to have Venus in its own sign of rulership, Taurus or Libra or its sign of exaltation, Pisces.

The second requirement is that the ruler of the 9th house must be strong as well as the ruler of the first house must also be strong. To be a strong planet, it must be in either a trikona house (1, 5 or 9) or an angle/kendra house (1, 4, 7, or 10).

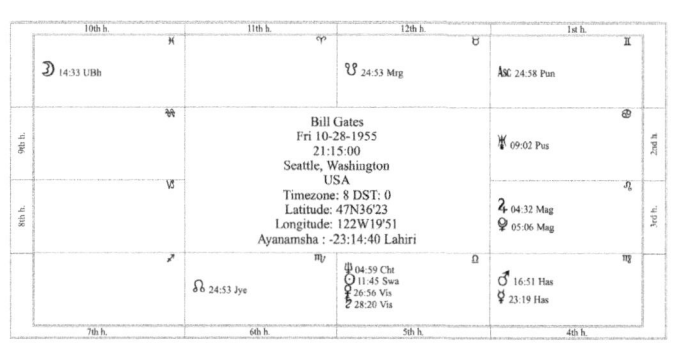

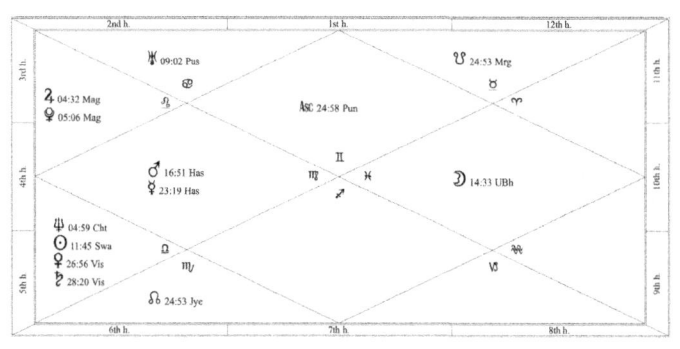

Bill Gates has a perfect Lakshmi yoga. He has Venus in Libra, its own sign of rulership. This fulfills the first requirement of Lakshmi yoga.

The ruler of the first house Mercury is strong as it is exalted in the 4th house a kendra, and the ruler of the 9th house is exalted Saturn in the 5th house in Libra. This completes the second requirement that gives Gates a perfect Lakshmi yoga, denoting great wealth.

Pancha Maha Purusha Yoga

Another powerful yoga is the Pancha Maha Purusha Yoga, meaning the five yogas of great men (people). This is when any of the five planets are in their own sign of rulership or exalted, in a kendra (angle) excluding the Sun and the Moon. This yoga makes whatever the planet rules a top priority and indication of what the individual is about. Its planetary energy will be accentuated in an individual's life.

Mercury: Bhadra yoga –Intelligent, witty, communicator

Venus: Malavya yoga -beauty, charming, artistic

Mars: Ruchaka yoga: aggressive, warrior, athletic,

Jupiter: Hamsa yoga – philosophical, teacher spiritual

Saturn: Shasha yoga – leader, organizer, disciplined, authoritative

In Gates chart he has a bhadra yoga in his 4th house, as Mercury is exalted in Virgo in a kendra (angle). Bhadra yoga represents someone of great intelligence and deals with communications. As creator of Microsoft software, he connects the world in mass communications which is all representative of Mercury which is in a bhadra yoga.

Sade Sati

Sade Sati means 7 ½ years and is when transiting Saturn is in the sign before the Moon, in the same sign as the Moon, and the sign after the Moon. Since Saturn stays in a sign for 2 1/2 years Sade Sati is said to last for 7 1/2 years. My take on this is that Saturn is more detrimental when it is transiting in the same sign as the Moon and is the most intense when it is the closest to the Moon by degree.

My personal experience with Sade Sati was extremely difficult, I had problems within the family, the death of my parents, relationship problems, and financial losses. I have come to realize that most people during the time of Sade Sati have difficult relationship problems.

In the chart of Jeff Bezos, he was going through Sade Sati at the time of his divorce. During this time, he had to split most of his profits from his business with his wife. This was an extremely difficult time in relationships and caused great financial losses for him even though at the time he was the richest man in the world. Bezos and his wife MacKenzie announced their separation on January 9, 2019. During this time, transiting Saturn was in Sagittarius around 18 degrees at the time of their announcement. But of course, they were in troubled times way before the announcement which puts Saturn in Sagittarius crossing over his natal Moon.

1st h.	2nd h.	3rd h.	4th h.
ASC 26:35 Rev ♃ 18:37 Rev			☊ 17:53 Ard
♀ 01:18 Dha	Jeff Bezos Sun 01-12-1964 11:33:00 Albuquerque, New Mexico USA Timezone: 7 DST: 0 Latitude: 35N05'04 Longitude: 106W39'04 Ayanamsha : -23:21:01 Lahiri		
♄ 28:18 Dha ♂ 06:16 USh			♅R 16:22 PPh ♆R 20:41 PPh
☉ 28:14 USh ☿ 17:53 PSh ♇R 11:42 Mul ☽ 04:48 Mul		♆ 24:06 Vis	
10th h.	9th h.	8th h.	7th h.

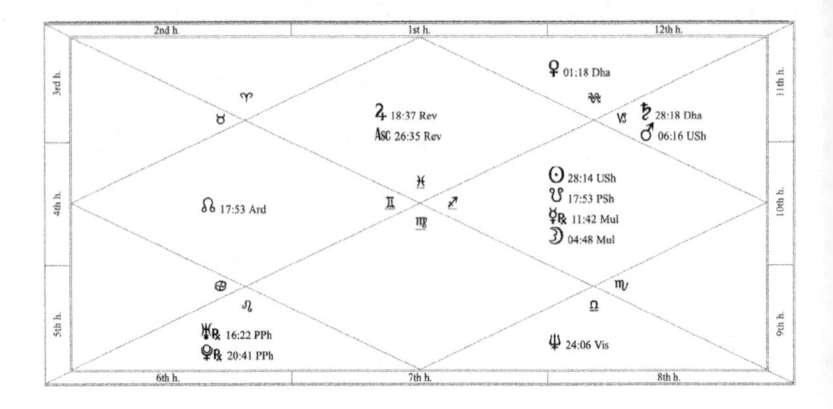

```
                2nd h.              1st h.                    12th h.
                                                    ♀ 01:18 Dha
                          ♉              ♒
                            ♃ 18:37 Rev        ♑  ♄ 28:18 Dha
                            ASC 26:35 Rev          ♂ 06:16 USh

                                    ♓                ☉ 28:14 USh
                ☋ 17:53 Ard    ♊        ♐           ☊ 17:53 PSh
                                    ♍                ☿℞ 11:42 Mul
                                                     ☽ 04:48 Mul

                          ♋                  ♏
                            ♌                  ♎
                      ♅℞ 16:22 PPh
                      ♀℞ 20:41 PPh      ♆ 24:06 Vis
                6th h.              7th h.                    8th h.
```

Sade Sati: Jordan Spieth won The Masters Golf Tournament

Transiting Saturn was 5 degrees Scorpio

Another interesting case involving Sade Sati is with pro golfer Jordan Spieth. He won the masters golf tournament in 2015 at the age of 21, the youngest to ever win this tournament. Transiting Saturn was 5 degrees of Scorpio less than two degrees from his natal Moon at 7 degrees of Scorpio.

How do I account for such a difficult planetary alignment as transiting Saturn is crossing over his Moon? Saturn does represent discipline, focus, and hard work. Saturn sometimes will give great rewards for those who have done the work. But as Saturn is usually a depressive force, I came to find out at the time of his win, his mother was ill. Luckily, she recovered, but the Moon does represent the mother, therefore there was a sense of loss and worry concerning his mother.

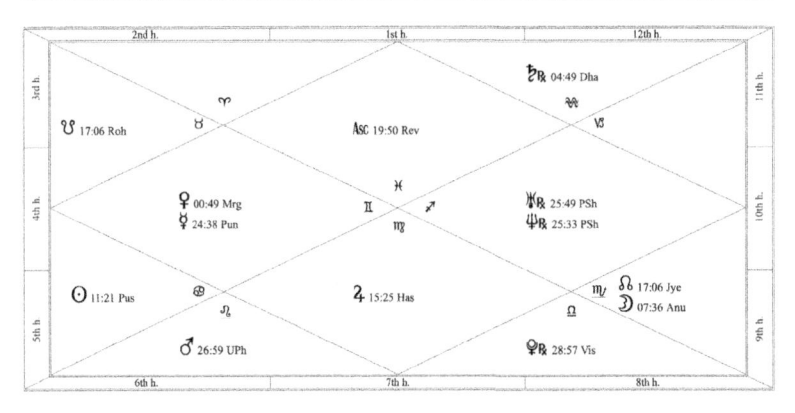

Saturn's Return

Many people speak of their experiences concerning the Saturn return. This is when Saturn transits through all 12 signs of the Zodiac to return to its natal position at birth. This always takes around 28 to 30 years because this is how long it takes for Saturn to transit through all 12 signs of the Zodiac. Therefore, everyone goes through Saturn's return around the same age, which is around age 28 to 30. The second Saturn return occurs when the individual is 58 to 60 years old.

Saturn is the planet that rules discipline and maturity, and the Saturn return is simply when the individual will realize the serious aspects of their life. Saturn is also a planet of karma and when Saturn returns to its natal position, we are made aware of our responsibility, duty and karma in this lifetime.

Around the age of 30 an individual must grow up and begin thinking about where their life is headed in terms of work, career and family. I believe that the Saturn return is simply a time when the individual grows up to become responsible in society. Many people believe that the Saturn return is a terrible thing, but nothing could be further from the truth because it is simply a time to become more aware, grounded and responsible with the realization of duty as to what you put into anything you will get the results out of it.

Around the age of 60 individuals begin to become more aware that their time is limited in this lifetime therefore they become more serious about accomplishing any goals that have been unfulfilled. Saturn is the planet that gives our just rewards, if we have worked hard around the age of 60 there will be great rewards and accomplishments for all the hard work put in a lifetime.

Many people confuse Saturn's return with Sade Sati, which are entirely different. Sade Sati as discussed before, is when Saturn transits close to the natal Moon, which in my opinion is far more difficult than the Saturn return.

Gandanta Planets

Gandanta Planets are when planets are the last few degrees of a water sign 27–29 degrees and the first degrees of a Fire sign 0–2 degrees.

Gandanta literally means a knot, indicating disruption and problems. I was always taught that it can indicate the effects of drowning, such as a feeling of being completely out of control. I have discovered that in many cases it does literally represent drowning.

Vedic Astrology Concepts that work!

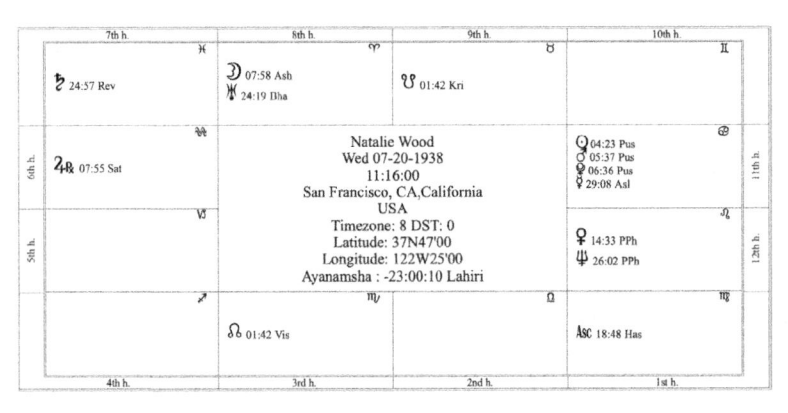

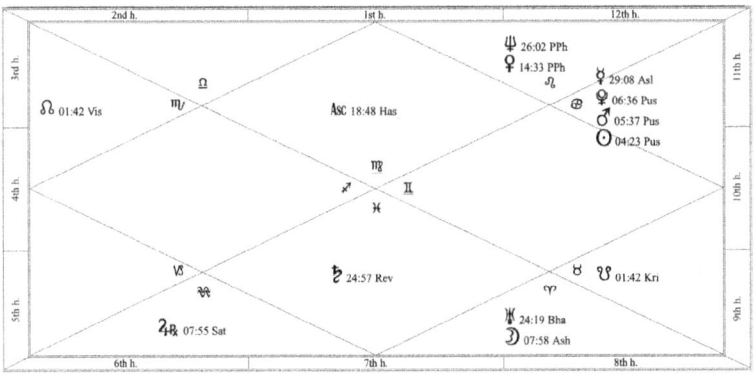

Chapter 17

	7th h.	8th h.	9th h.	10th h.	
	♓︎ ♄ 24:57 Rev	♈︎ ☽ 07:58 Ash ♅ 24:19 Bha	♉︎ ☊ 01:42 Kri	♊︎	
6th h.	♒︎ ♃℞ 07:55 Sat	Natalie Wood Wed 07-20-1938 11:16:00 San Francisco, CA,California USA Timezone: 8 DST: 0 Latitude: 37N47'00 Longitude: 122W25'00 Ayanamsha : -23:00:10 Lahiri		☾ 04:23 Pus ♂ 05:37 Pus ☿ 06:36 Pus ♀ 29:08 Asl ⊕	11th h.
5th h.	♑︎			♀ 14:33 PPh ♇ 26:02 PPh ♌︎	12th h.
	♐︎	♍︎ ☋ 01:42 Vis	♎︎	♍︎ Asc 18:48 Has	
	4th h.	3rd h.	2nd h.	1st h.	

Natalie Wood Drowned 11/29/1981
Natal Mercury 29 degrees Cancer
Transiting Ketu 29 degrees Sagittarius

In the case of the beautiful actress Natalie Wood, she died by drowning November 29th, 1981. There has been much speculation that her death was not an accident, nevertheless she was found in the water dead from drowning.

Wood's natal Mercury sits at 29 degrees of Cancer, Gandanta. When individuals have planets that are Gandanta especially in water signs, the last degrees of Cancer, Scorpio or Pisces they may have an experience of drowning in their lives.

181

She also almost drowned while filming a movie as a child and was terrified of water. On the day of her drowning in 1981, transiting Ketu was at 29 degrees of Sagittarius in an exact quincunx/shashtaka, an 8/6 relationship to her natal Mercury at 29 degrees of Cancer. As noted before the quincunx aspect can represent death and accidents.

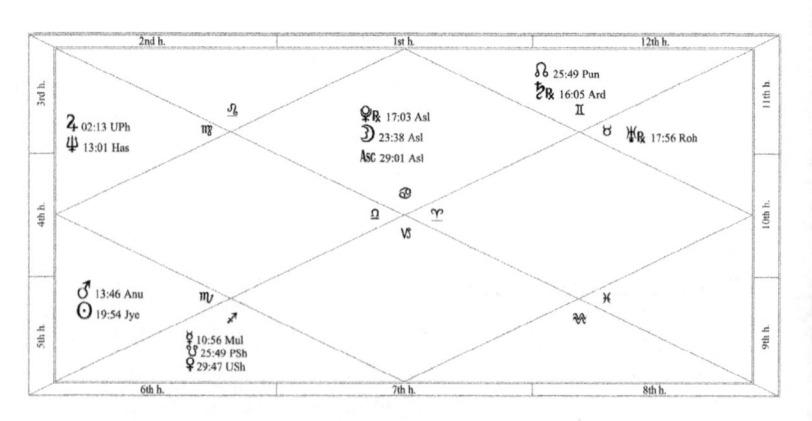

Dennis Wilson: Drowned: 12/29 1983
Natal Ascendant 29 degrees Cancer
Transiting Mars 29 degrees
Transiting Ketu 22 degrees Scorpio

Dennis Wilson, one of the legendary new rock sounds of the 1960's Beach Boys also died through drowning. His ascendant sits at 29 degrees of Cancer, gandanta. On that faded day transiting Mars was 29 degrees of Virgo, activating his 29-degree Cancer Ascendant. Another very interesting aspect that you will learn in this book is that when transiting planets are the same degree as natal planets or the ascendant it can represent an event in accordance to what the planet itself represents.

Another variable that happened on the day that he drowned was transiting Ketu was 22 degrees of Scorpio very close to his Sun representing the loss of the physical body.

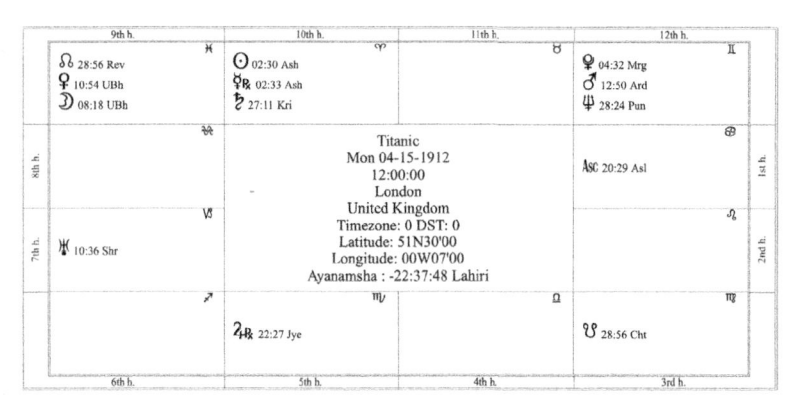

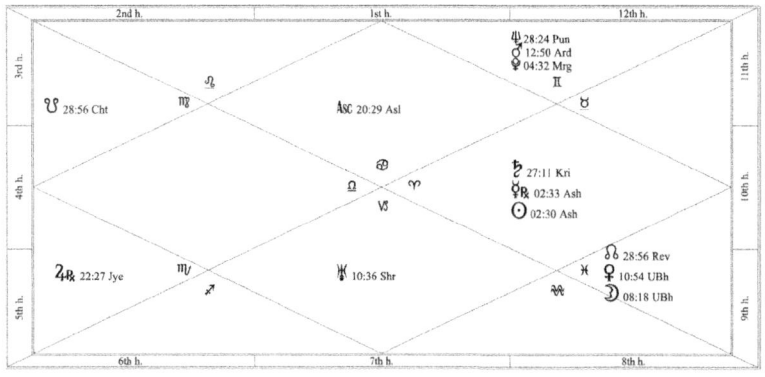

Titanic went down: 04/15/1912
Natal Rahu 28–29 degrees Pisces

When we think of drowning the Titanic is possibly one of the biggest mass drownings on record. On the day that the Titanic sank, transiting Rahu was at 28–29 degrees of the water sign Pisces, Gandanta.

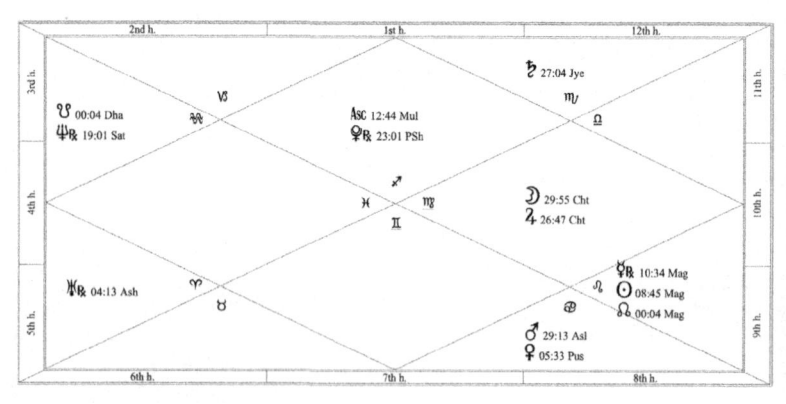

4th h.	5th h.	6th h.	7th h.
♓	♈ ♅℞ 04:13 Ash	♉	♊
♒ ♆℞ 19:01 Sat ☋ 00:04 Dha	Hurricane Harvey Fri 08-25-2017 16:30:49 Houston, Texas USA Timezone: 6 DST: 1 Latitude: 29N45'48 Longitude: 95W21'48 Ayanamsha : -24:06:03 Lahiri		♋ ♀ 05:33 Pus ♂ 29:13 Asl
♑			♌ ☊ 00:04 Mag ☉ 08:45 Mag ☿℞ 10:34 Mag
♐ ♇℞ 23:01 PSh ASC 12:44 Mul	♏ ♄ 27:04 Jye	♎	♍ ♃ 26:47 Cht ☽ 29:55 Cht
1st h.	12th h.	11th h.	10th h.

Hurricane Harvey
Mars and Rahu 0 degrees Leo

Gandanta planets represent not only drowning but massive flooding and storms. It was right before hurricane Harvey hit Houston, Texas that I noticed transiting Mars and Rahu were at the first few degrees of Leo, Gandanta.

Chapter 18

Outer Planets – Uranus, Neptune, and Pluto conjunct natal planets: Intense results according to planet they conjunct

Uranus conjunct Sun

	10th h.	11th h.	12th h.	1st h.
	☉ 22:58 Rev ♅ 22:27 Rev ☋ 21:28 Rev ♓	♈ ☿ 11:36 Ash	♉	♃ 18:59 Ard ASC 25:20 Pun ♀ 25:47 Pun ♊
9th h.	♀ 14:00 Sat ♒	Ram Dass Mon 04-06-1931 10:40:00 Boston, Massachusetts USA Timezone: 5 DST: 0 Latitude: 42N21'30 Longitude: 71W03'35 Ayanamsha: -22:53:44 Lahiri		♂ 09:00 Pus ♋	2nd h.
8th h.	♑			♆℞ 10:28 Mag ♌	3rd h.
	♄ 29:47 USh ♐	☽ 14:29 Anu ♍	♎	☊ 21:28 Has ♍
	7th h.	6th h.	5th h.	4th h.

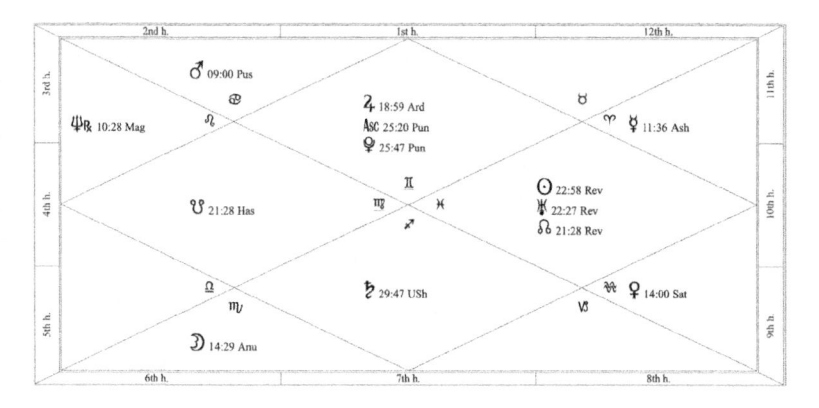

	2nd h.	1st h.	12th h.	
3rd h.	♂ 09:00 Pus ♋ ♆℞ 10:28 Mag ♌	♃ 18:59 Ard ASC 25:20 Pun ♀ 25:47 Pun ♊	♉ ♈ ☿ 11:36 Ash	11th h.
4th h.	☊ 21:28 Has	♍ ♓ ♐	☉ 22:58 Rev ♅ 22:27 Rev ☋ 21:28 Rev	10th h.
5th h.	♎ ♍ ☽ 14:29 Anu	♄ 29:47 USh	♒ ♀ 14:00 Sat ♑	9th h.
	6th h.	7th h.	8th h.	

Uranus/Rahu conjunct Sun: Unusual career

Ram Dass, who was Richard Alpert, was a professor at Harvard with Timothy Leary who experimented with LSD as a professor. He and Leary were both fired for their scandalous experimentation. Alpert upon being fired went to India to

185

find himself through spirituality, changing his name to Baba Ram Dass.

Dass was a spiritual teacher, guru of modern yoga, psychologist, and author. His best-selling 1971 book *Be Here Now*, helped popularize Eastern spirituality and yoga in the West. He authored or co-authored twelve more books on spirituality over the next four decades.

His Sun, Rahu and Uranus conjunction in the 10th house explains exactly his experience that occurred in his work in Harvard University as a professor. Uranus is the outer planet that represents rebelliousness, unconventional, and the unexpected. As this planet Uranus is conjunct the Sun in the 10th House of our work and career it seems likely that he would be unconventional and rebellious doing the unexpected within his work and career. Furthermore, the Sun in the 10th house will bring success through his career with Uranus and Rahu as this accentuated his work making him world famous from his work with LSD, his spirituality and his realization and enlightenment.

Uranus conjunct Moon

5th h.	6th h.	7th h.	8th h.
♓	♈ ☊ 13:49 Bha	♉	♊ ♀℞ 16:07 Ard
♒ ♅℞ 09:09 Sat ☽ 05:04 Dha (4th h.)	Timothy Leary Fri 10-22-1920 10:45:00 Springfield, MA, Massachusetts USA Timezone: 5 DST: 1 Latitude: 42N06'05 Longitude: 72W35'23 Ayanamsha: -22:45:13 Lahiri		♋ ♆ 20:50 Asl (9th h.)
♑ (3rd h.)			♌ ♃ 18:45 PPh ♄ 27:35 UPh (10th h.)
♐ ♂ 10:12 Mul	♏ ♀ 05:16 Anu ASC 16:58 Jye	♍ ☉ 06:08 Cht ☋ 13:49 Swa ☿ 29:57 Vis	♎
2nd h.	1st h.	12th h.	11th h.

186

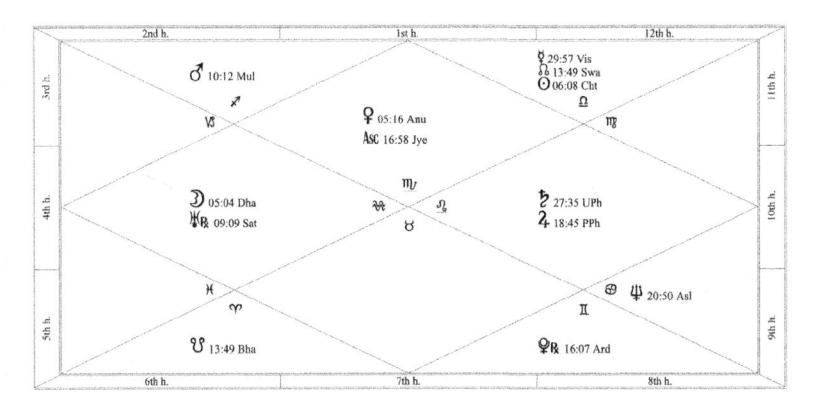

Outer Planets – Uranus, Neptune, and Pluto conjunct natal planets: Intense results according to planet they conjunct

Chapter 18

2nd h.	1st h.	12th h.
♂ 10:12 Mul ♐	♀ 05:16 Anu ASC 16:58 Jye	☿ 29:57 Vis ☊ 13:49 Swa ☉ 06:08 Cht ♎ ♍
☽ 05:04 Dha ♅ ℞ 09:09 Sat	♒ ♌ ♉	♄ 27:35 UPh ♃ 18:45 PPh
♓ ♈ ☋ 13:49 Bha		♊ ♆ 20:50 Asl ♇ ℞ 16:07 Ard
6th h.	7th h.	8th h.

Timothy Leary, who was the professor at Harvard and worked alongside Richard Alpert experimenting with LSD also has a very important planet conjunct Uranus, which is the Moon. Leary's Moon conjunct Uranus represents his unconventional ideas especially being in the sign of Aquarius which can be very unconventional all by itself. His Moon as ruler of the 9th house represents his unconventional, radical ideas about spirituality and truth.

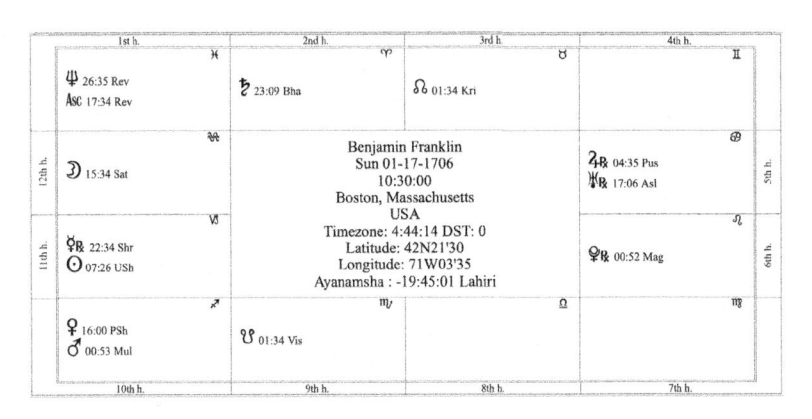

1st h.	2nd h.	3rd h.	4th h.
♆ 26:35 Rev ASC 17:34 Rev ♓	♄ 23:09 Bha ♈	☊ 01:34 Kri ♉	♊
☽ 15:34 Sat ♒	Benjamin Franklin Sun 01-17-1706 10:30:00 Boston, Massachusetts USA Timezone: 4:44:14 DST: 0 Latitude: 42N21'30 Longitude: 71W03'35 Ayanamsha: -19:45:01 Lahiri		♋ ♃ ℞ 04:35 Pus ♅ ℞ 17:06 Asl
☿ ℞ 22:34 Shr ☉ 07:26 USh ♑			♌ ♇ ℞ 00:52 Mag
♀ 16:00 PSh ♂ 00:53 Mul ♐	☋ 01:34 Vis ♍	♎	♍
10th h.	9th h.	8th h.	7th h.

187

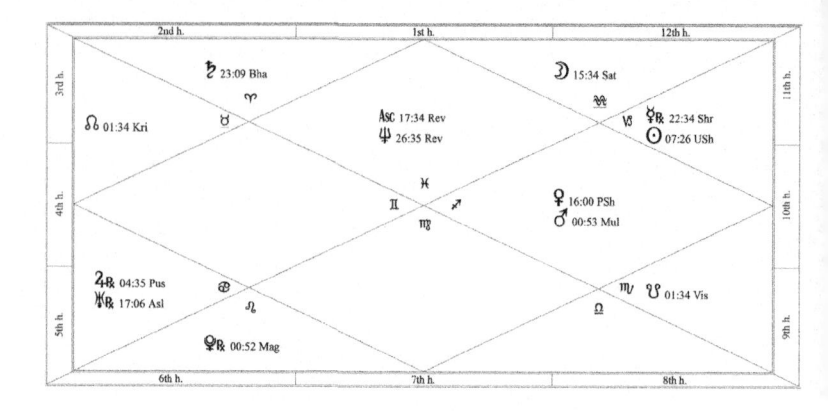

```
           2nd h.                      1st h.                    12th h.
          ♄ 23:09 Bha             ☽ 15:34 Sat
              ♈                       ♒
                                                              ☿℞ 22:34 Shr
     ☊ 01:34 Kri    ♉     ASC 17:34 Rev            ♑
                         ♆ 26:35 Rev                          ☉ 07:26 USh

                              ♓
                         ♊    ♐          ♀ 16:00 PSh
                              ♍           ♂ 00:53 Mul

     ♃℞ 04:35 Pus    ♋                            ♏  ☋ 01:34 Vis
     ♅℞ 17:06 Asl         ♌                  ♎

                         ♇℞ 00:52 Mag
           6th h.                      7th h.                    8th h.
```

Uranus conjunct Jupiter opposed Mercury/Sun - Brilliant Mind, Electricity

Benjamin Franklin was one of the Founding Fathers of the United States, a drafter and signer of the United States Declaration of Independence, and the first United States Postmaster General.

As a scientist, he was a major figure in the American Enlightenment and the history of physics for his studies of electricity. As an inventor, he is known for the lightning rod, bifocals, and the Franklin stove, among others. He founded many civic organizations, including the Library Company, Philadelphia's first fire department, and the University of Pennsylvania.

Uranus also rules over electricity as it can rule lightning and flashes of insight that fill the mind with genius ideas. Franklin has Uranus tightly opposing Mercury, the planet of the intellect and cognitive function. Individuals who have a tight orb conjunction or opposition of Uranus with Mercury will be very inventive, ingenious, and inventors. All of this describes the ingeniousness of Franklin and all his discoveries.

Pluto conjunct Planets: Betrayal, death

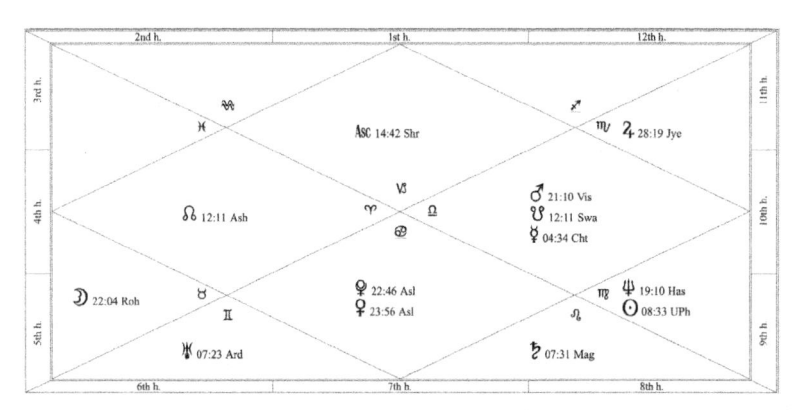

	3rd h.	4th h.	5th h.	6th h.
2nd h.	☋ 12:11 Ash	☽ 22:04 Roh	♅ 07:23 Ard	7th h.
	Phil Hartman Fri 09-24-1948 17:00:00 Brantford Canada Timezone: 5 DST: 1 Latitude: 43N08'00 Longitude: 80W16'00 Ayanamsha : -23:08:17 Lahiri		♀ 22:46 Asl ♀ 23:56 Asl	
1st h. ASC 14:42 Shr			♄ 07:31 Mag	8th h.
12th h.	♃ 28:19 Jye	☿ 04:34 Cht ☋ 12:11 Swa ♂ 21:10 Vis	☉ 08:33 UPh ♆ 19:10 Has	9th h.

Phil Hartman was a comedian known from Saturday Night Live who was murdered by his wife while she was in a drug induced state. She shot him in the head while he was sleeping. Pluto is a planet that can deal with deep dark issues particularly dealing with betrayal. I have found that when Pluto is tightly aspected Venus in a birth chart the individual will experience a deep dark betrayal.

In Hartman's chart he has Venus tightly conjunct Pluto in the 7th House of marriage. What could be a deeper betrayal than someone taking your life unexpectedly? Venus is also the indicator of the wife in a man's chart. The fact that they sit together, Venus and Pluto in the house of marriage tells everything about his wife and his death.

Another indicator for Pluto is death, Pluto's meanings are relative to all the meanings for the 8th house, which is the House of death. Literally, his wife murdered him causing his death. This in my opinion goes beyond betrayal.

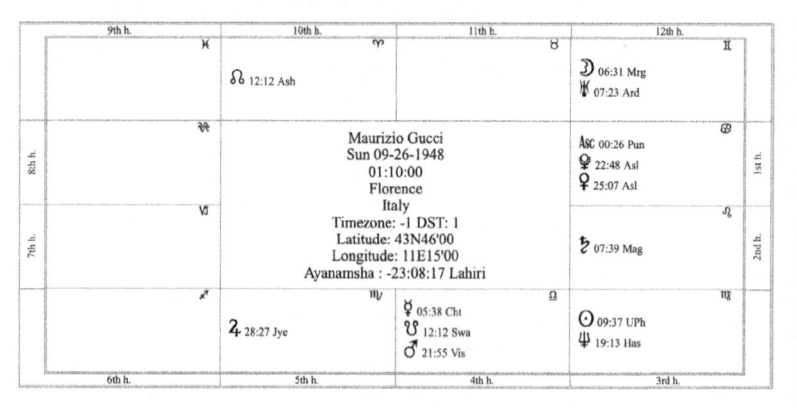

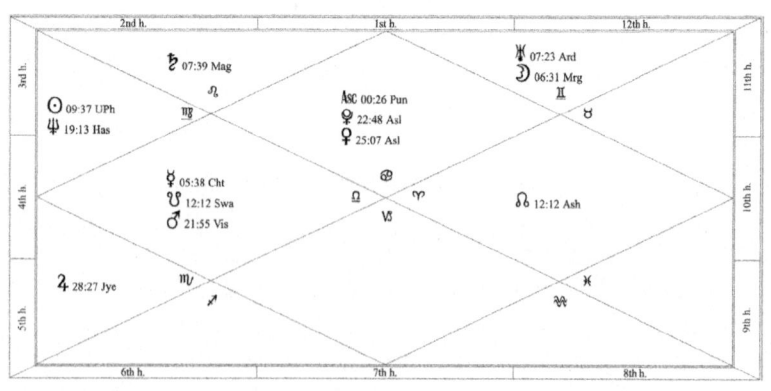

9th h.	10th h.	11th h.	12th h.
☿	♈	♉	♊
☊ 12:12 Ash			☽ 06:31 Mrg ♅ 07:23 Ard
8th h. ♒	Maurizio Gucci Sun 09-26-1948 01:10:00 Florence Italy Timezone: -1 DST: 1 Latitude: 43N46'00 Longitude: 11E15'00 Ayanamsha : -23:08:17 Lahiri		ASC 00:26 Pun ♀ 22:48 Asl ♀ 25:07 Asl ⊕ 1st h.
7th h. ♑			♄ 07:39 Mag ♌ 2nd h.
♐	♍	♎	♍
♃ 28:27 Jye	☿ 05:38 Cht ☋ 12:12 Swa ♂ 21:55 Vis	☉ 09:37 UPh ♆ 19:13 Has	
6th h.	5th h.	4th h.	3rd h.

2nd h.	1st h.	12th h.
3rd h. ♄ 07:39 Mag ♌	♅ 07:23 Ard ☽ 06:31 Mrg ♊	11th h.
☉ 09:37 UPh ♆ 19:13 Has ♍	ASC 00:26 Pun ♀ 22:48 Asl ♀ 25:07 Asl	♉
4th h. ☿ 05:38 Cht ☋ 12:12 Swa ♂ 21:55 Vis	⊕ ☊ 12:12 Ash ♎ ♈ ♑	10th h.
5th h. ♃ 28:27 Jye ♏ ♐		♓ ♒ 9th h.
6th h.	7th h.	8th h.

Maurizio Gucci was an Italian businessman and the one-time head of the Gucci fashion house. He was the son of actor Rodolfo Gucci, and grandson of the company's founder

Guccio Gucci. On March 27, 1995 he was assassinated by a hitman hired by his former wife Patrizia Reggiani.

Again, Pluto is tightly conjunct Venus, but in this case, they reside in his first house. His wife, represented by Venus, was extremely jealous and materialistic and killed him after he divorced her. Just like in Phil Hartman's chart Venus is tightly conjunct Pluto and represents death, deep betrayal and murder from the wife. With these two planets in the 1st house, they are fully aspecting the 7th house of marriage by opposition.

Most of all both Hartman and Gucci are born two days apart in the same year, so their Pluto is the same degree as Venus, a few degrees from Pluto. The nakshatra is Ashlesha for both planets, which can be very underhanded as the symbol is a snake. The degrees of 22–25 degrees Cancer must be watched as a very difficult placement for marriage, particularly for Venus and Pluto.

One more chart with Venus within a degree of Pluto is the chart of Robert Johnson, who was a blues musician and songwriter also killed because of a woman. His Venus/Pluto conjunction sits in the 1st house aspecting the 7th house of relationships just like Gucci.

Johnson was murdered by the jealous husband of a woman with whom he had flirted. In an account by the blues musician Sonny Williamson, Johnson had been flirting with a married woman at a dance, and she gave him a bottle of whiskey poisoned by her husband. When Johnson took the bottle, Williamson knocked it out of his hand, admonishing him to never drink from a bottle that he had not personally seen opened. Johnson replied, "Don't ever knock a bottle out of my hand." Soon after, he was offered another (poisoned) bottle and accepted it. Johnson is reported to have begun feeling ill the evening after and had to be helped back to his room in the early morning hours. Over the next three days his condition steadily worsened. Witnesses reported that he died in a convulsive state of severe pain.

His landmark recordings in 1936 and 1937 display a combination of singing, guitar skills, and songwriting talent that has influenced later generations of musicians.

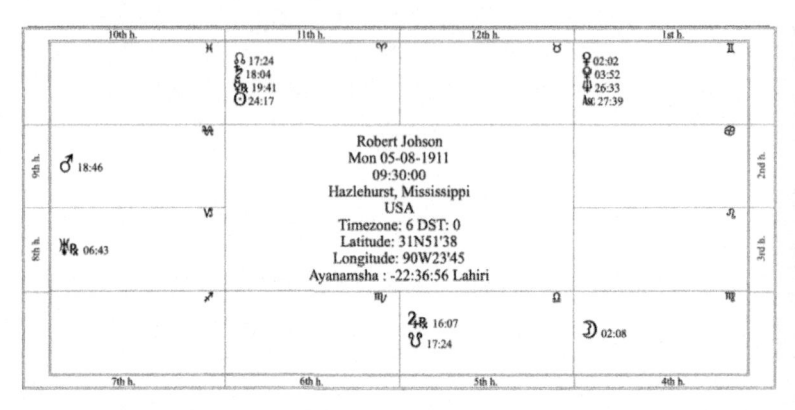

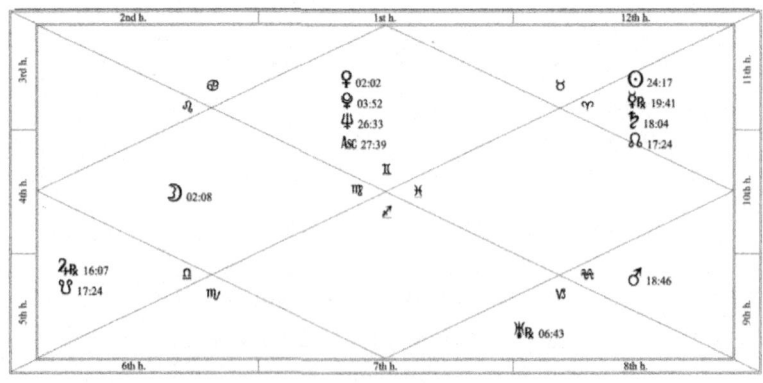

Uranus conjunct Venus: multiple marriages

Elizabeth Taylor was a beautiful actress from the 1950s to the 60s and was considered the most beautiful woman in the world at that time. Taylor was known for her many marriages as she was married to seven different men, but she married eight times because she married Richard Burton two times.

What is so interesting about her chart is that Uranus, the planet of change, unexpected behavior, and excitement is exactly conjunct her Venus in the 5th house of romance. And as expected Venus, which is the planet of relationships, is the ruler of the 7th House of marriage.

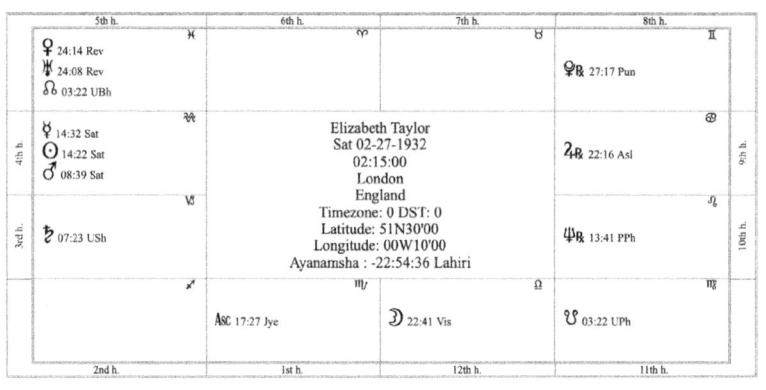

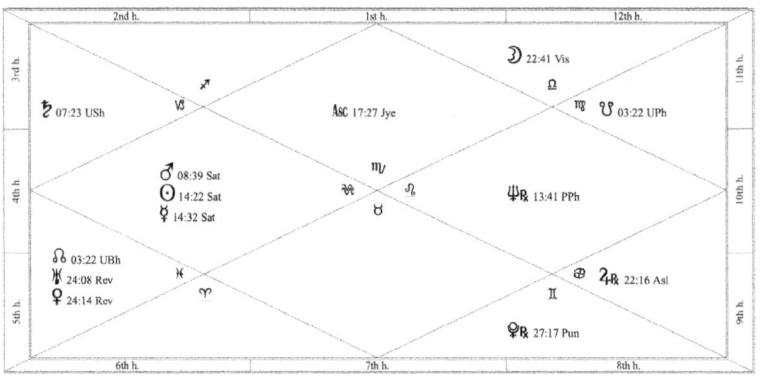

5th h.	6th h.	7th h.	8th h.
♀ 24:14 Rev ♅ 24:08 Rev ☊ 03:22 UBh ♓	♈	♉	♀℞ 27:17 Pun ♊
☿ 14:32 Sat ☉ 14:22 Sat ♂ 08:39 Sat ♒	Elizabeth Taylor Sat 02-27-1932 02:15:00 London England Timezone: 0 DST: 0 Latitude: 51N30'00 Longitude: 00W10'00 Ayanamsha : -22:54:36 Lahiri		♃℞ 22:16 Asl ♋
♄ 07:23 USh ♑			♆℞ 13:41 PPh ♌
♐ Asc 17:27 Jye	♍ 	♎ ☽ 22:41 Vis	♏ ☋ 03:22 UPh
2nd h.	1st h.	12th h.	11th h.

Mars Conjunct Neptune can be delusional

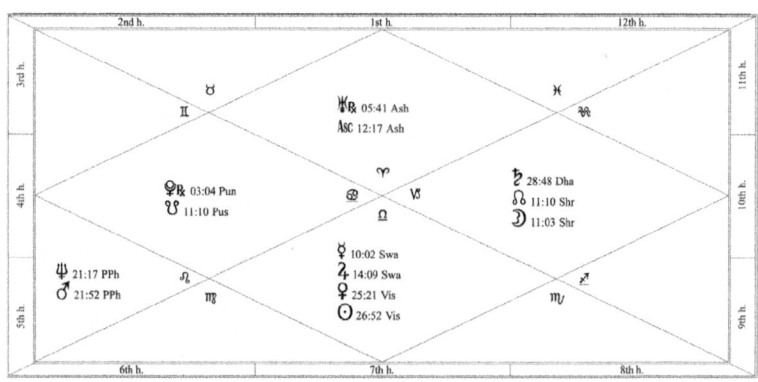

	12th h.	1st h.	2nd h.	3rd h.	
	♓	♈ ♅℞ 05:41 Ash Asc 12:17 Ash	♉	♊	
11th h.	♒	CHARLES MANSON Mon 11-12-1934 16:40:00 CINCINNATI USA Timezone: 5 DST: 0 Latitude: 39N09'43 Longitude: 84W27'25 Ayanamsha : -22:57:03 Lahiri	♀℞ 03:04 Pun ☋ 11:10 Pus	♋	4th h.
10th h.	♑ ♄ 28:48 Dha ☊ 11:10 Shr ☽ 11:03 Shr		♆ 21:17 PPh ♂ 21:52 PPh	♌	5th h.
	♐	♏ ☿ 10:02 Swa ♃ 14:09 Swa ♀ 25:21 Vis ☉ 26:52 Vis	♎	♍	
	9th h.	8th h.	7th h.	6th h.	

	2nd h.	1st h.	12th h.	
3rd h.	♉ ♊	♅℞ 05:41 Ash Asc 12:17 Ash ♈	♓ ♒	11th h.
4th h.	♀℞ 03:04 Pun ☋ 11:10 Pus	⊕ ♑ ♎	♄ 28:48 Dha ☊ 11:10 Shr ☽ 11:03 Shr	10th h.
5th h.	♆ 21:17 PPh ♂ 21:52 PPh ♌ ♍	☿ 10:02 Swa ♃ 14:09 Swa ♀ 25:21 Vis ☉ 26:52 Vis	♐ ♏	9th h.
	6th h.	7th h.	8th h.	

Charles Manson cult leader was very delusional as he controlled the minds of others to commit the mass Mason murders in Los Angeles in 1969. He is suspected of having murdered others as well.

Manson has Neptune exactly conjunct Mars. Neptune is the planet of deception, deceit denial, illusions and scandals. When it is conjunct Mars, it intensifies this delusional activity even more because Mars propels Neptune into action. The conjunction sits in the 5th house that can represent our mind and mental abilities. Mars is the ruler of the chart as well as the 8th house of death, scandals and deep dark addictions.

Neptune between Sun and Moon – Secrets and murder in Family

Neptune can represent deception, and delusions, as it also rules over secrets. An interesting finding was when I discovered that when Neptune sits between the Sun and Moon in a chart there can be deep deception and secrets. With the next two charts what occurs when Neptune is between both the Sun and the Moon in the 4th house it represents secrets within the family.

Shockingly, in both of these charts siblings were involved together with murdering their parents.

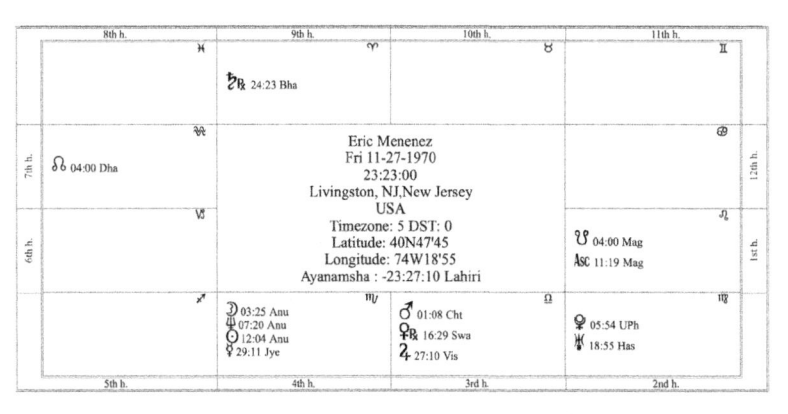

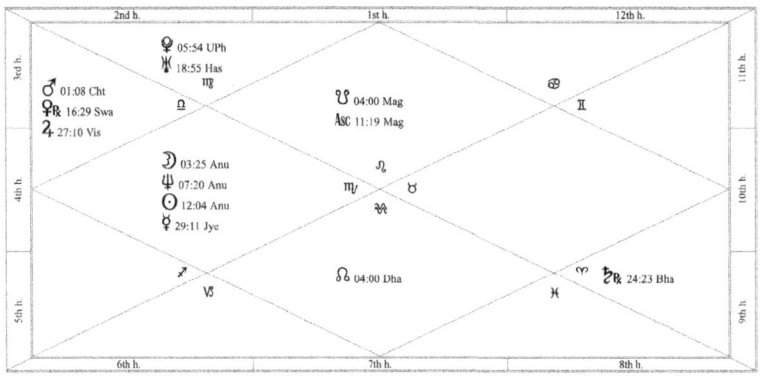

8th h.	9th h.	10th h.	11th h.
	♓ ♈ ℞ 24:23 Bha	♉	♊
7th h. ☊ 04:00 Dha	♒ Eric Menenez Fri 11-27-1970 23:23:00 Livingston, NJ, New Jersey USA Timezone: 5 DST: 0 Latitude: 40N47'45 Longitude: 74W18'55 Ayanamsha: -23:27:10 Lahiri		12th h.
6th h.	♑		♌ ☋ 04:00 Mag Asc 11:19 Mag 1st h.
	♐ ☽ 03:25 Anu ♆ 07:20 Anu ☉ 12:04 Anu ☿ 29:11 Jye	♍ ♂ 01:08 Cht ♀℞ 16:29 Swa ♃ 27:10 Vis	♎ ♀ 05:54 UPh ♅ 18:55 Has ♍
5th h.	4th h.	3rd h.	2nd h.

195

Eric Menendez with his brother Lyle conspired to murder their parents. After the murders they went on a spending spree as the parents were extremely wealthy in Beverly Hills CA. In his chart Neptune sits between the Sun and the Moon in Scorpio in the 4th house of the family. The dispositing planet of the Sun, Moon and Neptune is Mars which represents siblings and sits in the 3rd House of siblings.

Another lesson to be learned from this chart is that Mercury in the 4th House of family is Gandanta as it sits at 29 degrees of Scorpio. This represents an issue of losing control of the household and pertaining to family matters.

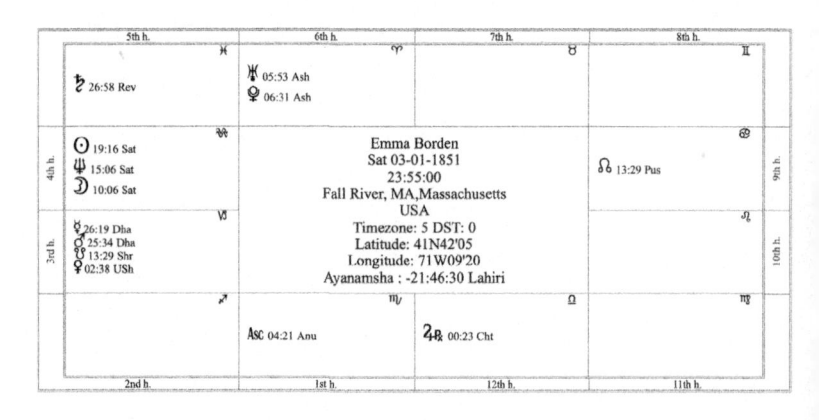

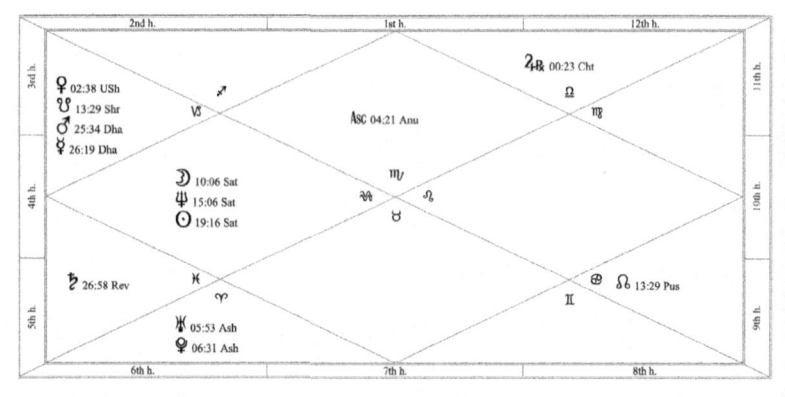

5th h.	6th h.	7th h.	8th h.
♄ 26:58 Rev	♅ 05:53 Ash ♀ 06:31 Ash		
☉ 19:16 Sat ♆ 15:06 Sat ☽ 10:06 Sat	Emma Borden Sat 03-01-1851 23:55:00 Fall River, MA, Massachusetts USA Timezone: 5 DST: 0 Latitude: 41N42'05 Longitude: 71W09'20 Ayanamsha : -21:46:30 Lahiri	☊ 13:29 Pus	
☿ 26:19 Dha ♂ 25:34 Dha ☋ 13:29 Shr ♀ 02:38 USh			
	Asc 04:21 Anu	♃ 00:23 Cht	
2nd h.	1st h.	12th h.	11th h.

Emma Borden along with her sister Lizzie were also involved in the murder of their parents. And in their case, they went to trial and got off with the not guilty charge, but later the maid admitted seeing the murder. Again Neptune, the planet of delusions and deception sits between the Sun and the Moon in the 4th house of the family.

In her third house of siblings, sits Mars exalted in Capricorn but conjunct Ketu which can cause injury and loss, this is a very difficult combination relating to siblings. The nakshatra the Sun, Moon, and Neptune sit in is called Shatabisha which can indicate hard to cure diseases such as mental disease.

Planets involved with Neptune can represent delusional behavior involving scandals, deceit, and illusions.

Chapter 19

Shastastaka
(6/8 Relationship)

- unfortunate relationship
- quincunx in western astrology
- life chaanging events
- combination of the 6th and 8th house
- 6th house: accidents
- 8th house change or transformations, extreme result is death

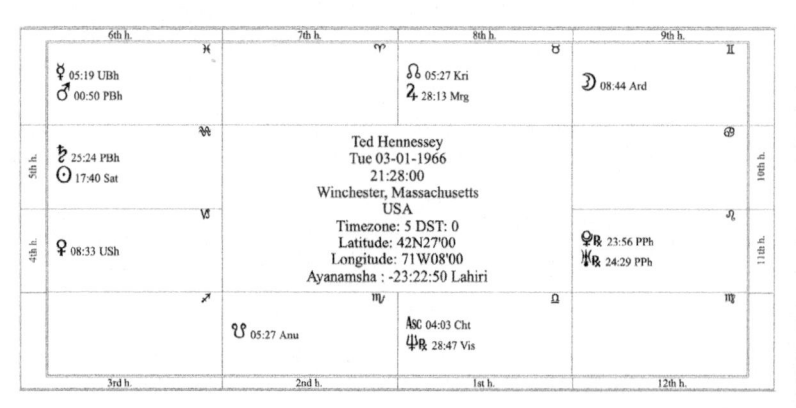

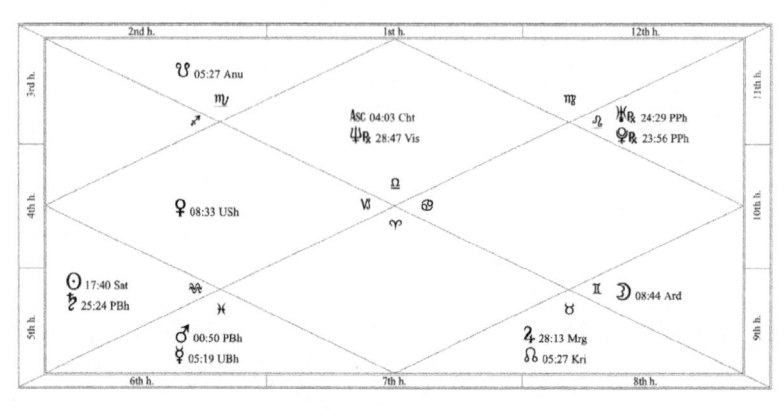

American Airlines Flight 11

Ted Hennessey was a passenger on American Airlines flight 11 that crashed into the World Trade Center on September 11, 2001.

The aspect most associated with life changing events that involve accidents and death is shashtaka (6 and 8 relationship between two planets), also called the quincunx in Western astrology.

In Hennessey's birth chart Venus is exactly 8 signs/houses from his Moon. If you count from Venus back to the natal moon it is six houses or signs away, this is the quincunx or shashtaka in astrology, 8/6 or 6/8 relationship.

At the time of the crash on September 11th, 2001, transiting Mars and Ketu were at 8 degrees of Sagittarius exactly opposing his Natal Moon at 8 degrees of Gemini. Mars and Ketu are known to represent injury and accidents. Transiting Mars and Ketu were in the 3rd house in opposition to the Moon in the 9th house and both houses represent travel.

Natal Moon 8/6 Venus
Transiting Mars/Ketu: 8 degrees Sagittarius

6th h.	7th h.	8th h.	9th h.
♆ ︎ ♓ ♀ 07:03 UBh ♂ 03:08 PBh	♈	♉ ♅℞ 12:21 Ard	♊
☊ 25:49 PBh ♃ 23:38 PBh ☉ 12:33 Sat ☿ 01:01 Dha ♒	John Ogonowsky Sat 02-24-1951 23:03:00 Lowell, Massachusetts USA Timezone: 5 DST: 0 Latitude: 42N38'00 Longitude: 71W19'00 Ayanamsha: -23:10:33 Lahiri	♀℞ 25:04 Asl	♋
♑		♌ ☋ 25:49 PPh	
♐	♍ Asc 18:19 Swa	♎ ♄℞ 07:33 UPh ☽ 23:18 Has ♇℞ 26:01 Cht	♍
3rd h.	2nd h.	1st h.	12th h.

199

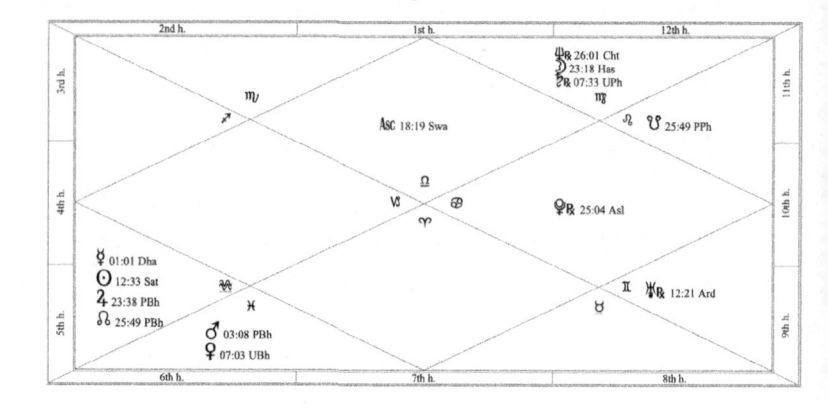

American Airlines Flight 11

Another passenger on American Airlines flight 11 was John Ogonowsky. In his birth chart the Moon and Jupiter are in an exact shashtaka 6/8 relationship. The Moon is at 23 degrees of Virgo six signs/houses from Jupiter which sits at 23 degrees of Aquarius, counting from Jupiter back to the Moon it is 8 signs/houses away, forming the Shashtaka or quincunx aspect 6/8. When individuals have this aspect in their birth chart, they are prone to accidents or injury.

On that tragic day September 11, 2001, transiting Mars was 8 degrees Sagittarius forming a full square aspect of Mars to natal Venus.

Transiting Saturn 20 degrees Taurus was in full third aspect to natal Jupiter, and it was in the 8th house of death aspecting Jupiter which ruled the 6th house of accidents.

Chapter 20

Dashas

The dasha calculation most used and discussed here is the Vimshottari Dasha system. The dashes are the planetary periods that represent our experiences throughout life. They are based on where the natal Moon sits according to its nakshatra. Each nakshatra is ruled by a planet and depending on the planet that rules the nakshatra of the natal Moon, this will be the dasha that begins the entire lifetime of the dasha cycles. For example, if the Moon is 20 degrees Leo, its nakshatra is Purva Phalguni, which is ruled by Venus, therefore the beginning life cycle begins in Venus maha dasha.

The sequential order that follows:

Venus, Sun, Moon, Mars, Rahu, Jupiter, Saturn, Mercury, Ketu

The maha dasha is the long main cycle that directs your life, it will give the big picture of life, but there are sub-cycles within the grand maha dasha, the 2nd level cycle, called the bhukti gives the more personal experience within the grand cycle. So, both the maha dasha and the bhukti are analyzed to understand what the life experience will be.

How maha dasha and bhukti are analyzed to predict life experience

Maha Dasha – big picture, like the country one lives in
Bhukti – personal experience, like home and personal life
Houses both planets are in are activated
Houses both planets rule are activated
Natal planets conjunct the dasha rulers are activated
Dasha ruling planets in the Divisional charts are activated

- Counting forward from the Maha dasha ruling planet to the bhukti reveals information about what the experiences will involve. This means the maha dasha ruling planet is counted as the beginning (like a new ascendant), then count the number of houses the bhukti is counting from the maha dasha ruling planet.

For example, If the individual is in the Jupiter maha dasha and the bhukti is Saturn, you would count the house that Jupiter is in as one, then count to where Saturn is from Jupiter. If Jupiter is in Pisces and Saturn is in Taurus, then counting from Jupiter, Saturn sits 3 signs/houses from Jupiter. This will give effects of 3rd house meanings, such as learning, travels and siblings, but counting back (always forward direction) from Saturn to Jupiter, they are 11 houses away, giving 11 house meanings, such as meeting groups, friends, and connections. This is a 3 and 11 spacial relationship. This process flavors the meanings of the cycles.

Chris Evert was the World Number 1 singles tennis player in 1974, 1975, 1976, 1977, 1978, 1980, and 1981.

When someone enters in a new maha dasha their life will change in accordance to how that planet is placed in their chart. This is always a big shift in life. Evert entered her Saturn maha dasha during the time that she made her world champion tennis accomplishments from 1974 to 1981. Saturn's maha dasha is 19 years, it was 1967 through 1986. She was in Saturn maha dasha and Venus bhukti 1974 through 1977 when she was the most successful.

Evert has both Saturn and Venus conjunct in her first house in Libra. Libra is the sign of Saturn's exaltation, while Venus is in its own sign of rulership. This indicates her great rise and success during this time. Both planets in the 1st house are a maha purusha yoga, Saturn is a Sasha yoga while Venus is a Malavya yoga. These two planets are incredibly powerful in the first house which represents the power of the individual. Furthermore, Saturn is the yoga karaka for Libra ascendant, as it rules the 4th and the 5th houses an angle/kendra and a trikona. The yoga karaka planet gives the power of a raja yoga to a single planet. This explains why the Saturn and Venus dasha brought her the greatest success.

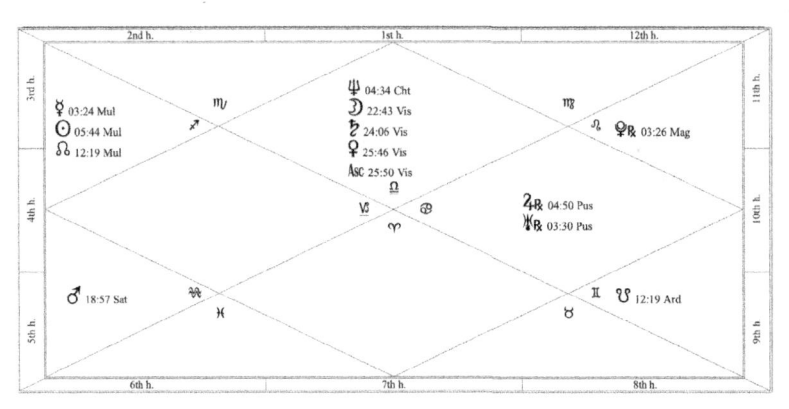

Dashas	Day	Begin date
♄ - ♄	Sat	09-16-1967
♄ - ☿	Sat	09-19-1970
♄ - ☋	Tue	05-29-1973
♄ - ♀	Mon	07-08-1974
♄ - ☉	Wed	09-07-1977
♄ - ☽	Sun	08-20-1978
♄ - ♂	Thu	03-20-1980
♄ - ☊	Wed	04-29-1981
♄ - ♃	Mon	03-05-1984

Maraka planets: Conor Clapton – Died in Jupiter Maha dasha Venus Bhukti

A Maraka planet is a planet that rules the 2nd and 7th houses as well as the planets that reside in the 2nd and the 7th houses. These planets are considered death inducing. When an individual is in the dashas of a Maraka planet it could be around the time of death. As we are in the dashas of Maraka planets many times and death does not occur, but at the time of death an individual is usually in a dasha that is a Maraka.

Conner Clapton, son of Eric Clapton, famous British rock star, was only four years old when he died. He accidentally fell from a high rise building in New York City.

This tragic event took place March 20th, 1991. He was in Jupiter's maha dasha and Venus' bhukti. In his natal chart Jupiter is in the 7th house and Venus is in the 2nd house, both houses are Maraka houses. Counting from Jupiter forward to Venus, they sit 8 signs/houses from each other. Since the 8th house is the house of death this is another indicator of this being a dangerous time that could be death inflicting.

8th h.	9th h.	10th h.	11th h.
☊ 28:28 Rev			
♃ɴ 26:47 PBh ☽ 22:47 PBh (7th h.)	Conor Clapton Thu 08-21-1986 06:20:00 London England		☿ 19:21 Asl (12th h.)
(6th h.)	Timezone: -1 DST: 0 Latitude: 51N30'00 Longitude: 00W10'00 Ayanamsha : -23:40:08 Lahiri	☉ 04:12 Mag ASC 07:33 Mag	(1st h.)
♂ 18:17 PSh ♆ɴ 09:31 Mul	♄ 09:33 Anu ♅ɴ 24:42 Jye	♀ 11:15 Swa	♀ 20:08 Has ☋ 28:28 Cht
5th h.	4th h.	3rd h.	2nd h.

Dashas

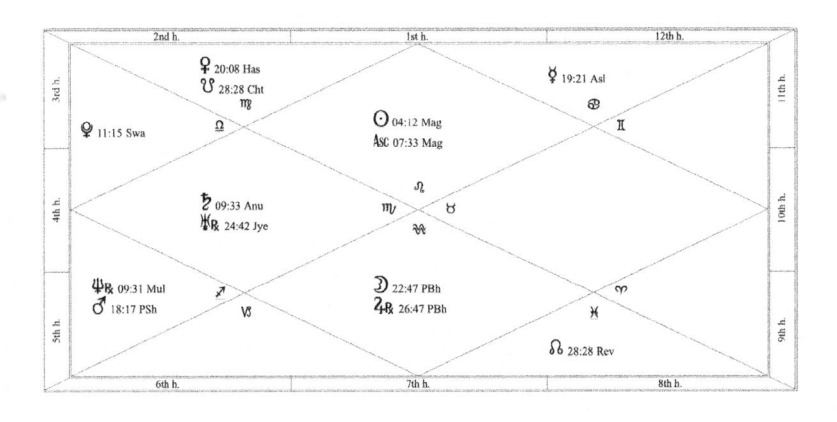

Chapter 20

```
                  2nd h.                    1st h.                  12th h.
          ♀ 20:08 Has              
          ☊ 28:28 Cht              ☿ 19:21 Asl
             ♍                        
                                       ⊕
  ♀ 11:15 Swa    ♎       ☉ 04:12 Mag              ♊
                         ASC 07:33 Mag
                              ♌
          ♄ 09:33 Anu       ♍   ♉
          ⛢℞ 24:42 Jye           ♒

  ♆℞ 09:31 Mul  ♐      ☽ 22:47 PBh         ♈
  ♂ 18:17 PSh           ♃℞ 26:47 PBh
              ♑                          ♓
                                ☋ 28:28 Rev
                  6th h.         7th h.          8th h.
```

Dashas	Day	Begin date
♃ - ♀	Fri	02-22-1991
♃ - ☉	Sat	10-23-1993
♃ - ☽	Thu	08-11-1994
♃ - ♂	Mon	12-11-1995
♃ - ☊	Sat	11-16-1996
♄ - ♄	Mon	04-12-1999
♄ - ☿	Mon	04-15-2002
♄ - ☋	Thu	12-23-2004
♄ - ♀	Tue	01-31-2006

Rahu 7th from planets: Rahu Dasha changes in relationships

Another interesting variable to be considered when looking at the maha dasha and the bhukti planet is when they are in opposition to each other. Counting from the maha dasha to the bhukti planet as they sit in the 7th house from each other these particular time frames will be indicative of relationships. When counting from the maha dasha ruling planet to the bhukti, if the bhukti planet is a natural benefic then at this time it indicates a possible new relationship or marriage, and if the bhukti planet is a natural malefic, it can represent the ending of a relationship. This very important concept is a powerful predictor for the beginning or ending of relationships based on the dasha and bhukti periods.

In the chart of actor Brad Pitt, it was during his Rahu maha dasha that he had a series of relationships. He was involved initially with Gwyneth Paltrow, then Jennifer Aniston, and then Angelina Jolie. Rahu sits opposite five planets and indicates the on and off time period of these relationships. Once he was in the marriage to Jolie, he then began to have children with her. During this time, he was in Jupiter's maha dasha. When an individual goes into Jupiter's maha dasha if they are in childbearing years, this is the time of having children. Furthermore, his Jupiter sits in the 5th house of children and rules the 5th house too. Through the understanding of the maha dashas and bhuktis one can predict the timing of marriage as well as having children in a lifetime.

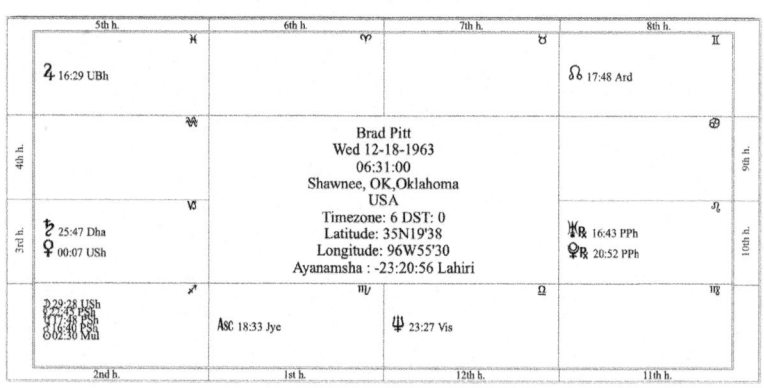

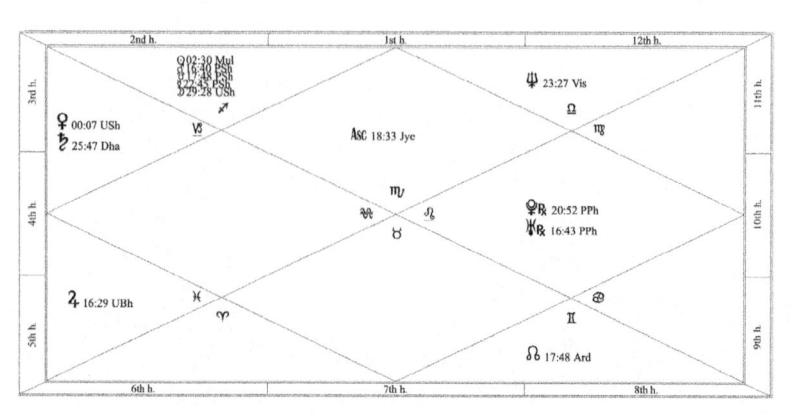

Dashas	Day	Begin date
☊ - ☿	Mon	08-23-1993
☊ - ☋	Tue	03-12-1996
☊ - ♀	Sun	03-30-1997
☊ - ☉	Thu	03-30-2000
☊ - ☽	Wed	02-21-2001
☊ - ♂	Fri	08-23-2002
♃ - ♃	Thu	09-11-2003
♃ - ♄	Sat	10-29-2005
♃ - ☿	Sun	05-11-2008

Here are some special features to remember when analyzing dashas. I have come to discover very specific events that occur during a certain maha dasha regardless of what houses they rule or are in.

Special Features of Dashas

- End of Jupiter dasha, which is Jupiter- overestimate- major expansion

    When someone is at the end of the Jupiter maha dasha the bhukti is Rahu, the individual will experience expansion and extremes within their life.

- Born in Ketu dasha- can indicate illness or problems in the family. When an individual is born into the Ketu cycle many times, they will experience illness as a baby, or the family or parents experience a difficult time around the individual's birth.

- End of Rahu-turbulent, Rahu/Mars

    Many individuals experience a very turbulent time when they are in Rahu maha dasha and Mars bhukti. This ends the 18-year cycle of Rahu, and it's said to be in many cases very difficult.

- Entrance into Rahu maha dasha – major changes, moves

When an individual enters Rahu's maha dasha most every aspect of life will change. It can indicate changes in relationships, careers and most importantly many times there will be a major change in residence.

- Rahu maha dasha and Venus bhukti or Venus maha dasha Rahu bhukti: Men meet their marriage partner or lover

  When an individual enters Venus' maha dasha and Rahu bhukti or Rahu maha dasha and Venus bhukti this can be an indication of a very intense relationship especially in a man's chart. As Venus represents the wife in a man's chart. Another interesting indication is when someone enters Venus maha dasha this can also be the time of marriage or relationship.

- If a planet is tightly conjunct Rahu or Ketu that planet will be greatly influenced. The planet will be magnetized and greatly exaggerated by the conjunction of Rahu. The same result will come when a planet is tightly conjunct Ketu. If the planet is a natural benefic it will produce good and positive results. But if the planet conjunct Rahu or Ketu is a natural malefic it will produce very difficult damaging results, especially when the individual is in the dasha of the planet tightly conjunct Rahu or Ketu.

- The divisional charts can be used with the dashas for prediction. When in a maha dasha or bhukti that is in the first house or the house that is most associated with the divisional chart, it can bring forth an event in accordance with what the divisional chart is good for. For example, if someone enters Saturn's maha dasha and Saturn is in the 10th or the 1st house of the D10 (Dashamsha chart) then this predicts activities relative to what the D10 chart is used for, which is career and purpose. If someone enters Jupiter's maha dasha and Jupiter is in the first house or the 5th House of the D7 (Saptamsha chart) then events concerning having children will occur during this time. Also, since the (D9) navamsha is used to predict marriage, if an individual enters a dasha or bhukti that is in either the first or the 7th House of the navamsha chart this is an indicator for a marriage or relationship.

- To tell if an individual is truthful or untruthful the 9th house, 9th house ruler, and Jupiter should be assessed. If the 9th house ruler is in the 8th house it is afflicted and or and if malefic planets aspect the 9th house or the 9th house ruler, or if natal Jupiter is afflicted by its house, sign or aspected by malefics. All these accounts would represent someone that is not truthful. If benefics aspects the 9th house, 9th house ruler and Jupiter, then the person tells the truth.

Transits during a maha dasha and bhukti

- The most important rule of a dasha and bhukti is that when in these dashas, the maha dasha ruling planet and bhukti ruling planet's transiting planet is more powerful at that time, and the natal planet of both the maha dasha ruler and bhukti is more important when hit by a transit. For example: If the individual is in Saturn maha dasha and Venus bhukti then the transits of both Saturn and Venus are more important while in those dasha ruling planets. Natal Saturn and Venus when hit by transits have a more powerful effect during their dashas.

- Rahu in a chart represents the future while Ketu in a chart represents the past. When transiting Rahu aspects a natal planet it will bring new things into life, but as Ketu aspects a planet it can bring people or things from the past. For example, if Ketu aspects a planet in the 7th House of relationship it could bring back an old relationship or memories of an old relationship.

- When the transit of Rahu conjuncts natal Ketu, and transiting Ketu conjuncts natal Rahu, I call this a nodal inversion. During this transit, the individual will go through a time of confusion not knowing what direction to go. But when Rahu and Ketu return to their natal positions every 18 1/2 years the individual is reminded of their purpose and their destiny and knows the right direction to move towards. The nodal inversion occurs nine years after the nodal return.

Chapter 21

Prediction with Transits

This very simple technique may be all you need to make astounding predictions no matter if you do Western tropical astrology or Vedic sidereal astrology. It is all the same because it involves numbers and not any system of astrology. You may not even need the time of birth, only the day and year of birth.

I am a Vedic sidereal astrologer but did Western astrology prior to Vedic for 20 years. The main reason why Western and Vedic astrology works in the same way is because the aspects are the same, meaning when a transiting planet aspects a natal planet in the birth chart it will happen at the same time, regardless of if you are using the sidereal or tropical system. In Western astrology the transits are 23 degrees backwards in the zodiac, but so are the natal planets. When transiting Saturn conjoins the natal Sun it happens in both systems. If the Sun is at 15 degrees Scorpio in Western astrology and Saturn transits over the Sun at 15 degrees Scorpio, then in Vedic sidereal astrology the Sun sits about 23 degrees backwards in the zodiac at 22 degrees Libra and the transit of Saturn which is also 23 degrees backwards in the zodiac will be conjoining the Sun also at 22 degrees Libra. The point is, that the zodiac is 23 degrees backwards in the zodiac due to the procession of the equinoxes. This is because of the procession of the equinoxes that the actual placements of the constellations and stars have moved. They move backwards 1 degree every 72 years, this movement is continual, and takes about 26,000 years to go through all 12 signs of the zodiac. This movement gives the sideral placements of the planets relative to the stars/signs. These placements are the true placements astronomically.

Aside from all this, you will not be focused on the signs or houses, just the number of placements of the planets to each other. But there must be an understanding of the numbers and the planets.

The planets will be connected by the exact degree, and you must know what the planets symbolize or represent, and what the numbers relative to the meanings of the houses represent. The exact degree is the most intense but the range of orb I allow is 3 degrees. So, we are looking at within only 3 degrees, but the more exact the more powerful.

I realized this technique from the use of the dashas in Vedic astrology as we look to the maha dasha ruling planet as the new ascendant, then count from that planet to the sub cycle planet (bhukti) and the number of houses gives the effect. The same principle is used here with the transiting planet to the natal planet.

Examples below will prove this technique.

Another very important variable that must be understood is that when a slow-moving planet aspects a natal planet due to the retrograde process the natal planet will be hit by the slow moving planet three times. The back-and-forth crossing gives three opportunities for events to occur. This happens with the three outer planets Uranus, Neptune and Pluto within a year or more. This also happens with transiting Jupiter and Saturn, but not always with these two planets.

Also, there may be three crossings of the faster transiting planets, Mercury, Venus, and Mars when they are retrograde. If a natal planet is within the degrees these faster moving planets are retrograde the natal planet will be aspected by their transit three times. This will indicate an event in accordance with the planet's energy and of course the houses they occupy and rule.

Another very important variable is the degrees a planet stations will most definitely activate an event if it stations on a natal planet. This will activate the house they are in most.

What the Planets Represent

Sun: Physical body, spirit, ego, father, yourself

Moon: Personal, feelings, emotions, mind, awareness, public, mother

Mercury: Intelligence, communication skills, travel, learning, connections

Venus: Love, beauty, relationships, creativity, attraction

Mars: Action, aggression, anger, accidents, war, weapons, fire

Jupiter: Opportunities, expansion, luck, fortune, excess

Saturn: Endings, contraction, death, discipline, depression

Uranus: Sudden unexpected, accidents, excitement

Neptune: Deception, deceit, denial, foggy vision, drugs

Pluto: Change, transformation, death, control, manipulation

Rahu: Very extreme for good or bad, can be extreme gains or death and sudden negative events

Ketu: Usually always bad and represents losses

Planets that are malefic and cause endings, loss, accidents and death are Mars, Saturn, Uranus, Neptune, Pluto, Rahu and Ketu.

The planets that attract positive events, gains and opportunities are Jupiter, Venus, Mercury and Uranus.

Another important variable to consider is the movement of the planets when in transit, in other words their rate of speed.

The slower a planet moves the more important and powerful it is to create an event. When they are retrograde, they are even more powerful because their rates of speed are slower. Remember the slower a planet moves the more powerful it is. When a planet stations to go retrograde or direct it almost stands still as it shifts directions. This is called a station, and a planet at its station is more powerful. These stationing degrees of all planets must be noted. They have a much more powerful effect on the natal planets that they aspect in transit. Also when a planet is retrograde it brings up things from the past, as they are moving backwards, Mercury past memories, Venus past relationships, and Mars past angers.

Planet's Speed

Moon: Changes sign every 2 ½ days takes 28 days to transit through all 12 signs

Mercury: Changes signs about every 28 days and transits through all 12 signs in one year with the Sun.

Venus: Changes signs about every 28 days and transits through all 12 signs in about one year with the Sun.

Sun: Moves one degree every day and changes signs each month taking I year to transit through all 12 signs. Mercury and Venus transit around the Sun from our vantage point, their orbit is inferior to the earth and orbit with the Sun.

Mars: Changes signs about every 2 months, and transits through all 12 signs every 2 years.

Jupiter: Changes signs in 1 year and transits through all 12 signs in about 12 years.

Saturn: Changes sign every 2 ½ years and transits through all 12 signs in about 28–30 years

Uranus: Changes sign every 7 years and transits through the entire zodiac every 84 years

Neptune: Changes sign every 12 years and transits through the zodiac every 260 years

Pluto: Has an elliptical orbit and stays in a sign from 12 to 30 years and takes about 244 years to transit through the entire zodiac.

From this you can see from fastest to slowest planets which ones are going to deliver a much more powerful punch when they aspect the natal planets. But to know when an event will truly happen you want to see more than one planet involved in a transiting aspect.

The houses are very extensive in meaning and all these meanings can be relative to the numbers of the houses. But one thing to always remember is that the planets are connected by the transits whenever the transiting planet is the same degree as the natal planet. Counting from the transiting planet to the natal planet when they are both the same degree this always connects the planets and the meanings of both the planets. For example, if transiting Mars is 12 degrees Scorpio and natal Sun is 12 degrees Gemini then they are connected because they are the same degree. Mars is the planet of action and aggression, and the Sun can represent the physical body, then there is intense energy towards the physical person, possibly even an accident.

But Mars is a faster moving planet, and this aspect happens every two years and we are not in an accident every two years. So, what to look for is when there are more than one of these exact aspects occurring around the same time then we can make a prediction that something will happen at this time.

Next the numbers are the consideration. Remember you are counting from the transiting planet as number one, regardless of what house it occupies. Therefore, it doesn't matter what house system Vedic or Western you are using. But make sure you are looking from sidereal to sidereal or tropical to tropical. We will be using sidereal in this book. Plus, besides just noting the planets, transiting and natal then the number they are located from each other we will also add in the meanings of the houses they are in in the Vedic sidereal charts, but this is not necessary, it is just added information for more details. I prefer the Vedic system for detail and accuracy.

Prediction with transits

Use in the same way you do with the dashas, meaning the transiting planet is the beginning or 1st house (ascendant) and the natal planet it aspects by exact degree, the number of houses the natal planet is placed from the transiting planet gives the clue as to what will occur. When an event occurs the exact degrees of planets must be observed.

Counting from the transiting planet to the natal planet

1/1 focus on the self and physical body

2/12 losses and gains possible from the losses

3/11 monetary gains as in the 11 house, drive ambition courage, getting known, communications

4/10 action, career

5/9 luck, creativity and procreation – children

6/8 death and accidents

7/7 marriage and relationships

The examples used here will convince you that this is the easiest and most accurate system for prediction available. Remember there must be more than one major transit to predict a major life changing event.

Events that predict accidents and death

These events involve the natural malefics with the 6/8 or 8/6 relationship.

Prediction with Transits

Chapter 21

Let me show you how it works!

4th h.	5th h.	6th h.	7th h.
☊ 03:27 UBh	☽ 17:47 Bha		
3rd h.	Koby Bryant Wed 08-23-1978 17:00:00 Harrisburg, Pennsylvania USA Timezone: 5 DST: 1 Latitude: 40N03'20 Longitude: 75W01'31 Ayanamsha : -23:33:32 Lahiri		♃ 03:57 Pus ☿℞ 28:12 Asl 8th h.
2nd h.			☉ 06:48 Mag ♄ 09:56 Mag 9th h.
Asc 16:21 PSh	♆℞ 21:59 Jye	♅ 19:14 Swa	☊ 03:27 UPh ♂ 18:43 Has ♀ 21:18 Has ♀ 22:47 Has
1st h.	12th h.	11th h.	10th h.

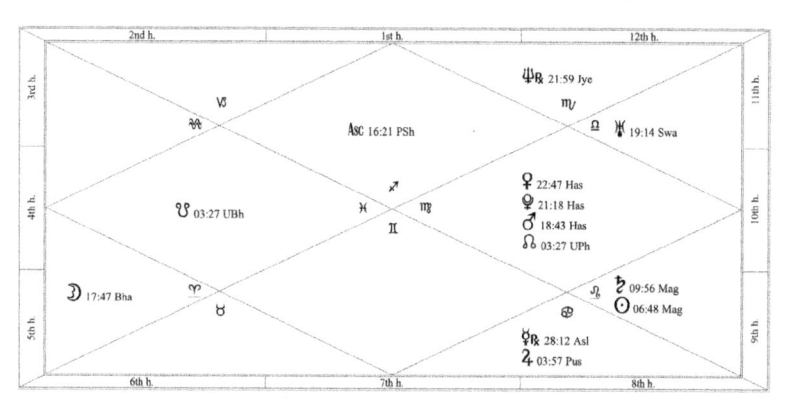

Death

Asc	11:14:55		Pis
☉	12:05:37		Cap
☽	02:50:30		Aqu
♂	21:40:26		Sco
☿	22:54:58	c	Cap
♃	18:22:56		Sag
♀	21:30:17		Aqu
♄	00:17:58	c	Cap
☊	14:04:24		Gem
☋	14:04:24		Sag
♅	08:37:24		Ari
♆	22:46:50		Aqu
♀	29:06:40		Sag

217

January 26, 2020, Bryant was on his way to a youth basketball game with his daughter Gianna Bryant, who was 13, when the helicopter crashed. Los Angeles County Sheriff Alex Villanueva said in a news conference that there were no survivors, and according to the flight manifest, there were nine people on board the helicopter.

On that fateful day transiting Neptune was 22 degrees Aquarius and Kobe's natal Pluto is 21 Virgo and Venus is 22 Virgo counting forward in clockwise motion from transiting Neptune to Venus/Pluto they are 8 placements exactly from each other. The number 8 relates to the 8th house of death. Neptune rules fog and not seeing clearly, and it was fog that caused the crash. Furthermore, transiting Mars was exactly 21 degrees Scorpio exactly conjunct natal Neptune. In the chart transiting Mars conjoins Neptune in the 12th house of loss and endings. There is more, transiting Pluto was 29 degrees Sagittarius and Mercury is 28 degrees Cancer within 1 degree orb of exact and Mercury is 8 placements away from Pluto. And lastly, transiting Ketu representing loss was 2 degrees off the 16-degree ascendant and Ketu was 14 degrees Sagittarius.

Transiting Mars was 21 degrees Scorpio while conjunct natal Neptune was also aspecting Pluto and Venus at 21 and 22 Virgo. They are connected by the exact degrees, counting from Mars to Pluto/Venus they are 11 placements away, counting back from Venus/Pluto Mars sits at 3 placements. Their relationship is 11/3 pertains to travel and Mars in the 12th is about loss.

With so many detrimental aspects indicating death occurring on that day you wonder if Kobe knew this information if the accident could have been prevented. I would like to believe so, but sometimes things are fated. We can be more cautious and not take risks especially when so many aspects like this are occurring in this time frame.

Prediction with Transits Chapter 21

He was in dasha Rahu/Saturn and Saturn sits in the 12th house of loss from Rahu.

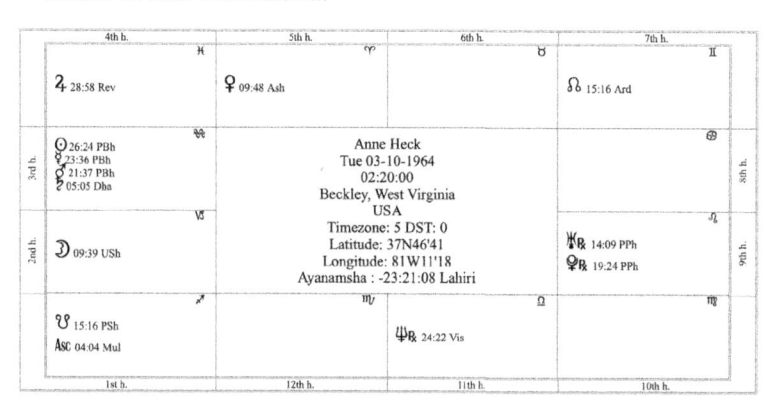

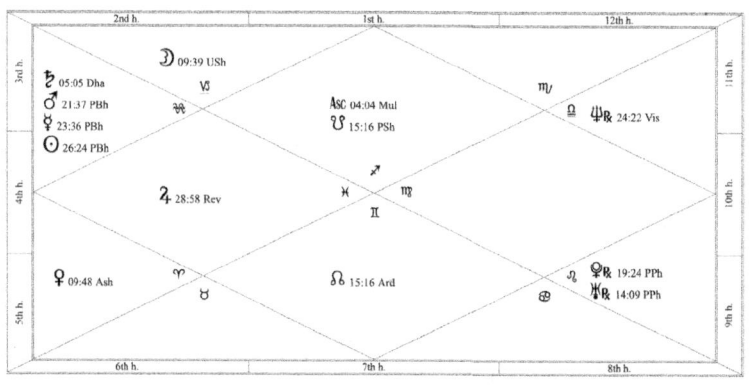

	4th h.	5th h.	6th h.	7th h.
	♃ 28:58 Rev ⊬	♀ 09:48 Ash ♈	♉	☊ 15:16 Ard ♊
3rd h.	☉ 26:24 PBh ☿ 23:36 PBh ♂ 21:37 PBh ♅ 05:05 Dha ♒	Anne Heck Tue 03-10-1964 02:20:00 Beckley, West Virginia USA Timezone: 5 DST: 0 Latitude: 37N46'41 Longitude: 81W11'18 Ayanamsha : -23:21:08 Lahiri		8th h.
2nd h.	☽ 09:39 USh ♑		♆R 14:09 PPh ♇R 19:24 PPh ♌	9th h.
	☋ 15:16 PSh Asc 04:04 Mul ♐	♏	♃R 24:22 Vis ♎	♍
	1st h.	12th h.	11th h.	10th h.

Accident		
Asc	25:01:38	Aqu
☉	19:29:39	Can
☽	27:55:22	Lib
♂	27:10:18	Ari
☿	08:52:51	Leo
♃	14:26:07 R	Pis
♀	28:56:30	Gem
♄	28:22:13 R	Cap
☊	24:12:19	Ari
☋	24:12:19	Lib
♅	24:36:36	Ari
♆	00:53:14 R	Pis
♇	02:47:08 R	Cap

Famous actor Anne Heche's car crashed into a Los Angeles home and erupted into flames on August 5, 2022. After the accident, Heche experienced a "severe anoxic brain injury," depriving her brain of oxygen following the crash. She died August 11, 2022, after being taken off life support.

Use in the same way you do with the dashas, meaning the transiting planet is the beginning or first house and the natal planet it aspects by exact degree, the number of houses the natal planet is placed from the transiting planet gives the clue as to what will occur. When an event occurs the exact degrees of planets must be observed.

On that fated day of the accident August 5, 2022, transiting Saturn was 28 degrees Capricorn aspecting natal Jupiter at 28 degrees Pisces. This is the full Vedic aspect of Saturn (Saturn's special aspects which are 3 and 10 signs from Saturn). Regardless of the aspect is the same degree – 3 signs/houses away pertain to traveling, indicating problems with travel. Transiting Saturn and natal Jupiter are 3/11 spacial relationship.

Transiting Mars (planet of accidents) was 27 degrees Aries, it is one degree from the natal Sun at 26 degrees Aquarius and the Sun is 11 placements from transiting Mars (11/3). The 3rd house represents travel. It is also one degree from natal Jupiter at 28 degrees Pisces, they are in a 12/2 relationship, indicating the 12th house of loss.

Transiting Uranus and Rahu were conjunct at 24 degrees Aries aspecting both natal Mercury and Sun within a three-degree orb also in a 11/3 spacial relationship, indicating problems with travel. Another very specific aspect of the slower moving planets is that Ketu at 24 degrees Libra is exactly on natal Neptune. Transiting Uranus and Rahu are opposed natal Neptune exactly. So, the energy of these planets must be considered regardless of the houses. This means the planet's meanings are connected and activated. Rahu expands and activates the meanings of Uranus, which rules unexpected sudden events such as accidents and both aspect Neptune which rules fog, lack of clarity and many times drug induced events, as she had issues with drugs and alcohol.

She was in Saturn's maha dasha and Venus bhukti. Saturn and Venus are in a 3/11 spacial relationship, which could be indicative of problems with travel again. Saturn by its ownership of the 2nd house is a Maraka, plus three malefics Saturn, Mars and Sun are in the 3rd house of travel and they surround natal Mercury which is the planet of traveling especially by car. Venus the bhukti also rules the 6th house of accidents. So, this was not a favorable maha dasha – bhukti.

The most important rule of a dasha and bhukti is that when in these cycles the maha dasha ruling planet and bhukti ruling planet's transiting planet is more powerful at that time and the natal planets of both the maha dasha ruler and bhukti is more important when hit by a transit.

Considering the rule of the activation of the bhukti Venus, transiting Venus was 28 degrees Gemini in a 10/4 relationship with Jupiter. Not a bad spacial relationship but Venus being ruler of the 6th house is not a good planet for Sagittarius ascendant, and the bhukti timing activates Venus' transit all the more.

This combination of transits with dashas was not good for travel or physical well-being at this time.

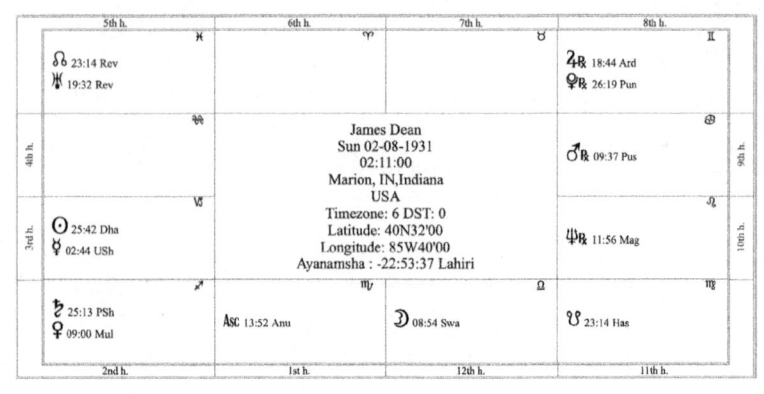

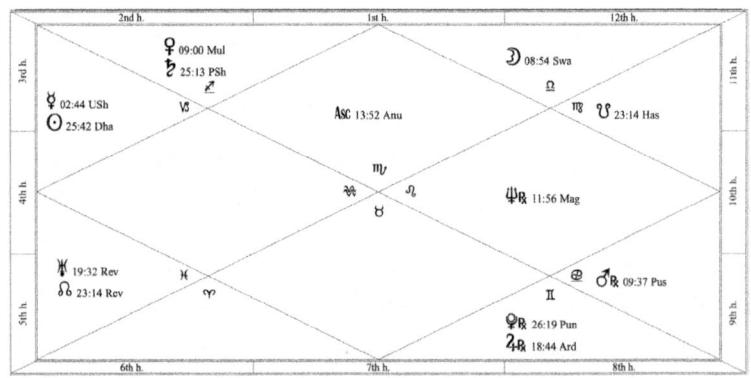

Astrologer's Secrets — My best Tools and Techniques

James Dean
Sun 02-08-1931
02:11:00
Marion, IN, Indiana
USA
Timezone: 6 DST: 0
Latitude: 40N32'00
Longitude: 85W40'00
Ayanamsha : -22:53:37 Lahiri

North Indian chart positions

- 5th h.: ☊ 23:14 Rev, ♅ 19:32 Rev
- 8th h.: ♃℞ 18:44 Ard, ♀℞ 26:19 Pun
- 9th h.: ♂℞ 09:37 Pus
- 3rd h.: ☉ 25:42 Dha, ☿ 02:44 USh
- 10th h.: ♆℞ 11:56 Mag
- 2nd h.: ♄ 25:13 PSh, ♀ 09:00 Mul
- 1st h.: Asc 13:52 Anu
- 12th h.: ☽ 08:54 Swa
- 11th h.: ☋ 23:14 Has

Death

Asc	05:04:02	Tau
☉	13:54:33	Vir
☽	04:59:04	Pis
♂	28:51:18 c	Leo
☿	05:22:47	Lib
♃	29:55:46	Can
♀	21:54:25 c	Vir
♄	25:17:20	Lib
☊	27:01:52	Sco
☋	27:01:52	Tau
♅	08:26:22	Can
♆	03:57:40	Lib
♇	04:29:51	Leo

September 30, 1955, 24-year-old actor James Dean was killed when the Porsche he is driving hits a sedan at an intersection.

Only one of Dean's movies, "East of Eden," had been released at the time of his death ("Rebel Without a Cause" and "Giant" opened shortly afterward), but he was already on his way to superstardom—and the crash made him a legend.

James Dean was in Jupiter maha dasha and Venus bhukti. His Natal Jupiter sits in the 8th House of death next to Pluto, another indicator of death. Venus the bhukti ruler is in the 2nd house, a Maraka – death inflicting, is aspecting Natal Jupiter by opposition and it is in Sagittarius which is ruled by Jupiter. Therefore, as he is in this maha dasha and bhukti ruling planets, the transits of both Jupiter and Venus plus their natal positions are more powerful during this time.

At the time of the accident, transiting Mars was 28 degrees of Leo within a three-degree orb of Natal Saturn, Sun, and Pluto. Mars' connection to Saturn is always difficult. Mars' aspect to the Sun is in a 6/8 relationship, and Mars is aspecting Pluto in the 8th house of death.

Transiting Saturn was 25 degrees of Libra aspecting exactly natal Saturn, Sun and Pluto. Saturn is the planet that most represents death along with Pluto. Rahu was 27 degrees of Scorpio in an 8/6 relationship with Pluto in the 8th house.

Probably the most death-defying aspect of all is that transiting Uranus at 8 degrees of Cancer was sitting on natal Mars and aspecting natal Venus. Mars is debilitated in the 9th House of travel and Venus is the bhukti ruling planet and a Maraka which sits in a 6/8 spatial relationship from each other. The 6/8 relationships are the strongest indication of death through accidents. Uranus as well is one of the strongest indicators of an unexpected accident happening suddenly.

Furthermore, transiting Uranus exactly aspects the natal Moon from 8 degrees of Cancer to 8 degrees of Libra. His natal Moon is in the 12th house of endings and loss and is hard hit by Uranus as it is in an exact square aspect. In Dean's case so many accident-prone aspects were occurring it is evident something of this nature would occur.

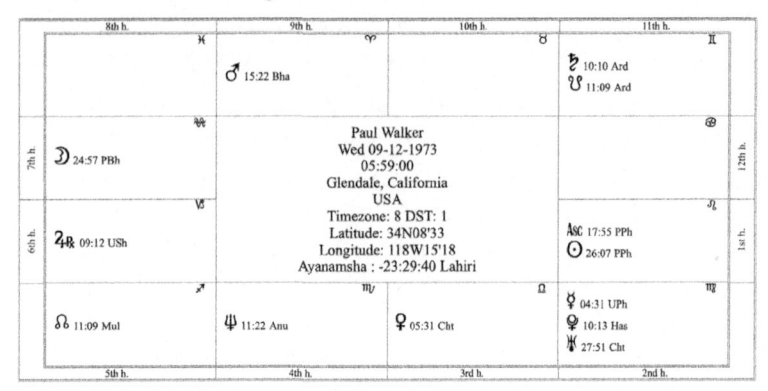

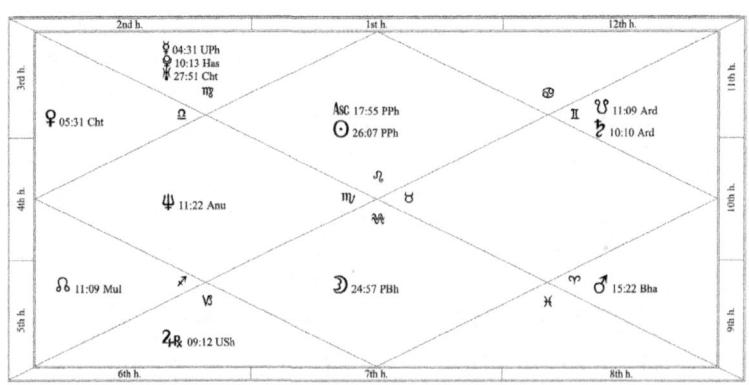

	8th h.	9th h.	10th h.	11th h.
7th h.		♂ 15:22 Bha		♄ 10:10 Ard ☋ 11:09 Ard
	☽ 24:57 PBh	Paul Walker Wed 09-12-1973 05:59:00 Glendale, California USA Timezone: 8 DST: 1 Latitude: 34N08'33 Longitude: 118W15'18 Ayanamsha: -23:29:40 Lahiri			12th h.
6th h.	♃ 09:12 USh			Asc 17:55 PPh ☉ 26:07 PPh	1st h.
	☊ 11:09 Mul	♆ 11:22 Anu	♀ 05:31 Cht	☿ 04:31 UPh ♀ 10:13 Has ♅ 27:51 Cht
	5th h.	4th h.	3rd h.	2nd h.

Death		
Asc	05:36:16	Leo
☉	15:07:15	Sco
☽	20:46:42	Lib
♂	02:28:42	Vir
☿	00:03:00	Sco
♃	25:30:36 R	Gem
♀	27:31:48	Sag
♄	23:06:16	Lib
☊	13:27:19	Lib
☋	13:27:19	Ari
♅	14:39:04 R	Pis
♆	08:36:45	Aqu
♀	16:09:46	Sag

Actor Paul Walker, who starred in the Fast & Furious series of action films, was killed in a car crash in California. Walker, 40, was a passenger in a Porsche sports car driven by a friend – who also died – when it crashed north of Los Angeles, November 30, 2013.

Walker was attending a charity event at the time when he jumped in for a quick test drive around the block when the unexpected accident occurred.

Walker was in Mercury maha dasha and Rahu bhukti. His Mercury is exalted in Virgo in the 2nd house, a Maraka, but is with both Pluto and Uranus which can indicate unexpected and possibly an untimely death. This is because during the time of his accident transiting Mars was within 3 degrees of natal Mercury. There were no exact same degree hits on his chart through transit, but they are within a three-degree orb which is very important to note.

Another very important transit concerns the bhukti ruler Rahu at 13 degrees of Libra within 3 degrees of Natal Mars. This means that transiting Ketu was conjunct Natal Mars in the 9th house which is a house of travel. This indicated a sudden loss.

Uranus which is the planet of accidents and sudden events was transiting at 14 degrees of Pisces in the 8th House of death which was in a 2/12 relationship with natal Mars. Remember no matter what the spatial relationship is, when the planets are connected within a three degree range the energy of the planets plays out and Mars is violence fire and accidents and is connected to Uranus which is also sudden accidents.

Transcending Neptune was 8 degrees Aquarius which was in a 2/12 relationship to natal Jupiter in the 6th house of accidents. Neptune rules things we cannot see or hidden as this event was something totally unexpected.

The final transit to be discussed is transiting Pluto was 16 degrees of Sagittarius within a degree of natal Mars in the 9th house. Although they may be in a trine aspect and both reside in good houses 5th house and 9th house, the degree marking connects both planets and Pluto is the planet that rules death and major transitions and Mars can rule fire and accidents. I have seen the 3rd and the 9th house and their spatial aspects to indicate travel. This will be noted in the next chart of John Kennedy Jr.

One important note from this chart is that aspects may not be exact for extreme events to occur, so realize a three degree orb is the what has to be focused on.

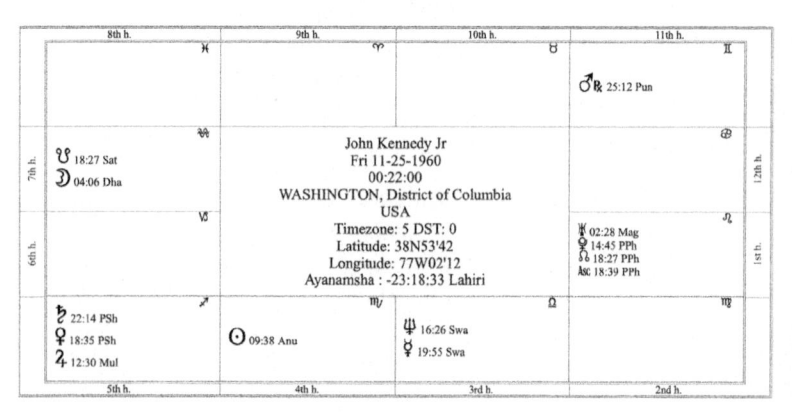

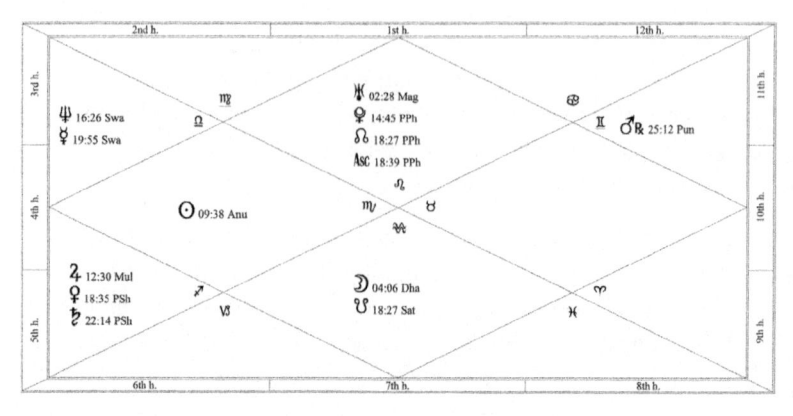

death		
Asc 09:49:08		Pis
☉ 00:19:53		Can
☽ 23:14:59		Leo
♂ 10:40:19		Lib
☿ 14:56:41	R	Can
♃ 08:45:34		Ari
♀ 08:21:29		Leo
♄ 21:41:53		Ari
☊ 19:10:58		Can
☋ 19:10:58		Cap
♅ 21:48:11	R	Cap
♆ 09:22:37	R	Cap
♇ 14:10:24	R	Sco

On July 16, 1999, John F. Kennedy, Jr.; his wife, Carolyn Bessette Kennedy; and her sister, Lauren Bessette, died when the single-engine plane that Kennedy was piloting crashed into the Atlantic Ocean near Martha's Vineyard, Massachusetts.

Kennedy was in Maha dasha Saturn and Mercury bhukti. On the day of his crash transcending Saturn was 21 degrees of Aries in his 9th house of travel aspecting natal Mercury which is his bhukti ruler in the 3rd house of traveling, plus Mercury is a planet that represents travels. So, he had both the transit of Saturn which was his maha dasha ruling planet making this transit more powerful aspecting natal Mercury, which when in a dasha of that natal planet produces bigger results when it is hit by a transiting planet.

Most importantly concerning the maha dasha and bhukti ruling planets, Mercury and Saturn are both Maraka planets, as Mercury rules the second house and Saturn rules the 7th house.

Transiting Mars was 10 degrees of Libra in a 2/12 relationship with natal Sun and Mars and was in the 3rd House of traveling. If we look at where bhukti ruling planet Mercury was transiting on that day, it was 14 degrees of Cancer in the 12th house of endings and loss.

Transiting Uranus was at 21 degrees of Capricorn in the 6th house of accidents aspecting natal Mercury within a three-degree orb and Saturn. Uranus and Saturn were in a 12/2 relationship, Saturn rules the 6th house of accidents.

Transiting Neptune which is a planet many times connected to death was 9 degrees of Capricorn in a 3/11 spatial relationship with the natal Sun at 9 degrees of Scorpio. Remember houses 3 and 9 commonly involve accidents dealing with traveling.

Concluding with these examples used, when there are many connections of planets within a three degree range regardless of their house location or spatial relationships these degree points simply connect the planets and what the planets energy concerns in combination. The connection of the two planets and their meanings result in the event. But there must be a group of events happening at the same time for a life changing event such as death to occur.

Chapter 22

Astrological realizations from my experiences

Sudarshan Chart, Bhava Chart, Declination and Out of Bounds, Aspects to the houses

- Sudarshan chart

    When looking at the birth chart not only is it important to assess the chart from the ascendant as to all the planets rulership's of houses and where they connect house to house, but remember it is so important to always look at a chart from the Moon as the ascendant, Chandra lagna. This gives the ability to see how an individual will feel about all aspects of their life. This means taking it in its entirety as the planets rule the houses and how they're all connected, there is no difference from looking at the chart from the natal Moon as the ascendant as looking at it from the birth rising sign or ascendant.

    Another ascendant that has great importance in viewing the birth chart is to look at the Sun as the ascendant. The Sun is our spirit and it has an important role when looking at career and work within our lives. When a chart is assessed from all three ascendants; Ascendant, Moon, and Sun, this is called the Sudarshan chart in Vedic astrology. Studying the chart from all three ascendants will give enormous depth and understanding to the individual's life and experiences.

    This means all the yogas in a chart must be assessed from all three ascendants looking at it from the ascendant, Moon, and Sun as the ascendant as these are the most important planets that must be assessed as the ascendant. When there is a yoga that is seen from all three ascendants you are guaranteed this yoga will produce enormous and powerful effects.

In reality, all the planets and houses can be viewed as an ascendant to further see the deeper intricacies in a chart, but for simplicity and to see the major points in a life the Ascendant, Moon, and Sun are enough, at least for now.

Realize also, in India they always emphasize that it is even more important to view the transiting planets from the Moon as the ascendant (Chandra Lagna) rather than the birth ascendant.

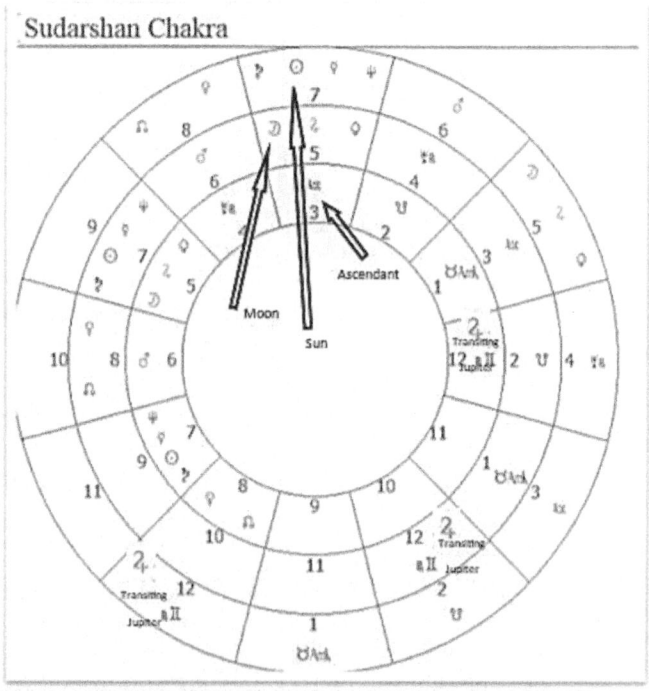

Sudarshan Chakra

If the transits are applied, you can see from the Sudarshan chart that a transit is in a different house simultaneously. For example, in this chart, if transiting Jupiter were applied today, (December 26, 2022) it would be in the 10th from the ascendant, 8th from the Moon and 6th from the sun.

- **Bhava chart**

    The bhava chart or sripati calculations do not use equal signs to a house. It uses the system closest to Placidus calculations in Western astrology. This means that some of the houses are longer and some are shorter depending on where the longitude and latitude is that a person is born on earth. If someone were born on the equator, then the houses would be equal but as they get into the northern or southern parts of the globe the houses will change in size. So, if the ascendant begins at a late degree of the sign, there will only be a portion of that sign in the first house. Sripati house system gives the same house cusps positions as the Western tropical astrology's Placidus system. I have seen this to work quite well, and I sometimes incorporate the house cusps according to this house system to get further details of how planets may affect certain houses. When someone's ascendant is on the cusp of changing signs, meaning it is the very end of a sign or very beginning of a sign, it is important to take note of this house system. The houses may have a variety of effects when they are on the cusp and can alter some meanings of the planets in accordance to what house they rule, but my experiences have been that both systems work.

- **Declination and out of bounds Planets**

Declination is the angular distance north or south from to the celestial equator, which is an extension of Earth's equator in the sky. The celestial equator divides the sky into the northern and southern hemispheres, just as Earth's equator does. The maximum possible declination of the Sun is 23 degrees 28' which occurs at the Solstices, when the Sun passes the Tropics (0 degree) of Cancer and Capricorn, the limit of the pole's greatest inclination from the plane of the Earth's orbit. The first degrees of Aries and Libra have no declination, since at these points the ecliptic intersects the equator. If it is north of the equator, it is positive and south of the equator it is negative. If planets are both aligned north or south of the equator, they are parallel, like a conjunction, but if they are aligned by degree and one is north and the other south, they are contra-parallel, like an opposition.

If planets are conjunct, this means they align according to longitude, but they may not line up according to latitude, which is declination. But when planets align in both longitude and latitude they are truly aligned and called an occultation, which is what occurs when there is a total eclipse. Natal planets that are both aligned in longitude and latitude give better results, but the transiting planets that align in this way also give much better results. The fact that a planet may be conjunct but not aligned in latitude as being parallel (means aligned by declination) may not give as powerful of effects and this is the reason why some transits miss their mark.

The main issue that I wanted to point out is that when a planet exceeds the maximum declination of 23 degrees 28 minutes the planet is considered out of bounds. Therefore, any planet that exceeds this degree mark is out of bounds. Out of bounds planets represent that their energy is out of control, in some way exceeds and stretches the limits in a normal way.

Planets in a birth chart whose declination is beyond 24 degrees are considered out of bounds and the definitions of what this planet represents will be extreme and out of control. The most important use of out of bounds planets is when we look at the transiting planets. When a transiting planet is out of bounds its energy will be extreme and out of control, for example whenever Mars exceeds 24 degrees it will produce violent and angry effects on planet Earth. So out of bounds planets can be looked at in terms of natal planets in a birth chart that are out of bounds as well as transiting planets that are out of bounds. This is a very important variable to be considered when looking at charts. For example, Mars was way out of bounds at the time of September 11, 2001. This played into the out-of-control event that caused the 9/11 attack.

Below is the chart of where the planet's declination was on September 11, 2001. Notice the declination degree of Mars-out of bounds. Mars' declination is South at -26:47:56. This is about the max a planet can be out of bounds, which a planet is considered out of bounds beyond when more than 23 degrees 28. The minus means it is south of the celestial equator; the ones without the minus are north.

Declination

Planet	Degree	Declination
Sun	144:58:09	04:24:49
Moon	64:11:33	22:58:51
Mars	247:33:59	-26:47:56
Mercury	170:24:40	-07:12:35
Jupiter	77:42:48	22:44:03
Venus	114:31:29	15:47:41
Saturn	50:52:32	20:47:17
Rahu	69:13:27	23:24:10
Uranus	297:57:43	-14:56:36
Neptune	282:28:00	-18:33:34
Pluto	228:45:41	-12:12:01

Aspects to a house

It is important to always recognize the Vedic aspects. The planets aspect not only the planets but the houses.

Here are the 100% in power Vedic aspects

All the planets aspect by the conjunction and opposition meaning in the same sign/house or opposing a sign/house.

But Mars, Jupiter, Saturn and Rahu and Ketu have special aspects as well.

Mars special aspects are four and eight signs/houses from its position.

Saturn special aspects are three and ten signs/houses from its position.

Jupiter's special aspects are five and nine signs/houses from its position.

Both Rahu and Ketu also aspect by five and nine signs/houses from its position just like Jupiter.

This is important to know the aspects because if a house or a planet is aspected by 2 natural malefic planets it is said to be afflicted and the house being aspected will have problems. But, if there are three natural malefics aspecting a house it will have severe problems concerning what that house rules. Such as if the 5th house is aspected by three malefic planets there will be issues with having children.

Likewise, if two or more natural benefic planets aspect a planet or a house that house is empowered for the good that it can produce in a person's life. Furthermore, when a planet aspects a house and the sign ruling that house happens to be the sign that planet rules, then the aspect will empower that house for the good that that house concerns. For example, if Mars aspects the second house and the 2nd house sign is either Aries or Scorpio which are ruled by Mars then Mars is aspecting a house that it rules which will empower that house for what it is good for, and the second house means Mars will empower the individual to make more money.

Chapter 23

Final Interesting Clues

Listed below are some very interesting findings I have practiced repeatedly to test the results over the years. Because these are some of my tried and true findings, I thought it valuable to share.

- Transiting Saturn on Ascendant can indicate the timing of the death of the mother.

- Both Mars and Saturn on Ascendant at the time of birth indicate problems at birth, baby or mother may almost die in childbirth, difficulty around time of birth.

- When transiting Jupiter is in the 3rd house before entering into the 4th house, individuals may move to a new house. As Jupiter is transiting the 4th house they are settling into a new home. Because the 3rd house is the 12th house from the 4th. Transits in the 3rd house can also indicate loss of parents.

- When you lose things during Mercury retrograde, you will find them.

- Strong and powerful Saturn in the birth chart and navamsha indicates the second part of life is better than the first half. Life is better when older.

- When the Moon is in the 5th house the individual usually has one child and it's a girl.

- Planets in the 11th house reflect the mother's mental health and death. Don't forget the 11th house is also the eldest sibling too. Transits of malefics here can indicate the death of the mother or the eldest sibling.

- The 2nd house is also a house of family affairs, but when malefics transit this house, it can represent divorce because it is the 8th house from the 7th, death of the marriage.

- The 8th house represents the marriage partner's wealth or money because it is the 2nd house from the 7th house. Natural benefics make them wealthy and natural malefic make them bad with money, maybe gamblers.

- The 2nd house represents the wealth from the previous house: 10th house is the father's wealth, 6th house is the children's wealth, 5th house is the mother's wealth, 4th house sibling's wealth.

- The 12th house represents foreign lands and countries, therefore traveling to foreign places. When transiting Jupiter is in the 12th house the individual will travel to foreign lands. The 12th house also represents the past, and issues will emerge concerning the past when planets transit here, malefics will bring hurtful memories and benefics happy memories.

- The first house represents the individual themselves and their ego and stamina, but it also may represent accidents to the individual or the death of a pet when malefics transit here as it is the 8 houses (death inflicting) from the 6th house. (Accidents and pets).

- Lastly, if you want to assess anyone in someone's life, even their future, turn the chart to the house that represents that individual in the chart and make it the ascendant and then read the chart as if it were the other person's chart in its entirety, even the transits. For example, if you want to know about the marriage partner you would make the 7th house the ascendant and read it as though it were the marriage partner's chart, even the transits. This works for everyone in a person's life, the mother (4th house), father, (9th house), siblings (11th and 3rd), children (5th house oldest, 7th house 2nd born, 9th house 3rd born, 11th house 4th born always moving 3 houses forward). This is a very important tool and works!

Look for positive in a chart

Astrology is for self-improvement. I believe the birth chart shows the accumulation of all our previous lifetimes of karma, good and bad combined. With this knowledge of the difficulties seen in a birth chart the individual can understand how to heal the past karmas the soul accrued and through conscious awareness change our behaviors to heal our past karmas.

In a birth chart we will be able to see an individual's greatest gifts, talents and goals, where they will excel the very most. As an astrologer I believe giving focus towards the individual's best combinations in a chart will develop their gifts and great skills therefore empowering that individual to be confident, happy and lessen the focus on the difficulties in a chart. It is everything to direct a person to discover their purpose in life, giving them a true sense of meaning, and the birth chart will reveal this.

Looking at the predictive aspects in a chart, it is very healing, to help individuals to know when the tough times will end, as this gives hope and light at the end of any dark tunnel. The inspiration to know when our suffering will end, and when good times will begin. This helps us get through these times and also to realize why we are experiencing the heart aches. Astrology gives us this timing and understanding.

But an awareness as to the difficult karmas and working to heal them will bring a life of success and healing. As an astrologer we must always focus on empowering the individual to be the best they can be, to heal the karma from the past, and focus on their happiness and success. But always remind the individual of the soul purpose in life, and that is to grow spiritually. Through all our life, career, relationships and family we will realize through all experiences in life that our purpose is to develop and grow intellectually, emotionally and most of all spiritually. Astrology is a tool to see our truth, heal and reach moksha, where we achieve spiritual liberation of the soul. Nothing is of more importance than this!

Closing

Astrology is the Science of Light – Jyotish, meaning it gives us sight into the darkness, and has given me an understanding of all aspects of this world from the elements, fire (spirit), earth (material), air (communications) and water (emotions), to the evolution of our soul essence to understand why we are here.

The understanding of the moksha houses (4, 8 and 12) gave me the understanding that through these houses, which are connected to the water signs (Cancer, Scorpio and Pisces) connect us to our emotions and feelings which are the pathway to healing. To heal our lives and break the cycle of the past (these houses reflect our past) we must feel our emotions to release the pain and hurt that keeps us in the chains of our past hurts and resentments. Realize these are the houses in astrology that will heal our past and give us what we all seek, which is our final liberation from the pain and sufferings of this world into our ultimate joy and happiness – enlightenment. Jyotish is the science that brought me this realization to heal my life and with this, all I want to do is alleviate the suffering in others through the healing understanding that astrology can bring to all of us and the world.

This book is a legacy of my forty-plus years of experience that I want to leave for all my students and those who see the wisdom of astrology. This book compiles all the magical combinations that I have experienced first-hand, that work and can help to give meaning to your birth chart and shine a light and understanding about the meaning and purpose of your life.

In my experience, I have found that in this information you can see the potential of all your personal talents and gifts and when the timing of events will occur throughout your life. I know this information helps us to make life decisions combined with using the power of our free will. To know astrology is the key to life's amazing journey. The information revealed in one's chart, allows us to make choices that will empower us to pursue a life of fulfillment, happiness, and the power to be who we have come into this life and world to be.

**With blessings and goodwill,
enjoy the journey of your chart!**

List of the charts

2016 US Election	172	Elon Musk	137
Aden Sanchez Chalino	146	Elvis Presley	80
Albert Einstein	108	Emeril Lagasse	94
Andrew Carnegie	135	Emma Borden	196
Anna Nicole Smith	149	Erdogan Recep Tayyip	132
Anne Heche Death	219	Eric Menéndez	195
Attack on America 9/11/2001	145	Ernest Gallo	96
		Farrah Fawcett	107
Barack Obama	99	Frank Sinatra	77
Barbara Wilson	57	Gloria Vanderbilt	127
Benjamin Franklin	187	Gloria Vanderbilt	138
Bhagwan Shree Rajneesh	105	Hillary Clinton	174
Bill Gates	136	Hurricane Harvey	184
Bill Gates	175	Jacqueline Kennedy Onassis	35
Brad Pitt	206		
Brian Epstein	147	Jacqueline Kennedy Onassis	160
Brigitte Bardot	124 & 126		
Brittany Spears	83	James Dean Death	222
Buddy Holly	55	Janis Joplin	159
Carla Bruni	164	Jayne Mansfield	166
Cary Grant	84	Jeff Bezos	177
Charles Manson	26	Jeff Bridges	21
Charles Manson	194	Jennifer Lawrence	75
Chelsea Clinton	173	Jimi Hendrix	101
Chris Evert	203	John D. Rockefeller Sr.	130
Christina Onassis	115	John Kennedy Jr. Death	226
Christina Onassis	60	John Kennedy Jr.	162
Clint Eastwood	23	John Ogonowsky	199
Conner Clapton	204	John Salvi	39
Dean Martin	78	John Travolta	151
Dennis Wilson	182	Jordan Spieth	179
Diane Creighton	155	Joseph Kennedy Sr.	123
Dolly Parton	143	Joseph Kennedy Sr.	152
Donald Trump	139	Julie Andrews	68
Elizabeth Taylor	193	Julio Gallo	118

List of the charts

Justin Bieber	140	Pope Francis	112
Kamala Harris	163	Priscilla Presley	90
Karen Carpenter	70	Priscilla Presley	153
Koby Bryant Death	217	Private Client Chart	113
Lindsay Wagner	93	Private Client Chart	129
Lisa Marie Presley	154	Private Client Chart	100
Madonna	73	Ralph Waldo Emerson	157
Maria Shriver	144	Ram Dass	185
Marilyn Monroe	102	Rena Krentkowski	156
Marion March	169	Robert Johnson	192
Mark Zuckerberg	86	Robin Williams	36
Mary Bell Vincent	142	Roman Polanski	122
Mary Wilson	67	Ross Perot	131
Mauricio Gucci	190	Serena Williams	53
Meryl Streep	17	Stephen King	88
Meryl Streep	45	Steven Spielberg	91
Michael Jackson	24	Sudarsha Chart	230
Michael Jordan	48	Susie Patterson	62
Michael Milken	148	Sylvester Stallone	141
Monica Lewinsky Scandal	171	Sylvester Stallone	150
		Tatum O'Neal	19
Natalie Wood	181	Ted Hennessey	198
Norman Wexler	41	Ted Kennedy	103
O.J. Simpson	28	Ted Turner	133
Oprah Winfrey	134	The Titanic	183
Oprah Winfrey	65	Tim Kaine	173
Oprah Winfrey	167	Timothy Leary	121
Paris Hilton	31	Timothy Leary	186
Paul McCartney	81	Tom Cruise	33
Paul Walker Death	224	Tonya Harding	119
Peter Lawford	165	Warren Beatty	89
Phil Hartman	189	Wilt Chamberlain	50

Printed in Great Britain
by Amazon